Robert Dew, Bill Russell, Cyrus Allen, and George Bej
**Lean CX**

Robert Dew, Bill Russell,
Cyrus Allen, and George Bej

# Lean CX

How to Differentiate at Low Cost and Least Risk

**DE GRUYTER**

ISBN 978-3-11-068368-4
e-ISBN (PDF) 978-3-11-068392-9
e-ISBN (EPUB) 978-3-11-068402-5

**Library of Congress Control Number: 2020948403**

**Bibliographic information published by the Deutsche Nationalbibliothek**
The Deutsche Nationalbibliothek lists this publication in the Deutsche Nationalbibliografie;
detailed bibliographic data are available on the Internet at http://dnb.dnb.de.

© 2021 Walter de Gruyter GmbH, Berlin/Boston
Typesetting: Integra Software Services Pvt. Ltd.
Printing and Binding: LSC Communications, United States

www.degruyter.com

# Acknowledgements

Any book like this is a team effort. Our team – Bill Russell, Cyrus Allen, George Bej and I – had a lot of fun creating this work together. When we first started talking about this idea, it seemed obvious to all of us that this topic could help with parts of the business strategy problem we had each been thinking about separately. All of us had seen companies invest in CX consulting and innovation only to stumble at the execution stage. Lean seemed like an interesting way to combat the issues. In practice, writing the book didn't unfold as effortlessly as we'd hoped, but we were able to get our act together and combine our thoughts in a meaningful way. Along the way it seemed ironic the book was not really evolving in an agile way. This turned out to be a pre-emptive judgement. Adjacent positioning and swarm algorithms were discovered as a result of research along the way and many other concepts ended up being refined as a result of sharing with readers in our network.

Our gratitude goes to the researchers and others who made such a rich heritage available to us. We sourced the understanding and knowledge from many academic and business journals. This has been good for frameworks. Beyond the cases we shared from our consulting practice, many real-life examples have come from people reporting online about their business experiences, or from journalists commenting about other people's businesses. This area may be one of the few domains where there is no requirement to report in a sensationalist manner.

Finally, as lead author, I need to thank the most important person in my life – my wife Sarah. The more time we spend together the more I appreciate her intelligence, grace, wisdom, and support. Recently her interest in how software can solve problems involving interactions with humans has been a catalyst to get me thinking more about systems and psychology. It is quite wonderful to watch a classically trained artist turn her formidable intellect and attention to using chatbots for internet marketing. Loving the adventure. Thank you.

-- Robert Dew

https://doi.org/10.1515/9783110683929-202

# About the Authors

Dr **Robert Dew** has evolved from physicist to manager to consultant over more than 30 years. He likes to recount the journey as starting from learned autism (undergrad), maturing through corporate cynicism (MBA) to finally getting some sense of what motivates people (PhD). Along the way he has done 50+ start-ups, lectured at eight universities around the world, and chaired the International Society of Professional Innovation Managers (ISPIM) advisory board. As one of the founding partners of CapFeather Global he enjoys helping companies grow by innovating customer strategy and CX.

Dr **Bill Russell** started out working in B2B and B2C sales, and now teaches innovation and marketing on the world's #1 MBA for sustainability – while juggling research, consulting, and writing. Some highlights have included five years working in motorsport, a stint as a sales director with Hallmark, and leading the international expansion of Emerald Publishing. He is a boundary spanner, bringing together diverse thinkers to see the world differently. An advocate of the Jobs-to-be-Done approach, he builds CX centred value propositions through researching the social, emotional and functional challenges of users and customers.

**Cyrus Allen** has been advising large corporates and government owned entities for 10 years on customer strategy and experience innovation. He has led and/or worked on nearly 200 projects across some 100 clients. Cyrus' deep interest in customer experience innovation emerged from his earlier years in product and brand marketing with organisations including Ericsson, Sony Ericsson, Telstra and ANZ. He wears the scars of having designed and deployed experience innovation and customer-centric change programs with pride. Those scars are what lends Cyrus a pragmatic view to customer experience innovation, and what helps him drive real change with clients.

**George Bej** has successfully implemented customer focused programs that have led to revenue growth, improved retention and bottom line results. He specialises in accelerating business performance, bringing tools and insights that underpin successful transformation programs. His approach draws on disruption theory, design thinking, entrepreneurialism and innovation. He has worked in senior executive roles in tough markets and has more than 30 years' commercial experience across a range of industry segments and organisations. Career highlights include roles as CEO of the Australian National Cyber Institute and CREST ANZ, as well as Executive Director of Strativity Group.

https://doi.org/10.1515/9783110683929-203

# Foreword

When you reflect on this time in our history, how will you mark it?

There will be businesses, large and small, that will never recover, others will adapt and survive, and some will thrive.

Shareholders, customers and suppliers are watching revenue plummet, EPS dive, dividends evaporate, and they already know that profits, if there are any, will be hard to come by. Such generational challenges are devastating and will have far-reaching, long term resonance. Still, within this incredibly difficult time, there will be opportunities, to take a risk, accelerate change, repair, or adapt and set for the future. In this future, the consumer holds enormous power. So perhaps a better question is this:

How will you use the opportunity COVID presents you?

These powerful external influencers are driving massive change in customer behaviour. Differentiating and capitalising in the moments that matter for customers and responding, quickly, isn't easy. Harder still, if you don't have an aligned and committed leadership supporting the change, and a motivated, incentivised front-line staff to deliver on it.

In this book, *Lean CX*, Robert Dew, Bill Russell, Cyrus Allen and George Bej tackle the problem that many CX leaders confront every day – to convert what appears to be almost common sense into business practice and priority. As Drucker said, the real reason for a business to exist is to create and keep customers. So simple, so then why isn't this simple truth at the very heart of our organisations?

Some of the largest and most influential business leaders in the world regularly gather to discuss why corporations exist, most recently on August 19, 2019. The 181 American CEOs that make up the American Business Roundtable came together and announced a new purpose for the corporation: that it exists to create value for all stakeholders. Namely customers, employees and shareholders alike – undoing in a single meeting the Milton Friedman approach that the corporation exists only to serve shareholders.[1]

So leaders are ready, customers are impatient, and the external conditions present us with a once in a generation chance to drive significant and systemic change. The only real question that remains is how will you do it? But something seems to be in the way.

*Lean CX* is an exciting evolution and a timely response to this worthy challenge; it is the practice reboot needed, delivered through the application of agile management techniques to the problem of improving the customer experience for real cut-through.

Dew et al. contend that within our largest corporations and government entities, the language of CX is not yet crisp enough to be sustainable, and the bell is tolling for practitioners that don't, or won't, seek to make the commercial dialogue the beating heart of the CX practice.

https://doi.org/10.1515/9783110683929-204

Stop trying to be the best, strive to be the only, is undoubtedly a galvanising and rousing call to arms, but it needs the support of the practice, commercial acumen and the strength of a robust process. *Lean CX* delivers the framework, supports a crisp commercial dialogue and has a laser-sharp focus on adjacent markets and value creation.

At its essence, the *Lean CX* approach provides an entrepreneurial approach and useful new ways to think about market engagement, iteration and value creation. It demonstrates how to get to actual customer observation via market testing as quickly as possible. In doing this, the *Lean CX* approach may reduce the risk of stalling at the point of planning and listening by reducing the time and resource investment compared to waterfall approaches.

As a CX practitioner or senior marketer it is important to deal directly with a lack of alignment around the customer, value and even go to market. *Lean CX* helps to address this by creating a common language for the organisation; by suggesting that the organisation needs to be an ambidextrous firm, that is, a firm that creates a difference every day by being able to exploit and explore at the same time. This approach stretches the boundaries of contemporary thinking about how CX can be applied to develop innovative solutions to complex organisational and market problems.

This book will re-energise your love of customer experience and sharpen the way you go about creating value for your customers, stakeholders, employees and yourself.

*Lean CX* is an original, intelligent and practical work, and I recommend you take the time to learn more from it.

**Macgregor Williams**
VP Strategy and Marketing, Asia Pacific
Pearson Asia Pacific

# Contents

# List of Cases

https://doi.org/10.1515/9783110683929-206

# List of Figures

https://doi.org/10.1515/9783110683929-207

# List of Tables

https://doi.org/10.1515/9783110683929-208

# Introduction

Mice, Monkeys, and Gazelles.

More than two decades ago in 1998,[2] Spencer Johnson wrote a business fable about two mice and two people who all lived in a maze and essentially spent their lives looking for cheese. After successfully finding some cheese, both the mice and the humans had to deal with the challenge of what to do when the cheese runs out. Johnson's genius was in describing the differences between the responses to this problem: the mice realised their cheese supply was dwindling and set off on a search to find more, even before their stash was gone. The humans were less open to change and one almost perished because of an inability to stray from the cheese pile they had found. Even though the humans could see their store was running out, the prospect of leaving their comfort zone in favour of the unknown almost proved too daunting.

The problem of being unable to invest in the only viable option for long-term survival against short term incentives is the major strategic issue for most businesses today. We call this problem a 'monkey jar' problem. This comes from another fable about how to catch a monkey: You put a banana in a heavy, clear glass jar. The jar must be the correct size. Ideally the bottleneck is wide enough so the monkey can get a hand inside to grab the banana, but not so wide that while holding the banana the monkey can pull its hand back out. You leave the banana jar seemingly unattended (but hide in wait nearby) until a monkey comes along. Once the monkey grabs the banana, it is a simple matter to walk up and catch it, because the weight of the jar prevents it from getting away. Of course all the monkey should do is let go of the banana to get away free. But not being able to give up the banana means the monkey is trapped and caught. We see many businesses are trapped in a monkey jar of their own making.

Every business begins its life as a start-up. During this phase, its founders are on a quest to find a profitable, sustainable market. The odds are that most fail and perish before they are successful in finding their 'cheese.' Those that are successful then try to scale. This can take years. Success in this scaling phase comes down to learning how to switch from an entrepreneurial modus operandi to a more corporate management approach. Entrepreneurs are driven by opportunity and characterised by exploring. Corporate managers are characterised by exploiting a proven business model increasing efficiency and consistency. Efficiency and consistency are necessary (but not sufficient) to scale. During this transition some businesses fail because they can't solve the efficiency problem and end up with too many costs. Others fail because they can't solve the complexity problem and delivery poor quality at volume. Some fail simply because they grow too fast and become insolvent. Despite the triple threat scaling involves, it is less risky than the start-up. But it is in the scaling phase that businesses somehow lose their ability to explore. It's almost as if their owners don't believe in their team's underlying capability or

https://doi.org/10.1515/9783110683929-209

the systems in the firm. They operate as if the business has achieved its market position and profitability by luck. All too often the switch from entrepreneurs to corporate managers means explorers become exploiters.

Nothing lasts forever, and ultimately whatever market opportunity the business originally found erodes. This could be due to competition, technological changes, regulatory reform or market preference shifts. The change can be gradual as the market environment evolves, or rapid if caused by disruptive innovations. Businesses unable to adapt as their market environment changes will ultimately fail. Ironically, the research suggests most managers in large business failures were not surprised by their fate. They saw the decline coming. In every case, they were simply unable to switch from exploiting mode to exploring mode in time to find a new profitable and sustainable market. Their very success was the monkey jar of their downfall. This problem of how to balance the conflicting strategic focus across different time horizons can be simply stated: "Do we stay with the current dwindling pile of cheese or venture out in search of a new cheese source?"

Twenty years on from Johnson's elusive cheese, business markets are more like mazes than ever. Now they are just harder to navigate. The walls of the maze move as technology advances. The size of the maze increases as globalisation links different markets together. Globalisation increases both opportunity and competition. Firms are no longer mice. Many have become predators. They build ever more clever traps to catch their customers. It is consumers who are the unwitting Mice wandering around the maze of the market. The predators bait their traps with evermore enticing cheese with the end goal of locking in their prey for as long as possible. These predators want to extract as much from their prey as they can. Sophisticated traps include things like:

- Subscription contracts designed to compel overconsumption
- Finance products with exit penalties for early repayment
- Requiring the use of overpriced genuine parts to maintain product warranties
- Proprietary connectors to prevent compatibility with rivals' products or add-ons
- Using two-factor authentication to prevent customers sharing log in details
- Building product ecosystems as mini-mazes to confound customer churn
- Designing shopping spaces with hard-to-find exits
- Locating commonly sought products far from exits to compel more time in the store
- Including in-game bonuses to prompt social media sharing to attract more players
- Offering free drinks to patrons to get them to stay longer and gamble more
- Delaying food service to diners to get them to order more pre-dinner drinks
- Increasing 'hurry-up-and-wait' delays at airports to coerce impulse spending as a relief

- Lobbying for laws that restrict free market competition to hold up prices
- Building 'confusopolies'[3] where changing features and prices hinder finding the best value

Businesses doing things on the list above have disappointingly shifted their focus away from earning their keep through providing customer value. Instead, they focus on tricking customers into making a poor purchase decision in favour of their firm. They avoid innovating to create more value. This attitude is the worst amongst executives in large corporates who single-mindedly pursue performance bonuses with an 'ends justify the means' philosophy. Ironically, it is this group who become the most trapped as Monkeys locked into a jar of their own making. Instead of exploring for new ways to add value, they erect more of the same type of trap, in the same part of the maze, perhaps with new types of cheese and more subtle snags. They hope to catch more unsuspecting and careless Mice. They get most excited when they can find rich, dumb customers.

*$U^4$- Could algae or seaweed replace oil, gas, and coal for energy generation?[5]*
*One of the best examples of the Monkey Jar problem is the energy industry. The big players in oil, gas, and coal have huge sunk investments in maintaining the status quo. The problem is twofold. Firstly, oil, gas, and coal will eventually run out. Secondly, it seems before they do, the continued use of fossil fuels will have an adverse effect on our climate. There has been a lot of effort to get solar and wind power generation to work at scale. These technologies kind of work, but they are more expensive, less reliable, and need far more land than fossil fuels (assuming you leave out the cost of climate change like most markets during our history using oil).[6] According to a report published by Reuters,[7] the largest 24 oil companies invested 1% of their capital budgets in wind, solar, and battery technologies. In the same report, critics assert the investment is much less than spending to block climate initiatives and regulations and fossil fuel projects. Shell is one of the largest players and most forward-thinking in terms of investment, but even it is apparently stuck in a Monkey Jar. Here is copy from their Energy Future website:[8]*

> *"As the energy system evolves, hydrocarbons will continue to play a vital role in the coming decades, providing much-needed energy to fuel transport, in particular aviation, and make everyday products from plastics to steel . . . Today, natural gas – the cleanest-burning hydrocarbon – makes up more than half of our production. We believe it will be vital to building a sustainable energy future, especially in power generation, where it produces around half the $CO_2$ and just one-tenth the air pollutants that coal does. We are involved in several projects to safely capture and store $CO_2$ to mitigate the use of hydrocarbons. These depend on government support to be financially viable and to become more widespread. Replacing a coal-fired power plant with a gas-fired plant that has CCS can cut $CO_2$ emissions by up to 90%. We also have a decade of experience in wind power, with involvement in nine projects in North America and Europe."*

*The sector is shifting more to natural gas. Natural gas is cleaner than other fossil fuels and is often used to help manage reliability issues with solar and wind energy. However, there are other clean energy alternatives worth considering.*

A range of companies are now exploring algae or seaweed for their potential to replace oil. These fast-growing plants produce lipids. The lipids can be refined to make diesel, petroleum, and aviation fuel with by-products of food and fertiliser. Algae systems are freshwater and can be based on land or sea. They are typically enclosed and need carbon dioxide and wastewater input. There are both land-based and ocean setups. Typically, the land-based systems need to be near a power station to exploit its $CO_2$ emissions. The ocean setups need to be near sewerage outlets to exploit wastewater. In contrast to algae systems, seaweed systems are usually unenclosed and use natural $CO_2$ and fertiliser runoff from farming. But they still require infrastructure to support the seaweed and additional machines for harvesting. Several different companies are pursuing scaled trials with algae or seaweed, but right now the cost seems to be uncompetitive compared to fossil fuels.

In 2016, Global Algae Innovations was producing fuel at around 10x the price of oil using acres of algae raceways installed beside a power plant in Kauai. They have managed to reduce production costs from $30 per gallon of oil in 2013 down to projecting possibly $2–$3 per gallon at scale.[9] At the time of this writing, crude oil costs around $60 per barrel (one barrel = 42 US gallons) or about $1.40 per gallon. Sapphire Founder and director of the California Center for Algae Biotechnology Stephen Mayfield points out algae was already a $US 10 billion global industry in 2015. He asserted replacing 40% of US corn farmland with algae could yield 200 billion gallons of oil. This would have been enough to cover all of the US of annual diesel and petroleum consumption at the time.[10]

Project OMEGA is NASA's attempt at algae energy farming for aviation gas. OMEGA uses plastic tubes of algae located at sea. Like most sea-based installations, energy is only part of what the project is set up to produce. Focusing solely on energy production is uneconomical. NASA is focused on showcasing pollution reduction benefits and the lack of adverse impact on marine life.[11] Smith asserted himself as one of the world's first 3D Ocean farmers.[12] He presented his farm as part of the solution to overfishing, unemployment, and clean energy problems. The vertical farm grows a mixture of shellfish and seaweeds to produce local food, organic fertilizer, and biofuel. Both algae and seaweed have a way to go to become economically viable. The suboptimal strategic decision from the major oil companies is not to be exploring these and other technologies beyond just natural gas, wind, and solar to solve our looming energy and climate challenges. It is clear big oil's customers want cheaper energy.

Over the last decade we have seen examples of businesses trying to improve their customer experience (CX), but still trapped in their own monkey jars. These Monkeys try new CX when their traditional ads fail, online campaigns stall, their investment in the new digital platform or tech widget doesn't pay out, they realise a lower cost challenger is about to eat their lunch, or they suffer several consecutive periods of revenue contraction. Suddenly they decide they need to work out how to seem more attractive to their customers. Their process is generally the same: They create or 'steal' some budget, hire experts (consultants or executives), do some customer research, build a journey map, create a change roadmap, fail to fix most pain points, fail to meaningfully identify their ideal customers, fail to implement major CX change initiatives, and then they run their 'experts' out of town. Their failures are almost always at the execution stage. There are many possible causes of these failures: Returns take too long, cross-silo coordination is too hard, key supporters move, politics intervene, and the changes are too extreme. But the root cause comes down to a single issue. These businesses are not customer-centric at their core. They operate to perpetuate their own existence first and consider dealing with customers only as the means to get there.

As consumer goods organisations strive to rejuvenate growth, they face the task of satisfying changing definitions of consumer value. More customers now prioritise purpose-led brands. Research indicates over 65% of consumers are ready to pay more for sustainable products. Apparently 90% are ready to change to sustainable products if price and quality are the same. Danone has developed a "One Planet. One Health." organisational-level manifesto and the purpose-led brands at the food giant are growing three times faster than the rest of the firm's portfolio. Unilever's 28 sustainable living brands are growing faster than the firm's other product ranges. These products are driving 75% of the company's growth.[13]

Growth has been hard to find for consumer products companies over the last decade. The majority of established firms have focused on cutting costs to shield margins. They have avoided developing innovations to connect with the higher purpose so many consumers now value. Almost three-quarters of the leading consumer brands reduced their R&D and innovation spending between 2006 and 2017, and only 2% of sales are dedicated to these vital investments in the future.[14]

When consumers or professional buyers evaluate any product or service, they are usually assessing the perception of the product or service versus its asking price. The people involved with the overall process of developing an offering and taking it to market are typically more comfortable with the price side of the equation than they are with the value side. Consumers and buyers all find the value equation is amorphous, psychological, and complex. Developing value propositions for target segments is a challenge. This includes how to identify value and figure out how to deliver more of it. This value can be functional (cost reduction, time saving, increased reliability) or emotional (reducing anxiety, providing entertainment, facilitating social connections). Investing in CX is all about managing customer value.

It turns out the biggest waste for companies trying to do CX is investment in research and design instead of market testing. Instead of replacing their trap with something better for their Mice customers, all they end up doing is lining their current trap with fur. At the end of the day this is less bad for the Mice, but still ultimately bad. Fur-lining the trap includes lowering customer effort scores, increasing transaction security, ensuring invoice accuracy, and everything else related to delivering consistently around hygiene factors. *Hygiene factors* are the things customers expect because they simply should be there anyway. A vehicle should be safe. A restaurant should have clean toilets. A valid refund request should be honoured immediately. Customer-facing staff should be polite and know what they are doing. Forms should only have to be filled out once, ever.

This is certainly (and only) the minimum, but effective CX is just not about making your experience less bad than nearby rivals' CX. You need more than just a softer lining. You need a *silver* lining. More than ever before customers warn each other about businesses who seem out to get them – they do this face to face and through social media. But they also share standout customer experiences. This is the ultimate goal of CX management. It is about being remarkable. To offer a remarkable experience, a business must meet conflicting requirements of being both safe enough and novel enough to achieve *cut-through*. Cut-through occurs when your business grows because your customers share their experiences with others to refer, recommend, or endorse what you do. Happy customers are not just satisfied customers, happy Mice don't feel less trapped, they feel free. In return they help create business growth for free by spreading the word!

There are many examples in this book showing companies growing fast in crowded markets because they have used lean methods (explicitly or intuitively) to discover new profitable market niches across all parts of their market maze. These are the *Gazelles*,[15] who seem to be able to magically leap the walls of the maze and explore more of the market faster, cheaper, and with less risk than the Monkeys stuck with their jars. This book is about what the Gazelles do differently.

The key difference between the Monkeys and the Gazelles is that the Gazelles are customer-centric. They start with a focus on how to create more value for customers instead of scheming how to exploit them more efficiently. This is an *abundance* mindset as opposed to the Monkeys' *scarcity* mindset. Gazelles have empathy for customers and intuition about what might attract them and get them talking. So they go right out and test their ideas for real in the market. As they learn, they adapt and change on the fly. Once they have enough proof of what works, they scale. Many of the Gazelles in this book are start-ups recently grown to scale, but there is no intrinsic reason larger corporates can't copy the Gazelles to grow fast as well. They can certainly afford to in the short term and can't afford not to in the long term. They just need to learn why and how. For smaller firms, Lean CX offers a repeatable process to search for their first source of cheese with more of a system, so they too can transform into Gazelles.

Despite its title and focus, this book is actually about ambidexterity. The content covers a range of lean management processes validated in real world organisations. If you apply the tools outlined in this book, you will learn how to find and implement cut-through for your business. While there are many ways you might get cut-through, this book is specifically about achieving growth through delivering a superior customer experience. But more than that, the book is about how companies can simultaneously exploit their existing market opportunities and explore new ways to add value. The most common way to achieve organisational ambidexterity involves a structural fix where a firm splits into two parts. One part is for business as usual and the other is for so-called 'skunk works' to do innovation.[16] Lean CX offers an alternative: Instead of a structural change, which creates resource allocation conflicts, use the tools outlined in this book. Instead of trying to squeeze more out of customers, search for ways to innovate and create more value to share in. The CX part helps both with where to search and what to look for. The Lean part lower the risks and costs of the traditional CX management approaches we have seen over last decade. To help you navigate more easily to topics relevant to your size of business, the book is divided into sections:

Chapter 1 provides reasons why changing the approach to CX is critical. It covers the issues of how and why many firms' CX investments have not been as successful as they had hoped. It also outlines the potential of CX to transform businesses and move the needle on performance for a comparatively small, low-risk investment compared to other innovation options. Read this chapter if you are looking to get traction to try some, more, or any CX improvements in your business.

Chapter 2 is a primer on lean management. It covers Lean's primary objective of eliminating waste and how this applies to the execution problem for innovation generally. This is expanded to show how reversing the traditional processes companies use to improve their CX can lower the costs and risks involved. Finally, the core process of Lean is introduced. This is the agile management cycle. Read this chapter if you are not familiar with lean or agile management. You should read this chapter and the first chapter if you believe the traditional waterfall process for CX improvement is still the way to go.

Chapter 3 covers creating cut-through. Businesses that grow rapidly do so because they have spare capacity matched to a previously unmet or unrealised market potential. The chapter introduces two places to search for such sweet spots. The external search involves the idea of adjacent market positioning. The internal search involves applying the *MAYA* design principle.[17] MAYA means Most Advanced Yet Acceptable. If you are into high-level strategy, this chapter is foundational and conceptual. You can skip it if you just want to get directly into what is it is you need to actually do.

Chapter 4 introduces *Human Centred Design* (HCD). HCD is not so much a discipline as a philosophy based on empathy for the user or customer. The core HCD values are close to the ideals of customer centricity with the main difference being the latter is explicit about commercial considerations. To deliver more customer-centric experiences, this chapter presents a practical model of applied customer psychology and an introduction to the complexities of three-level cognition. Three design methods for CX innovation are shared: the TERMS transaction framework, the Kano quality framework, and the CAPFUL personal needs framework.

---

*How to quickly find relevant cases and examples*
*We have formatted the mini case studies in the book like this section so it is easy to find concrete examples. There is also a list at the beginning of the book, so you can see examples from specific companies or industries you might know. Each of the formatted examples is coded first for*

CAPFUL needs (explained in more detail in Chapter 4) and then for whether the CX is positive or negative for customers. The CAPFUL acronym includes six different psychological needs:[18]

C +|- Certainty and safety
A +|- Advancement and growth
P +|- Prestige and status
F +|- Fulfilment and meaning
U +|- Uncommon and novel
L +|- Love and belonging

This makes it easy to look up examples to help with inspiration in improving your own CX. For example, a C- case is one where the experience tends to reduce customers' feelings of certainty (not normally a way to foster goodwill). In contrast, a case coded N+ is an example where something novel in the experience tends to pique customers interests in a good way.

Chapter 4 also suggests an inherent reversal in how lean management applies to CX. In order to reduce experience-related waste in a business, you should work on how to actually reduce the waste on the customer's side. However, reducing the waste customers experience can increase the costs required on the business side of the transaction. Balancing the two sides can be non-trivial. Generally we find managers are much better at cost management than experience management. HCD is important to cover if you have never tried to design a CX improvement, or been involved in something like new product development or identifying potential new *customer value propositions* (CVPs).

Chapter 5 presents a modified version of the Kanban method from lean as it applies to CX. This chapter includes the templates for creating testing plans for individual CX initiatives. The summary is critical for being able to conduct split testing for optimisations and identifying when pivots are appropriate to consider for cut-through. At its heart, the lean CX process uses empathy to design a CX innovation and outline it in two pages, then conducts small-scale market tests, pivoting until you find what cuts through. Finally, split testing is conducted to optimise before scaling. This chapter contains the nuts and bolts of how to manage Lean CX innovation.

Chapter 6 switches focus from B2C to B2B market contexts. CX is still relevant in B2B with some additional considerations. Individual customers become client organisations with multiple decision makers and users. This creates differences in B2B marketing, delivery, service, and support. A framework for dealing with the different buyer types inside client organisations is presented and the concept of client centricity is compared and contrasted with the customer centricity concept introduced in Chapter 4. You can safely skip this chapter if you don't work in a B2B context, unless you want to get an additional perspective on providing CX for organisations.

Finally, Chapter 7 concludes the book with a discussion of how future organisations might evolve to apply Lean CX to solve the organisational ambidexterity problem. This chapter is perhaps the most aspirational (and risky) because it presents new ideas about how organisations might simultaneously exploit and explore. The approach is inspired by hive insects (like bees and ants). These creatures allocate resources between harvesting known food sources and searching for new food sources without centralised management controls. The 'swarming' paradigm presented builds a case for episodic roles, slack resources, and decentralised controls. These concepts tend to conflict with much of the accepted best practices about how to run a corporation with good corporate governance. So this chapter (unlike the previous) is more of a guess about a new organisational form than a description of current best practices. In short, it is an interesting possibility. Read this chapter to get ideas on how to integrate Lean CX in your business in an (almost) unprecedented way; however, consider the ideas with a grain of salt as they are largely unproven in the market at the time of this writing based on our research. More than the other chapters, this one represents the frontier of Lean CX thinking.

It is our hope as authors that as you read this book you will make a choice to transform your Monkey firm into an elegant Gazelle. This is because we are all customer Mice of the many businesses out there and enjoy or suffer the CX they offer us. It would be much nicer to be talking about the value great companies offer us, instead of warning other Mice about the traps we have fallen foul of in the market. Don't you think?

## Endnotes

**1** *Businessroundtable.org*

**2** Johnson (1998). *Who Moved My Cheese? An Amazing Way to Deal with Change in Your Work and in Your Life*, Putnam Adult, https://en.wikipedia.org/wiki/Who_Moved_My_Cheese%3F

**3** Scott Adams coined this term in his famous Dilbert cartoon see https://en.wikipedia.org/wiki/Confusopoly

**4** See box 'How to quickly find relevant cases and examples' later in this Introduction.

**5** Mayfield (2015). *Food and Fuel for the 21st Century – Algae and the Green Revolution 2.0 with Stephen Mayfield* [from https://www.uctv.tv/shows/Food-and-Fuel-for-the-21st-Century-Algae-and-the-Green-Revolution-2-0-with-Stephen-Mayfield-Cavendish-Global-Impact-Forum-29682 last accessed 14/7/19]. Mayfield asserted oil (then at $200/barrel) would never return to $20/barrel, and peak oil production had occurred in 2007.

**6** Shellenberger (2018). *Why Renewables Can't Save The Planet* [from http://www.tedxdanubia.com/videos?performer=2888, last accessed 14/7/19].

**7** Bousso (2018). *Big Oil Spent 1 percent on Green Energy in 2018* [from https://www.reuters.com/article/us-oil-renewables/big-oil-spent-1-percent-on-green-energy-in-2018-idUSKCN1NH004, last accessed 14/7/19].

**8** See https://www.shell.com.au/energy-and-innovation/the-energy-future.html [last accessed 14/7/19].

**9** See Global Algae Solutions press releases [from http://www.globalgae.com/news, last accessed 14/7/19].

**10** Ibid., footnote 3.

**11** NASA (2012). *NASA Showcases Innovative Method to Grow Algae-Based Biofuels* https://www. nasa.gov/centers/ames/news/features/2012/omega_algae_feature.html (accessed 14/7/19).

**12** Smith "Vertical Ocean Farming – The Least Deadliest Catch" *TEDxBermuda* https://www.you tube.com/watch?v=j8ViaskDSeI (accessed 30/7/20).

**13** Gadiesh et al. (2019). "The Power of Delivering Elements of Value® in Consumer Products" https://www.bain.com/insights/the-power-of-delivering-elements-of-value-in-consumer-products/ (accessed 5/8/20).

**14** Ibid.

**15** Birch (1987) *Job Creation in America: How Our Smallest Companies Put the Most People to Work*, Free Press. A Gazelle is a high-growth company with at least 20% year-on-year revenue growth for four years or more, starting from at least $100,000 sales in year one. Birch contended Gazelles (around 4% of all companies) created 70% of new jobs in the US economy.

**16** Skunk works are separate divisions inside a company created to do innovation without having to comply with the normal KPIs and processes of business as usual. See Chapter 7.

**17** See https://www.interaction-design.org/literature/article/design-for-the-future-but-balance-it-with-your-users-present for an overview of MAYA and its creator Raymond Loewy.

**18** This list of needs is adapted from Tony Robbins' concepts of basic human needs, which in turn seemed to be a reformulation of Maslow's Hierarchy of Needs from Maslow (1943). "A theory of human motivation," *Psychological Review* Vol 50 Iss 4 Pages 370–396. We first came across Robbins' work at a live event, but check out https://www.tonyrobbins.com/mind-meaning/do-you-need-to-feel-significant/ for an overview. All we did was create the CAPFUL acronym to make them easy to remember.

# Chapter 1
# The Case for Change

Some two decades since its inception, the global Customer Experience movement finds itself in a perilous state. Inside many organisations, the executive support and sponsorship of CX that once underpinned investment in CX resources and programs, is being replaced by CX fatigue. The promise of CX transformation once heralded as 'central to our strategy' is no longer heard in the corridors and meeting rooms of organisations around the world. Instead, CX finds itself a potential line item on the cost cutting list, the subject of a quiet and considered executive discussion about evacuating costs and reinvesting elsewhere.

## CX Under Threat

Forrester Research, Inc., attests to this onset of fatigue and offers the 'plateauing of CCOs' as evidence.[1] Few respondents to a 2016 survey held a chief customer officer (CCO) title amongst C-suite leaders who are responsible for CX efforts. Half a decade ago, CCO roles seemed poised for growth as more companies invested in their customer experience efforts. At that time just 10% of Fortune 500 companies had one and 10% of enterprise-level respondents volunteered that their firms planned to hire one. Now CCO roles are under threat. In its predictions for 2020, Forrester forecast that one in four CX leaders would lose their jobs against a background of buoyant economic conditions with increased expenditure on CX. COVID-19 changed that picture and it now appears conservative as budgets are slashed in the face of reduced demand. A figure of one in three CX leaders losing their jobs now looks more likely. Forrester's original prediction rejected the increasing levels of pushback by senior executives against CX that it is 'fluffy' and 'not commercially-oriented.' In a recent exchange, an industry pundit made the same point using more colourful language:

*The CX industry is drowning under the weight of its own BS at the moment.[2]*

In its Predictions 2020 report,[3] Forrester argues even more dramatically that customer experience professionals will either quantify their business impact or find themselves in a tenuous position. CEOs will demand CX initiatives move out of the experimental phase and prove their contributions to top and/or bottom-line growth verified by measurement, metrics, and analytics.

As the Sword of Damocles dangles precariously over the heads of CX executives, the onset of tragedy is restrained only by a delicate chance of survival. We are reminded about the long list of management fads that were once announced with fanfare and now relegated to corporate history. Those fads promised outcomes such

https://doi.org/10.1515/9783110683929-001

as greater effectiveness, more motivated and productive workers, and deeply satisfied customers.[4] Matrix Management became big in the 1980s where everyone had several different bosses. Matrix Management was phased out as organisations realised it made office life one long turf battle.[5] Management by Objectives also failed because priorities change over time. In fast-moving sectors, defined objectives can be rendered as meaningless within a week.[6] Theory X was based on the premise that workers inherently dislike and avoid work and must be driven to it. Once used in human resource management, organisational behaviour, organisational communication, and organisational development, Theory X was replaced in some sectors by its exact opposite (Theory Y).[7] The list is long.

## CX Transformation

While CX is exposed to imminent risk, the bell has not yet tolled. Because leaders and employees are themselves customers, there is still a daily quest for (and sometimes a discovery of) truly differentiated customer experiences. These are the experiences that are both surprising and delightful. The abundance of inherent hope CX will prevail exists because we know customers no longer base their loyalty exclusively on price, product, or brand. Instead, they stay loyal with companies because of the experience they receive.[8]

CX must pivot to survive, prosper, and escape its potential inclusion on the long list of defunct management fads. Changing the approach to CX is critical inside many organisations where CX investments have not been as successful as first hoped. The potential of CX to transform businesses and shift the needle on performance relies on first understanding the gaps, inadequacies, and blind spots.

Three critical vulnerabilities are common across the landscape of government and enterprise CX programs today:
1. Inability to demonstrate CX returns
2. Inadequately differentiated CX
3. Lack of CX execution

### Inability to Demonstrate CX Returns

Reflecting on the lack of bottom-line CX outcomes, some CEOs are beginning to exhibit early symptoms of CX fatigue. The CEO, struggling to identify an ROI (return on investment) on several years of CX investment, questions the economic upside created from customer experience improvement. The silence from many CX practitioners is deafening.

Developing and selling the conceptual story of why customer experience is important has proven relatively easy. Executives in many markets realise they must differentiate their organisations through compelling customer experiences. From the early 2000's to the present day, leadership teams have demonstrated their support for the notion of improving the experience their customers have by incorporating CX in their articulation of strategy. This articulation was sometimes followed by investments in customer research, current state journey mapping, and target state design. Sadly, in most cases, the advancement came to a grinding halt. CX groundwork headed for the filing cabinets of informed, but largely unconvinced, leadership teams. Others remained steadfast in their commitment to investment and progressed into CRM implementation, Voice of Customer program design, and experience reporting and dashboard creation. Fewer still progressed beyond strategy, design, and other internally focused programs to creating new and/or differentiated experiences for customers. This is an alarming but not entirely surprising outcome.

The inability of CX leaders and teams to link CX to the top- and bottom-line fortunes of an organisation is a fundamental contributor to its decline and potential destruction. CX has always been a strategy for growth and profit. It has never been about putting journey maps up on a wall to showcase understanding. A relatively small investment might be adequate for some journey maps and co-design workshops; however, real transformation will only be realised if it is underpinned by a credible, financially driven, business case highlighting the economic benefits of customer experience. In the absence of a financially driven business case, leadership teams may be approaching a time when they are no longer willing to fund the CX experiment. The reason is simple: they cannot see the clear linkage between the experience delivered and creation of financial value.

So why, after many investment seasons, are most CX teams still unable show the ROI attached to their CX program? It would seem to be an amazingly simple question. Despite the importance of customer experience economics, few executives know even the basic numbers that are so critical to establishing a financially driven customer experience business case. Companies struggle to tie customer centricity directly to business performance because many executives feel customer centricity is more of a *qualitative* measure than a *quantitative* one.[9] In the words of William C. Taylor:

*Most organisations know the cost of everything but the value of nothing.*[10]

A big part of the problem is the use of Net Promoter Score (NPS) as the cornerstone metric for CX. NPS was first developed in 2003 by Bain and Company. Today the metric is used by millions of businesses as a measure of customer perception and loyalty. It is often held up as the gold standard CX metric. NPS measures customer perception based on a simple question: "How likely is it that you would recommend our [Organisation/Product/Service] to a friend or colleague?" Respondents provide a rating between 0 (not at all likely) and 10 (extremely likely). Customers are categorised by their response into three groups: (1) Promoters, with a score of 9 or 10 are typically loyal and enthusiastic customers; (2) Passives, with a score of 7 or 8

are customers satisfied with service but not happy enough to be considered promoters; and (3) Detractors, with a score of 0 to 6 are unhappy customers who are
unlikely to buy again and may even discourage others from buying. The actual NPS
score determined from the difference between Promoters and Detractors is scaled to
100 responses.

Bain's original research showed companies with positive NPS scores grew faster
than their lower scoring rivals. However, NPS scores do not vary consistently across
markets, and the rate of growth is not consistent with NPS across sectors. A bank
with a small positive NPS could not be compared to Apple's remarkable NPS to determine a proportional level of growth. NPS purports to measure customers' desire
to stay with a company and whether they will recommend others to that company.
It does not do that. NPS is a measure of immediate sentiment like customer satisfaction. The difference with NPS is in providing a way for customers to signal they
were more than just satisfied. Companies with positive scores can know they have
created experiences resulting in more than just satisfied customers. The resulting
revenue is not predicted by this score. The cost of this sentiment is also ignored.
NPS must be connected to return metrics to be totally effective – frequently it is not.

The problem with NPS is it is only an accurate measure of sentiment. It is an inaccurate measure of intent. Asking customers about their likelihood to recommend is
different from tracking if they did actually recommend someone, who was referred,
and when. It is tantamount to the billions of all too frequent discussions about weight
loss. Being on a diet may or may not account for something on the bathroom scales.
Stating you are on a diet and intend to slim down only indicates a sentiment about
body image and a desire to lose weight. But it is the scales that provide unambiguous
evidence about your actions. If you have ever tried to lose weight and failed, you will
know the scales do not seem to listen to your stated intentions. Scales are not senti-
mental! Intention to purchase research is notoriously inaccurate (see Table 4.1 in
Chapter 4). Tracking NPS for CX effectiveness has the same inherent issue.

CX ROI is not measured by NPS. CEOs are not typically seen running through
the office demanding to know the firm's NPS score. Those same CEOs will not often
be heard or seen demanding today's Customer Satisfaction (SAT) or Customer Effort
Scores (CES). Customer satisfaction measures the way customers feel about a company or its products and services. Satisfaction is customers' attitude toward a company in the context of trying to get something done. Customer effort defines the
amount of work customers experience during any part of their lifecycle while doing
business with a company. Neither SAT nor CES are measures of actual customer behaviours resulting in retention or loyalty. While NPS/SAT/CES may be correlated
with financially relevant customer actions, the variance across markets and businesses matches the range of customer experiences on offer.

The most important metrics for the CEO are EBITDA (earnings before interest,
taxes, depreciation and amortisation), ROFE (return on funds employed), and other
financial ratios valued by shareholders. Business is about revenues and costs and

building any CX program to exclusively pursue improved levels of referral, advocacy, and NPS scores ignores the real and potential financial upsides created by improved CX. Those upside revenues and cost savings are summarised below.

## CX ROI Revenue Upsides

Unlike NPS, the following financial outcomes of improved CX are unambiguous and bankable[11] (see Table 1.1).

**Table 1.1:** CX Revenue Upsides.

| CX ROI metric | Description |
|---|---|
| Portion | The increased share of wallet of the customer's total budget realised by delivering superior customer experiences. This includes cross-selling and upselling other products and services. Cross-selling describes the ability to sell additional, related products and services to current customers. Cross-selling helps to create sticky customers who want to stay with a company because of convenience. Upselling describes the ability to sell upgraded products and services to current customers. |
| Premium | The price difference charged over competitors because of superior customer experiences. A price premium signifies customers perceive the product or service as superior and differentiated. |
| Permanence | Permanence is the financial value of extending the length of the organisation's customer relationships due to delivering superior customer experiences. This is also described as customer retention, customer renewal, and customer tenure. Permanence is a measure of loyalty demonstrated by how long they stay, whether they continue buying products and services, and if they recommend or refer other customers. Retention rate is defined as the percentage of customers who stay with a company and continue to buy products or services for a specified period. Customer retention rate is a standard key performance metric used to measure performance by month or year. Renewal rate describes the number of customers who re-sign up for contracted products or services in one year. |
| Promotion | The upside revenue derived from *actual* referrals to friends and peers as well as *actual* public support. This includes endorsements, press interviews, sharing opinions through blogs, social networks, and public and private forums due to superior customer experiences. Customer referrals or customer advocacy describes a company's ability to provide such high value to their current customers that they refer new customers and advocate for the company. |
| Pull | The financial value of the product or service-related purchases by new customers entering the market because of the superior experiences of other customers in the segment. This is often transmitted by word of mouth. |

There are more measures[12] organisations would do well to consider as principal CX metrics including:

- **Average order size** describes the average dollar amount customers spend each time they place an order, on a company's products and services.
- **Average order frequency** is the average number of times customers purchase a company's products or services.
- **Customer profitability** is the amount or percentage of profits from a given customer, customer segment, customer cohort, or company.
- **Customer lifetime value** totals the dollar value that customers spend on products and services across their entire relationship with a company.
- **Conversion rate** refers to converting prospects who are using a free/limited product or service into fully paid subscriptions beyond the trial period. In this instance, customer experience affects whether customers will decide to pay for the full scope of services.
- **Product or service adoption** is helping customers to extract value from purchased products and services from effective use. Effective use supports customers to achieve their goals and directly impacts perceived value and performance, causing customers to buy a company's products and services more frequently.

---

**U+ L+ The Ritz-Carlton customer fund**

*Every Ritz-Carlton employee is given an allowance of $2,000 per guest to spend each day to enhance their experience or to immediately resolve any problems, effectively "wowing" the guest. Because of their son's food allergies, a family vacationing at the Ritz-Carlton, Bali, was always careful to bring their own supply of specialised eggs and milk. In this instance, however, the food was ruined en route. The Ritz-Carlton manager could not find any of the special items in town, but his executive chef recalled that a store in Singapore sold them. The chef contacted his mother-in-law who lived in Singapore to purchase the items, and then fly to Bali (about 2.5 hours) to deliver the items.[13]*

---

## CX ROI Cost Improvements

Increased revenues are not the only bankable benefits from CX innovation. Cost improvements also apply. NPS, CSAT, and CES measures fail to capture these potential and real cost savings. These savings measure business efficiency. They define how streamlined and efficient it feels from a customer and/or company perspective to do business with a company. Designed experiences should at least deliver simplicity to simultaneously reduce customer effort and company costs.

While this appears logical, CX cost units are often unknown within organisations. The data is spread across multiple departments that treat each transaction or interaction with a customer as an isolated event. As a consequence, the true cost of serving a customer, the cost of a generated lead, the cost of a new customer acquisition, and the cost of a complaint are difficult if not impossible to find in corporate records.[14] Achieving an ROI on CX involves not only understanding these cost units but being able to apply them both collectively and effectively to the organisational benefit (see Table 1.2).

**Table 1.2:** CX Cost Improvements.

| CX ROI | Description |
| --- | --- |
| **Corrections** | The cost savings due to error reduction and elimination programs. This is often an outcome of purposely designing improved customer experiences to prevent errors. |
| **Complaints** | The cost savings due to complaint reduction and elimination, often the outcome of an optimally sequenced customer pain point reduction program, root cause analysis, and resultant actions. |
| **Complexity** | The cost savings derived through process simplification, moving from historical operating models to leaner, more intuitive, more customer centric, target operating models. |
| **Coaxing** | The lead generation and customer acquisition cost savings due to superior customer experiences. Current investment in sales, marketing and brand can be redeployed because word of mouth about the firm spreads. |
| **Churn** | Customer churn refers to customers lost due to poor experiences or in response to rival promotions. Customer-centric firms spend less on last chance initiatives to retain customers. Permanence (Table 1.1) measures the additional revenue from keeping a customer. Churn is about reducing the costs to retain customers when the customer signals they are about to switch to a competitor. |

The quality and consistency of the experiences an organisation delivers to customers has both a direct and indirect impact on value creation (e.g., share of wallet, price premium, retention, referral) or, conversely, the destruction of that financial value. Simultaneously, poorly designed customer experiences create costs (e.g., errors, complaints, workarounds, and increased acquisition and retention costs). From the organisation's perspective, an inability to grow and/or command a price or margin premium is combined with a relentless escalation in the cost of servicing and acquisition. This creates the perfect storm.

CX practitioners must link CX to business economics if they are going to successfully recruit allies in the organisation for transformational growth. They must speak in the language of profit and loss, of EBITDA and ROFE, of risk and reward. Within our largest corporations and government entities, the language of CX is not yet crisp enough to be sustainable. Arguably the single most significant challenge for CX practitioners is shifting from the warm and fuzzy motherhood statements about CX visions and values to a more hard-nosed dialogue about returns.

To avoid irrelevance, the CX industry must move to robust quantitative analysis. This must validate the economic value of various customer interactions and allow the organisation to determine where an investment in experience improvement will deliver the greatest return. New capabilities alone do not guarantee success. Most CX measurement systems fail to link business impact to the elements driving customer satisfaction improvements.[15] Value realisation requires measurement of both upside and cost. It is that simple. A compelling financial story is necessary to secure funding and executive buy-in. CX is on notice that the nice story is no longer enough. Executives expect an actual demonstration proving money spent on CX delivers positive business results. Otherwise the future is bleak: CX budgets will shrink and CX jobs will get cut.[16]

## Inadequately Differentiated CX

Compounding the inability of most CX functions to link their activities to financial impact is that fact that the CX programs observed in most major organisations are largely ill-defined. Most CX practitioners certainly understand that today's battlefield of hypercompetition is about winning customer preference and loyalty by consistently delivering against a differentiated promise. Despite this, most CX programs only aim to deliver to minimum customer expectations. There is rarely any surprise and delight and frequently no clear evidence of specific customer experiences that genuinely differentiate the firm in the eyes of its customers relative to its competition.

The reality for many organisations is consumers can buy the same product or service from different businesses. Markets tend toward commoditisation over time. When there is no significant difference in quality or in how consumers access these products, commoditisation has well and truly set in. In many segments, organisations now face a lonely and desolate future in this barren wasteland of commoditisation. The price of their goods and services cannot be easily increased, yet costs are going up relentlessly. This is in large part because customers have shifted to a brand-agnostic mindset. With increasing frequency, customers simply ignore offers not fit for their purposes and are quick to switch when suppliers are not consistent and reliable. But fitness for purpose, consistency, and reliability are not remarkable. The only brands we talk about with our friends, families, and colleagues are the ones where a business or an individual within a business has gone above and beyond what everyone else would do and created a memory that is truly personal and unique. Hopefully this is a uniquely good experience because we are even more likely to share uniquely bad experiences.

This market reality drives organisations to invest in 'customer experience' to escape commoditisation. Often CX is a last resort to escape being disrupted, digitised, or commoditised. Leaders postulate how to wrap a highly differentiated and consistently delivered experience around a product or service. They hope customers will reward them with increased share of wallet or increased prices if their CX improves. They expect removing customer pain points will create a sustainable competitive advantage.

But to advance beyond postulation, leaders need to understand that pain point removal is simply not enough. Every organisation has specific experience attributes. When CX practitioners map the customer experience to understand differentiation within an organisation, they look at these elements and try to categorise them into either dissatisfiers (pain points that need to be removed) or experience creators (to be designed). Unfortunately, a disproportionate degree of early and immature focus in CX has been on current state experience mapping to identify pain points. More aspirational CX improvements are considered too expensive to design, develop, and deploy.

### Parity is Inadequate

When most CX programs only aim to deliver to the parity of the customer's expectations, there is no surprise and delight. There is no clear evidence of anything to genuinely differentiate the firm for customers relative to its competition. Instead, organisations need to build a CX program based on both differentiated and excellence attributes as depicted in Figure 1.1.[17] The parity line is where customers stop looking for reasons to reject the firm because it does not meet their requirements or is just one of many other firms able to do the job.

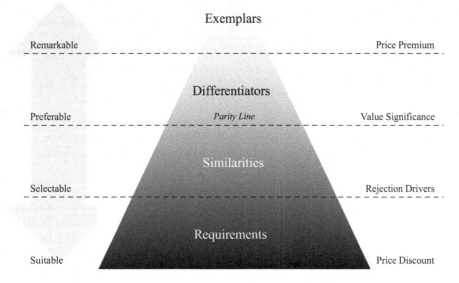

**Figure 1.1:** CX Spectrum.

> **F+ L+ Zappos walks a mile for the customers shoes**
> A customer's mother had recently had some medical treatment that left her feet numb and sensitive to pressure, rendering most of her shoes totally useless. She ordered her mother six pairs of shoes from Zappos, hoping that at least one of them would work. After receiving the shoes, her mother called Zappos to get instructions on how to return the shoes that did not work, explaining why she was returning so many shoes. Two days later, she received a large bouquet of flowers from Zappos, wishing her mother well and hoping that she recovered from her treatments soon. Two days later, the customer, her mother, and her sister were all upgraded to "Zappos VIP Members," which gives them all free expedited shipping on all orders.[18]

The focus on pain points or dissatisfier removal effectively guarantees a below-the-parity-line performance. Merely meeting customers' minimum expectations of what the product or service is expected to do is not enough. Firms failing to achieve *Requirements* level CX can only win customers by offering a price discounted below rivals who do meet their minimum needs. A focus on the basic CX elements an organisation shares with competitors will not lead to preference. Firms meeting *Similarities* level CX are only capable of avoiding rejection. A lack of differentiation forces customers to look for reasons to not choose that firm. Commonly this relates to price, availability, or awareness of complaints. Similarities do not encourage customers to want to share experience with others. Similarities do not create preferences or attract price premiums. They merely prevent the firm from being excluded from the customer's consideration set.

Everything below the parity line are customer expectations. Evolved customers recognise this as a ticket to the game, a hygiene factor, an existence requirement. There is nothing the customer did not expect to experience from what is necessary, and they have seen it offered by a competitor. The failure of many CX practitioners to dig themselves out of the mire of pain point removal and incremental improvement adds to CX fatigue, threatening future resource allocation. The alternative is excellence creation.

> **C+ Nike provides fast service for busy shoppers**
> Nike has long been known for its customer experience, but it is taking things to the next level at its new New York City flagship store. The Speed Shop allows customers to order shoes online and try them on in the store. Customers use a special entrance to find their shoe locker, which is unlocked via smartphone. After trying the shoes on, they can check out on their mobile phone without having to interact with a person.[19]

Above the parity line are the differentiated attributes setting an organisation apart. Ideally these underpin a premium price position because the firm is considered as the market *exemplar*. It is possible to be above the parity line without being an exemplar. Such firms are recognised for being different to their competitors. Customers who value this difference may pay a premium or simply preferentially select the *differentiated* firm provided they are not expensive. Without such differentiated attributes, organisations are compelled to compete on price.

Excellence attributes, consistently above the parity line experience, are seldom observed, much less experienced by the customers of most organisations. Excellence attributes are defined as attributes that are so unique that the competition cannot rival the offer. It is almost impossible to do this at the product/service level and that is why organisations invest in creating unique, differentiated, and memorable experiences. Author and consultant Lior Arussy argues that organisations regularly make the mistake of confusing excellence and consistency.[20]

Consistency is about removing dissatisfaction, meeting customer expectations. It is about hygiene factors like eliminating inaccurate invoices, ensuring uniform product quality, and standardising response timeframes. In a consistency-driven environment, optimised processes are emphasised and the role of employees are de-emphasised. Consistency is an uninteresting place to settle because customers do not celebrate consistent performance.

Excellence on the other hand, is about going above and beyond, surprising the customer, exceeding expectations. Excellence often requires human intervention to individualise and humanise the interaction, demonstrating and delivering authenticity. In excellence environments, processes are a tool, but employees focus more on their discretion to get the job done and exceed expectations.

*C+ L+ U+ Southwest Airlines provides comfort through the turbulence*
*When Garrick, a Southwest Airlines flight attendant, found himself in the position to help a passenger in need, he went above and beyond the call of duty.*

*Nine-year-old Gabby, a Type 1 diabetic, was severely anxious about being on an airplane. Garrick, a Southwest crew member, worked throughout the flight to make her more comfortable, bringing her special drinks and trying to make her laugh after he noticed her struggling during take-off.*

*When the plane hit a serious patch of turbulence, he let her sit in the empty seat next to him, talked to her about his daughter (the same age as Gabby), about her pets, her school, and even let her grab his arm for comfort.*

*At the end of the flight, Garrick used the PA to tell the whole plane that his friend Gabby had just overcome her fear of flying, and that she deserved a round of applause from the whole plane. "The whole plane clapped for her," her mother reported afterward, "It was a wonderful experience on Southwest. We are forever grateful to have met such a beautiful, selfless soul."[21]*

Fast Company co-founder William C. Taylor believes firms should "stop trying to be the best, strive to be the only." This aspiration encourages businesses to reconsider their automatic assumptions about processes and customers. This gives rise to core principles focused on striving to be the only ones doing what they're doing instead of competing in crowded fields. Customer do not expect us to be consistent at every touchpoint. They want us to focus on excellence in the moments that matter.[22]

Most CX practitioners certainly understand that today's battlefield of hypercompetition is about winning customer preference and loyalty by consistently delivering against a differentiated experience. Unless a customer thinks we are remarkable, we are not. The reality for many customers is that their experience has not changed and is less differentiated than ever. The corporate CX model is biased toward internal work programs, generating information, data, and systems to inform decision making. Activating and delivering utterly unique customer experiences relies on empowering the front line to go above and beyond the customers parity line and create memories, not just complete transactions.

Across the business landscape there is not a lot of evidence of 'wow' in most traditional corporate models and customer experiences. Customer experience is a sustainable competitive differentiator, but the focus is often on those features that can be replicated by competitors like price, stock availability, convenience, and self-service. By comparison, a business's history and interpersonal relationships between employees and customers cannot be easily replicated or reverse-engineered.[23]

It is by no means easy, but for CX investment to be sustainable, customers as well as executive sponsors need to see more 'wow' and less 'how.' The accountability sits with the CX team, not just to design it, but to ensure that the organisation delivers it.

## A Lack of CX Execution

There is a difference between activity and action. Strategy, research, insights, pain points, and transformational roadmaps are typically not problems for organisations with established CX programs – these staple CX ingredients are usually found in abundance. Instead, the sad reality has been these organisations invest in CX only to fall over at the execution stage. Characterised by a disproportionate focus on research and design instead of market testing, many CX programs are internally biased, not externally oriented. Investing in everything except execution exacerbates CX fatigue.

Achieving financial success with CX innovation relies on the ability to get quickly and directly through or past those obstacles that block or impede change. Cutting through to the heart of the problem is about being both agile and decisive. Cutting through requires both innovation and experimentation as a management mindset. MIT published a list in 2019 of the biggest megatrends that will impact the world by 2030.[24] The work was completed by a researcher having worked with clients including McDonald's, Apple, Bank of America, Walmart, HP, Disney, and Cisco. Among the common characteristics of the nine megatrends are two valuable observations directly relatable to implementing and activating CX. First, innovation is speeding up exponentially. Second, the will to execute known solutions for many of the megatrends is absent. The reasons for this are systemic.

Forrester surveyed CX professionals and chief marketing officers (CMOs) to better understand the challenges holding back CX leaders and how to overcome them.[25] Despite greater customer focus and increased CX budgets for the past two years, respondents reported significant challenges:

- *Lack of customer-centric cultures.* More than 50% of these professionals believed organisational culture impeded their success.
- *Counterproductive organisational structure and processes.* Around 45% cited organisational structure as a major challenge to success and 40% said the same about company processes.
- *Lagging technology capabilities.* More than 30% reported technology capabilities as a challenge. More than 60% attested to CX technology either hindering or having no impact on the competitiveness of their offerings.
- *Insufficient influence, support, and alignment with peers.* Almost 40% complained peer support and alignment were challenges.

Of these, peer support is perhaps the most insightful observation. While many executives have jumped on the CX bandwagon, many senior leaders have not come around. This reflects the fact CX has not delivered results in many organisations. In most companies, the success of a change initiative hinges not on knowing what to do but on developing the ability to do it.

Rigby, Sutherland and Takeuchi[26] argue agile innovation methods have revolutionised information technology over the past 25 to 30 years. They assert that taking people out of their functional silos and putting them in self-managed and customer-focused multidisciplinary teams using agile methodologies has accelerated profitable growth. They also believe this has helped to create a new generation of skilled general managers.

They ask how companies can achieve better results. Results such as positive returns on more than half of the new products they introduce; marketing programs prompting 40% greater customer enquiries; human resources programs succeeding in recruiting 60% more of their highest priority targets; and organising to have twice as many workers emotionally engaged in their jobs. Similar aspirations apply for CX.

McKinsey[27] argues that one of the most effective ways to boost momentum among middle managers is to spotlight those who are championing transformation. While the practice is referenced as a best-practice foundation for lean management behaviours (measured by change-oriented performance indicators and managers' evaluation metrics built into easy-to-read dashboards) the acceleration of an organisation's CX trajectory can be similarly enhanced, particularly when coupled with unleashing entrepreneurialism (in a guided way), so that the economic value gains accrue more broadly across the enterprise.

Rising CX stars are rare and exotic creatures in many corporate contexts primarily because of the absence of empowerment. Empowerment is one of those concepts that managers claim to provide but most employees fail to see eventuate. Employees are often encouraged but rarely empowered to consider "what's the right solution for the customer?" when performing day-to-day tasks. That is, employees are acutely aware of what they *can't do* (and what the consequences are) but rarely is there an accompanying list of things that the employee *can do* to go above and beyond the customers' expectations without fear of repercussion.

Whether it is a budgeted and delegated authority, an outcome of employee empowerment or a simple act of human kindness, systemising CX performance relies on creating memorable and valuable experiences for customers. They may include some of the following:[28]

- Inviting customers to test new features first
- Replacing a lost part at no cost
- Sending thoughtful gifts through the mail
- Personalising the experience for customers and the community
- Offering research that customers can trust
- Proactively creating conversations with customers
- Rewarding loyal customers with premium gifts
- Going the extra mile with detractors
- Improving the experience in unexpected ways
- "Speed dating" with customers to determines likes and dislikes
- Reducing customer support response time

While all these examples are helpful, it is the knock-on effect of a systematic implementation of these examples which is often invisible within corporate contexts. Companies ultimately judge transformations by whether they produce improvements in customer and business metrics.[29] Without actual customer outcomes there are no measurable 'results' and CX fatigue is not far away.

> **A+ C+ Money Management International (MMI)**
> Money Management International (MMI), a non-profit credit counselling agency, struggled to get more of the people who contacted its call centre to use its counselling services. To understand why so few calls led to follow-up sessions, MMI implemented a call analytics platform from Nice Systems. It learned that offering a wide range of service options all at once overwhelmed consumers, so consumers passed on them all. MMI coached call centre reps to consider the difficulty that customers face in selecting from a broad range of options and to focus instead on recommending a single best course of action. The change led to a 45% increase in first-time callers signing up for a session and a 56% decline in the number of customers who never received service.

Above-average returns on investment are non-linear by nature. Accordingly, they require game changing thinking and execution. But innovation is hard, it requires a lot of capital to build another thing that either 'we don't need' or 'may not work.' Leaders typically seek lowest variability in terms of potential returns driven by their inherent aversion to risk. Achieving a guaranteed return above the weighted cost of capital is desirable, but simultaneously dangerous. Avoiding this danger is built in to corporate DNA. It is a large part of the reason for a lack of CX execution.

## Competing Values and CX

The Competing Values Framework (CVF) defines a classification of four corporate cultures, and provides powerful leadership and cultural change insights[30] (see Figure 1.2). It outlines how a company may operate, how employees may collaborate, and what the corporate values are; and explains how these may come into conflict inside organisations. The four classifications are Clan, Hierarchical, Market, and Adhocracy.

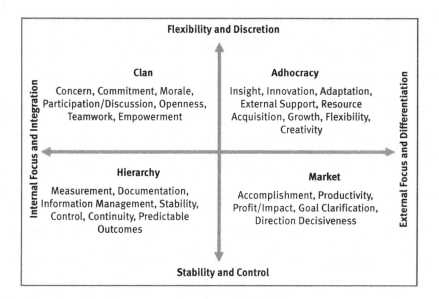

**Figure 1.2:** Competing Values Framework.

*Clan* characteristics stem from an underlying belief that people are an organisation's greatest asset. Other stakeholders including shareholders and customers are secondary. These firms tend to be dominated by the HR Function and are defined by the following attributes:
- High degree of flexibility and internally focused
- Centrality of friendly relationships between people
- Great value placed on teamwork, participation, flexibility, and consensus
- Leaders are easily approachable mentors or even mother/father figures.
- Held together by loyalty, tradition, and mutual commitment
- Strong loyalty and morality
- Customer satisfaction is a basis of success

*Hierarchical* firms prioritise the efficiency of the organisation above all else, stakeholders (employees, shareholders, and customers) are secondary. These firms tend to be dominated by the Operations function. This includes the associated reporting functions like Accounting and Quality Assurance and have the following traits:
- Internally focused with a high degree of controlling behaviour
- Extremely formal, structured working environment
- Procedures determine employee actions with focus on managing control systems
- Clearly structured hierarchical layers are present
- Work processes are efficiently organised
- Formal rules and policies stabilise the organisation
- Reliable supply, tight scheduling, and low costs are the basis of success

*Market* culture organisations operate from the theory of the firm. Shareholders are given paramount consideration over employees and customers. Corporate Governance provides an overarching direction. These firms tend to be dominated by the Finance function and are defined by the following features:
- Externally focused with a high degree of controlling behaviour
- All about results and the completion of work
- Competitive and goal-oriented employees
- Employee activities closely followed by managers
- Emphasis is on reputation, success, and winning to stay ahead of the competition

*Adhocracy* cultures assume that the most successful firms are the ones best able to customise their offerings for customers. Other stakeholders (employees and shareholders) are secondary. These firms tend to be dominated by the Marketing function or Innovation divisions in R&D focused firms and are defined by the following tendencies:
- Externally focused with a high degree of flexibility
- Innovation is key
- Dynamic, enterprising, and creative work environment
- Employees encouraged to strive for innovation and use creativity to create new ideas
- Encourage individual initiative and allow the freedom to determine what tasks to execute

Classifications in the CVF come down to two trade-offs: control/flexibility priority and external/internal orientation. Our experience is that firms failing to transform to customer centricity are characterised by a control priority, internal orientation, or both. These organisations typically suffer from adhocracy deficit where innovation is not part of their core operating model. These workplaces lack the sorts of dynamism, entrepreneurship, and creativity that represent the foundations of a customer-centric culture. Not surprisingly, this creates a major impediment to CX execution. Without an element of adhocracy, CX transition is much more likely to end in mediocrity than magnificence.

For Clan, Hierarchical, and Market culture types to develop and sustain a customer-centric focus, their challenge is to build a workforce that welcomes change, and an environment in which leaders stop building systems for risk defence and instead promote dynamic product, service, and experience development. The result is an urgency to set trends, not follow them.

Consider a clinical healthcare company where most staff believe they know what is best for the patient. How can this organisation hope to deliver great experiences until these beliefs are challenged? A mindset that focuses on helping patients achieve their best outcomes and considers their chosen provider would go further toward improving the experience.[31] The dominant mindset is centred on task instead of experience. This often leads to patients developing lasting memories (and sometimes stories for friends and families) about clumsy, uncoordinated teamwork amongst clinical and care personnel. An all too frequent characteristic of a hospitalisation stay occurs when different clinical and care staff repeatedly ask the patient the same question throughout the course of treatment. Team members who are biased (through their education and training) to treat their patient with condescension can increase anxiety and suffering.

Similarly, imagine a prestige hotel brand where employees do not understand the expectations of high-end customers and, even worse, resent their customers (some of whom are wealthy, arrogant, and demanding). There are no journey maps that will underpin excellent experience delivery until these employee belief systems are addressed and reshaped and accordingly. Unless these are addressed, any investment in CX will never deliver the maximum return and economic value.

Inherent in this pursuit of cut-through is the capture of value. Taylor proposed, "Nobody wins unless everybody wins, create more value than you capture.[32]" The distribution of benefits cannot be one sided for CX cut-through to occur. The firm, the customer, and the employees all need to share in the upside for CX transformation to be realised in a sustainable way. Taylor argues, "The organisations that inspire the deepest sense of commitment are the ones whose members receive a fair share of the value they help to create." If your organisation finds itself struggling to execute CX improvements for results, it is time for Lean CX.

# Endnotes

**1** Stern (2016). "The Challenges Holding Back CX Leaders and How to Overcome Them Results from Our Survey of More Than 250 CX Executives and CMOs," Forrester Research Inc.
**2** Forrester (2019). "Predictions 2020," Forrester Research Inc. https://go.forrester.com/press-news room/forrester-releases-2019-predictions/#:~:text=CX%20performance%20was%20flat%20and, methods%20for%20short%2Dterm%20gains, accessed 25 July 2020.
**3** Forrester (2019). "Predictions 2020," Forrester Research Inc. https://go.forrester.com/press-news room/forrester-releases-2019-predictions/#:~:text=CX%20performance%20was%20flat%20and, methods%20for%20short%2Dterm%20gains, accessed 25 July 2020.

**4** Miller and Hartwick (2002). "Spotting Management Fads," *Harvard Business Review*. https://hbr. org/2002/10/spotting-management-fads, accessed 25 July 2020.

**5** Kellaway (2013). "Where others failed: Top 10 fads," *Financial Times*. https://www.ft.com/con tent/3c7f1e40-a03e-11e2-88b6-00144feabdc0, accessed 25 July 2020.

**6** James (2019). "17 Management Fads Almost as Dumb as the Open-Plan Office," *Inc*. https://www. inc.com/geoffrey-james/17-management-fads-almost-as-dumb-as-open-plan-office.html, accessed 25 July 2020.

**7** Wikipedia (2020). "Theory Z." https://en.wikipedia.org/wiki/Theory_Z, accessed 25 July 2020.

**8** Kulbytė (2020). "37 Customer Experience Statistics You Need to Know for 2020," *SuperOffice*. https://www.superoffice.com/blog/customer-experience-statistics/, accessed 25 July 2020.

**9** "Making Customer-Centric Strategies Take Hold," *Harvard Business Review*, 2015.

**10** Taylor (2016). *Simply Brilliant: How Great Organizations Do Ordinary Things in Extraordinary Ways*, Portfolio Publishing.

**11** Arussy (2010). *Customer Experience Strategy – The Complete Guide from Innovation to Execution*, Strativity Group Media Company.

**12** Carr (2015). "Customer Experience Metrics," Lori Carr & Associates. http://loricarrassociates. com/Customer_Experience_Metrics.pdf, accessed 25 July 2020.

**13** Conradt (2015). "11 of the Best Customer Service Stories Ever," *Mental Floss*. https://www.mental floss.com/article/30198/11-best-customer-service-stories-ever, accessed 25 July 2020.

**14** Arussy (2010). *Customer Experience Strategy – The Complete Guide from Innovation to Execution*, Strativity Group Media Company.

**15** McKinsey and Company (2019). "What matters in customer-experience transformations." https:// www.mckinsey.com/business-functions/marketing-and-sales/our-insights/what-matters-in-cus tomer-experience-cx-transformations, accessed 25 July 2020.

**16** McKinsey and Company (2016). "Linking the customer experience to value." https://www. mckinsey.com/business-functions/marketing-and-sales/our-insights/linking-the-customer-experi ence-to-value#, accessed 25 July 2020.

**17** Arussy 2014 'Principles of Customer Experience Chapter 4', Strativity Group (internal document, not published).

**18** Ibid., footnote 29.

**19** Morgan (2019). "20 Fresh Examples of Customer Experience Innovation," *Forbes*. https://www. forbes.com/sites/blakemorgan/2019/10/21/20-fresh-examples-of-customer-experience-innovation/ #3f108c9b7c41, accessed 25 July 2020.

**20** Arussy (2017). *Creating Amazing Customer Experience – Excellence or Consistency*, Strativity Group Media Company.

**21** Ciotti (2020). "These 13 Stories of Remarkable Customer Service Will Put a Smile on Your Face," *Help Scout*. https://www.helpscout.com/blog/remarkable-customer-service/, accessed 25 July 2020.

**22** Taylor (2016). *Simply Brilliant: How Great Organizations Do Ordinary Things in Extraordinary Ways*, Portfolio Publishing.

**23** Springman (2020). "The Myths Putting the Future of Customer Experience in Peril," *MYcustomer*. https://www.mycustomer.com/customer-experience/engagement/the-myths-putting-the-future-of-cus tomer-experience-in-peril, accessed 25 July 2020.

**24** Winston (2019). "The World in 2030: Nine Megatrends to Watch," *MIT Sloan Management Review*. https://sloanreview.mit.edu/article/the-world-in-2030-nine-megatrends-to-watch/?gclid= CjOKCQjwjer4BRCZARIsABK4QeWT1FgrauZOMFtayMkazd6Zc65Dk46cWhWiFZV356VbfPQnvUDrm2 YaAuxoEALw_wcB, accessed 25 July 2020.

**25** Stern (2016). "The Challenges Holding Back CX Leaders and How to Overcome Them Results from Our Survey of More Than 250 CX Executives and CMOs," *Forrester Research Inc*. https://www.

forrester.com/report/The+Challenges+Holding+Back+CX+Leaders+And+How+To+Overcome +Them/-/E-RES119915, accessed 25 July 2020.

**26** Rigby, Sutherland, and Takeuchi (2016). "Embracing agile," *Harvard Business Review*. https:// hbr.org/2016/05/embracing-agile, accessed 25 July 2020.

**27** Various authors (2014). "The Lean Management Enterprise: A system for daily progress, meaningful purpose, and lasting value," *McKinsey and Company*. https://www.mckinsey.com/business-functions/operations/our-insights/the-lean-management-enterprise-a-system-for-daily-progress-meaningful-purpose-and-lasting-value, accessed 25 July 2020.

**28** Keck (2018). "11 Examples of Exceptional Customer Service from Companies That Walk the Walk," *Promoter*. https://www.promoter.io/blog/great-customer-service/, accessed 25 July 2020.

**29** Stern et al. (2017). "Leading Indicators of An Effective Culture Transformation," Forrester Research Inc. https://www.forrester.com/report/Leading+Indicators+Of+An+Effective+Culture +Transformation/-/E-RES115512, accessed 25 July 2020.

**30** Cameron and Quinn (2005). *Diagnosing and Changing Organizational Culture: Based on the Competing Values Framework*. John Wiley & Sons.

**31** Dempsey (2017). *The Antidote to Suffering – How Compassionate Connected Care Can Improve Safety, Quality and Experience*, McGraw-Hill Education.

**32** Taylor (2016). *Simply Brilliant: How Great Organizations Do Ordinary Things in Extraordinary Ways*, Portfolio Publishing.

# Chapter 2
# Defining Lean CX

*Lean CX* is the application of agile management techniques to the problem of improving customer experience for cut-through. At a minimum, Lean CX improves a company's current go-to-market approach. At its best, Lean CX simultaneously explores new adjacent opportunities. This is a new use of agile management because lean approaches were not originally developed for this purpose.

## Lean Management Reduces Waste

Lean management is the evolution of the Toyota Production System (TPS) developed in the 1970s to reduce waste.[1] In combination with Six Sigma (management to eliminate defects) and Kanban (management to drive execution), lean approaches have been so successful that they have spread to other fields. In lean's original application, Toyota's Chief Engineer, Taiichi Ohno, identified seven sources of waste. There are now eight. The 'unused talent' waste was introduced by other lean practitioners later on (see Figure 2.1).[2]

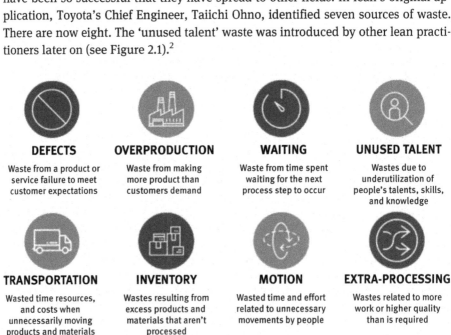

**DEFECTS**
Waste from a product or service failure to meet customer expectations

**OVERPRODUCTION**
Waste from making more product than customers demand

**WAITING**
Waste from time spent waiting for the next process step to occur

**UNUSED TALENT**
Wastes due to underutilization of people's talents, skills, and knowledge

**TRANSPORTATION**
Wasted time resources, and costs when unnecessarily moving products and materials

**INVENTORY**
Wastes resulting from excess products and materials that aren't processed

**MOTION**
Wasted time and effort related to unnecessary movements by people

**EXTRA-PROCESSING**
Wastes related to more work or higher quality than is required

**Figure 2.1:** Sources of Waste.

The waste categories above apply explicitly to production within a firm. Lean CX expands beyond production to consider the waste occurring for customers at

https://doi.org/10.1515/9783110683929-002

touchpoints. Customers are directly concerned with waste relating to defects, waiting, transportation, and motion. The other wastes identified in the TPS are an indirect concern for customers when they translate into higher prices. In the short term, customers may perceive these other wastes as benefits. For example, overproduction and inventory can lead to discounting. Bad for the firm but good for customers. Extra-processing can result in getting higher quality goods than expected – again bad for the firm but beneficial for customers.

The concept of the key wastes relevant to CX is explored by David McLachlan.[3] However, his view of lean management as it applies to customer experience seems incomplete because it is focused on wastes only on the customer side. Some substantial wastes remain on the company side, especially when innovating to improve CX is considered. The most common example of this is when firms try to introduce new products.

## New Product Failure is Wasteful

Joan Schneider and Julie Hall highlighted the difficulties introducing new products:

> According to a leading market research firm, about 75% of consumer packaged goods and retail products fail to earn even $7.5 million during their first year. This is in part because of the intransigence of consumer shopping habits. The consultant Jack Trout has found that American families, on average, repeatedly buy the same 150 items, which constitute as much as 85% of their household needs – it's hard to get something new on the radar. Even Procter & Gamble routinely whiffs with product rollouts. Less than 3% of new consumer packaged goods exceed first-year sales of $50 million – considered the benchmark of a highly successful launch. Products that start out strong may have trouble sustaining success. We looked at more than 70 top products in the Most Memorable New Product Launch survey (which we help conduct) for the years 2002 through 2008. A dozen of them are already off the market.[4]

Noted innovation management researcher Clayton Christensen has been quoted as suggesting 95% of new products fail.[5]

Schneider and Hall are essentially describing the problem of achieving cutthrough in a crowded market. It's about getting customers to churn from their existing preferred product solution to the innovation. New products must be innovative enough to attract customers' attention and consideration, but not so innovative as to be perceived as risky. This is the concept of MAYA (Most Advanced Yet Acceptable) first proposed by Raymond Loewy.[6] In contrast Clay Christensen defines this cutthrough problem differently. He suggests the root cause is not understanding the job the customer buys the product to do. He describes a customer buying a milkshake not to solve a thirst or a hunger problem, but to cheaply solve the problem of a boring commute to work. Christensen is describing the problem of cut-through from inside the customer's head. Car makers struggle to achieve cut-through every time they introduce a new model.

Nissan has sold around 100,000 of their Juke model in Europe each year since 2011, but sales have always been poor in Australia. Registrations in 2019 were down more than 25% in Australia, with only 266 Jukes sold through to November that year. Something about the Juke just doesn't work for Australian customers. In contrast 10,345 Mitsubishi ASX cars were sold in Australia during the same period. Interestingly, Nissan has suddenly experienced a similar issue in the US, with only 731 Jukes sold in 2018, compared to between 20,000 and 30,000 per year between 2011 and 2016. It seems the Juke used to suit US buyers and suddenly it has become obsolete. When a big company produces a product the market doesn't warm to, it is similar to a start-up.

### Waste in Start-ups

Eric Ries described how to solve the cut-through problem for start-ups with lean approaches.[7] The start-up search problem is clearly an exploration problem. In contrast, Toyota set out to solve an exploitation problem: cutting costs and improving quality to earn more from making cars. Unlike a start-up, Toyota already had found its profitable sustainable marketing and simply wanted to mine profit from it more efficiently. It didn't need to systematise the start-up's search for market traction. Taiichi Ohno probably didn't countenance the idea Toyota would ever try to sell a product the market didn't want and hence this waste was not identified. However, we commonly see companies producing products and services the market is less than enthusiastic about. Ries' most valuable contribution was in repurposing lean from exploitation to exploration.

Ries asserts that the greatest waste in a start-up is offering a product or service the market doesn't want to buy. At the time of this writing, statistics from the Ewing Marion Kauffman Foundation suggest around 20% of US start-ups in 2018 did not make it to their second year.[8] However data from the latest Global Entrepreneurship Monitor (2018) suggests lower annual mortality rates varying by country (see Figure 2.2). GEM respondents reported only 1%–5% discontinuation rates across Europe and the US.

GEM numbers may be understated. Eurostat 2017 data[9] suggests the survival rate of European start-ups founded in 2014 was around 58% and for those founded in 2012 survival chances were around 44%. This suggests that in Europe more than half of all start-ups don't survive to year five. This would correspond to a 15% per year failure rate (much higher than European GEM data, but lower than comparable US numbers produced by the Kaufmann Foundation). Perhaps the discrepancies are due to sampling differences – Kauffman Foundation is based on US companies, Eurostat is based on European companies, and GEM is based on entrepreneur surveys and not company data. Despite the differences in the data, it seems Ries did hit a nerve with his characterisation of waste in start-ups being mostly related to product-market fit. The rate of start-up failure seems close to new product

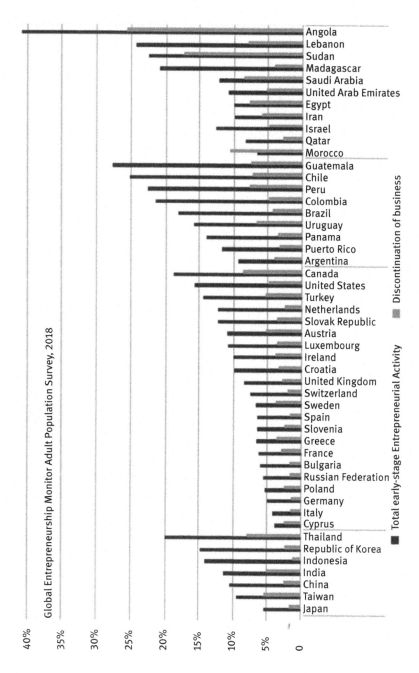

Global Entrepreneurship Monitor Adult Population Survey, 2018

**Figure 2.2:** Early Stage Entrepreneurial Activity and Discontinuation Rates.

failure rates. This suggests that the waste Ries identified for start-ups also exists in the corporate innovation space.[10]

## Confusing Cost Reduction with CX Improvement

Part of the problem with innovation in traditional corporates is a priority focus on cost reduction before innovating to add value. Consider the case adapted from a 2018 report on the banking sector by EY:

> *C- A- P- L- Banks duplicate identical digital deployments*[11]
> *An EY survey of 221 major financial institutions across 29 markets (including Europe, North America, BRIC countries, developed APAC countries, and the Middle East) showed 85% prioritis-ing a digital transformation program in 2018. The respondents accounted for at least 50% of the total balance sheet assets in each market. The majority of banks expected their revenues and profitability to improve over the next 12 months to 3 years, despite rising costs. EY asserted suc-cess required switching from regulatory-driven transformation to innovation-led change and achieving 'digital maturity' (see Figure 2.3).*
>
> *EY's version of digital maturity apparently means investing in 'a more digitally enabled exter-nal ecosystem' and 'more efficient infrastructure' instead of 'tactical projects' and 'front-end customer interfaces.' Internally, the banks frame mobile and online banking as fast, all hours, easy, consistent, everywhere, and safe for customers (the bank version of FAECES). Most of the time they are right, until their systems fail. Then the lack of human help to hand is negative mo-ment of truth (C- A- P- L- for customers).*
>
> *Digital maturity sounds and looks good when presented externally by a credible consulting global consulting firm like EY. A different reality emerges when you discuss with executives in-side these companies what they intend to do to achieve 'digital maturity.' Their primary focus in digital is in automating their business to further reduce staff costs (C+ A+ for the bank). In Asia, ING is an online-only bank, considered the industry exemplar for avoiding the costs of a branch network. But cutting staff costs is not the only reason to upgrade bank systems. Bank execs we talked with also explained how a digital platform can automate marketing messages to try and drive more enquiry (U- for customers). They also were focused on how to use the mountain of big data on customer transactions to extract more value. One bank for example was using learn-ing algorithms (a version of AI) to evaluate around 400 different customer transaction behav-iours. They claimed to be 60% accurate in predicting churn 90 days before the customer took real steps to switch their mortgage. This allowed the bank to try and intervene to dissuade the customer from leaving. Other banks were analysing tenure rates to maximise the value of differ-ential pricing between current customers and new customers. Banks offer deals all the time available only to new customers. Eventually this prompts some current customers to switch, so finding the most profitable exploitation pricing is critical. This relies on being able to use the data tangled up inside the bank's digital platform. Both the churn intervention and differential pricing are about exploiting customers to extract as much value out of them as possible (C- for customers, A+ for the bank in the short term).*

This case shows how the inside perception of digital maturity is more profit from less staff, more effective spam, and more complex data analysis to extract more out

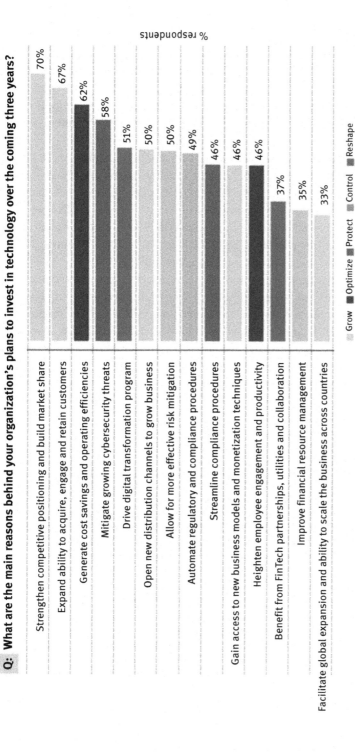

**Q:** What are the main reasons behind your organization's plans to invest in technology over the coming three years?

% respondents

Strengthen competitive positioning and build market share — 70%
Expand ability to acquire, engage and retain customers — 67%
Generate cost savings and operating efficiencies — 62%
Mitigate growing cybersecurity threats — 58%
Drive digital transformation program — 51%
Open new distribution channels to grow business — 50%
Allow for more effective risk mitigation — 50%
Automate regulatory and compliance procedures — 49%
Streamline compliance procedures — 46%
Gain access to new business models and monetization techniques — 46%
Heighten employee engagement and productivity — 46%
Benefit from FinTech partnerships, utilities and collaboration — 37%
Improve financial resource management — 35%
Facilitate global expansion and ability to scale the business across countries — 33%

Grow · Optimize · Protect · Control · Reshape

**Figure 2.3:** Digital Maturity Drivers.

of customers via pricing strategies. This is hardly customer-centric. And since every bank is doing the pretty much the same thing, none will get a differentiation. This suggests that pursuing digital maturity as a growth strategy is at best idealistic. At worst it is a strategic error. Digital platforms can deliver cost reductions, but it would be surprising if they directly delivered real market share growth for financial institutions. It is also hard to see how digital maturity is actually innovation. It seems more like incremental improvement leading to a race to the bottom.

Some firms have built CX-based advantages through digital innovation. In the US, Charles Schwab was able to grow its online share trading business as a cost-effective and fast alternative to stockbroker trades. It was most appropriate for the segment of the market wanting to advise themselves on stock trading. Commsec similarly enjoys a leading market share for online trading in Australia. In Europe, a quick online search uncovered 22 online brokers relevant to someone living in the UK (7 UK firms, 6 based in the US, and the others in various other European countries).[12]

For companies trying to create more value rather than just cutting costs, the challenge is getting the innovation approach to the right level. Corporate management has traditionally taken a first order thinking approach to the new product cut-through problem. First characterised by Theodore Levitt as 'Marketing Myopia,'[13] organisations are most attracted to exploitation. This causes them to define the scope of their market opportunity too narrowly. Marketing myopia limits solutions, products, and CX improvements to Fast, Assured, Easy, Close, Efficient and Simple options.[14] The older the firm the more likely it is to struggle to create new value and the closer it gets to obsolescence.

*P+ For sale: the oldest winery in France*
*Chateau de Goulaine is a vineyard established around 1000 AD in the Loire Valley in France. It is possibly the oldest operating winery-chateau in the world. It is also one of the 10 oldest companies in the world (the majority of top ten oldest are Japanese).[15] Today Marquis de Goulaine Muscadet wine retails online for around $AUS 20 per bottle. The Muscadet grape is a cross between Pinot and the nearly extinct grape called Gouais Blanc. It is believed the grape came from the east and was perhaps imported to the Loire/Nantes area from the Kingdom of Burgundy when it was part of the Holy Roman Empire (starting around 1000 AD).*

*In 1997, the winery innovated beyond the Muscadet, Sancerre, and Vouvray wines it had been known for to produce a Chardonnay.[16] Not much of a first for the world of wine, but still a first for producers in the Loire Valley. At the time, the owner was hoping to expand wine production from about 30,000 cases a year to 40,000. Even before 2000, the estate was not profitable and received funding from the French government as a historic monument. Back then upkeep was covered by charging the 25,000 visitors per year to see the estate. Today this has expanded to include a biscuit museum and a hire venue for weddings. It seems this is all at risk now with the estate up for sale. Incremental innovation may not have been enough to sustain this beautiful historic icon beyond 1020 years.*

Managers with an incremental innovation mindset believe innovation is limited to asking customers what they want and them giving it to them. This is *first order* thinking. The problem with first order thinking is it is only superior to no thinking at all. If all the market players are using first order thinking then there is no advantage to applying it. To put it another way, it is like a solution to the problem of choosing the fastest line to join with multiple options available. This is a common problem at restaurants, theme parks, and airports. If anyone worked out a way to reliably identify which queue was the fastest-moving to join, soon everyone would know the solution and then there would never be a fastest queue remaining to join! This realisation comes from applying *second order* thinking. In this case, the approach is simply an example of systems thinking.[17] Applying second order thinking to the problem of finding out what customers want involves solving design problems using lateral thinking instead of thinking linearly.

*C+ Improving train CX in Europe and Australia*
*In his 2009 TED Talk, Rory Sutherland described how the engineering solution to improving the Eurostar journey was to spend £6B to reduce 40 minutes from a 3½ hour duration journey. Despite admitting the investment in new track is a perfectly adequate solution, Sutherland asserted the improvement is suboptimal from a CX perspective. Instead he suggested having supermodels walk the length of the train serving complimentary fine wines for the whole journey. He estimated this would save £3B and prompt passengers to ask for the trains to be slowed down! Sutherland's thought experiment highlights the limited mindset of the engineering designers tasked with coming up with a better train journey.*

*We found a similar engineering mindset working with an urban rail operator in Australia. Charged with the problem of improving CX for city commuters, the firm was initially limited to considerations around how to upgrade rolling stock and platforms to improve service frequency. As the operator was incentivised to run trains to their termination stations on time, they would occasionally skip stopping at stations if running behind on a service. This occurred without warning the passengers on board. This would anger the affected passengers who would have to exit at the next stop and take another train back to their intended arrival station, often arriving late to work. Focusing on meeting the timetable for most customers disproportionately annoyed other customers.*

*The operators believed they could run on time more efficiently if they had the capability to use all trains on all lines. When they took over the train services, they inherited three different types of trainsets. Some trains couldn't run on some parts of the network due to varying platform heights and/or visibility issues. The main problem with upgrading platforms and rolling stock was the cost. Beyond the timetable issue was the problem of crush loading on some morning commuter services. Commuters would frequently experience travelling with more than 1000 people on a train designed to carry only around 700.*

*We proposed some CX innovations for the operator to reduce these pain points. To reduce the crush loading we suggested supplying commuters with a simple Wi-Fi device designed to help with a choice to avoid crush loaded services. This device would be something like an active refrigerator magnet. Commuters would choose the time they intended to travel and in return would get an estimate of the congestion on their service. It was hoped that this information would prompt travellers with flex in their schedules to travel earlier or later and reduce the crush loading.*

A second innovation was based on the idea of offering different fare classes (common in Europe). All of our client's train services offered four cars with the same general use design. A business class car could help fund rolling stock upgrades. Unfortunately, policy constraints enforced by the public transport agency meant differential fare pricing was not allowed. Instead we proposed to split services into different types of cars – a priority standing room car for commuters in a hurry that would stop closest to the exits and have its doors opened before the other cars. A quiet car for commuters who wanted to read, and a noisy car for commuters who wanted to socialise during their journey (like school children). The costs for these changes were comparatively low – decals to identify general/priority/quiet/noisy cars, mobile phone inhibiting paint on the quiet car, and a Wi-Fi modem for radio station access on the noisy car. They also provided a way for commuters to somewhat customise their travel experience within the same ticket price.

Ultimately the operator did present innovations to the public transport agency as part of a successful bid to extend their management contract. Disappointingly the different car idea was rejected due to safety concerns related to different door opening times for the priority cars. The Wi-Fi device has never been implemented and crush loading remains an issue most weekday mornings. The operator has at least reduced their station skipping policy however.

Henry Ford was famously renowned for saying if he had asked what customers wanted they would have said "faster horses."[18] Even if Ford didn't say this, the idea customers don't know all of what they want seems true when a new product or service achieves substantial market penetration. In most cases, this new product or service involves some 'method step of inventiveness,' or 'eureka moment,' or 'customer insight' the market had previously missed, ignored, or overlooked. So prevalent is the idea of innovations as unprecedented things that managers describe these phenomena as *disruptive*. It is only disruptive for incumbents who prefer to increment. For entrepreneurs innovation/disruption is axiomatically the path to business success. Lee Iacocca was considered a standout because of his entrepreneurial approach to finding new value by intuiting customer needs.

**P+ C+ L+ Iacocca re-segments the car market, twice**
Lee Iacocca took the reins as vice president and general manager of Ford in 1960. In 1964, he brought out the Mustang, a car designed to appeal to buyers who had dreamed of owning a sports car, but had never been able to afford one. At the time, America was enthralled in the possibility of space travel. Astronauts owned Mustangs, and so many men who dreamed of having 'the right stuff' were suddenly able to validate their status claim by buying the same car. The Mustang earned Ford record profits of more than $US 1.1 billion in just two years.[19]

At its core, this innovation seems like a product innovation. However it can also be seen as a segmentation innovation. Prior to the Mustang, car makers segmented their markets using demographics. They built cars for income level, family size, and targeted based on the suburbs where customers lived. Iacocca pivoted from this approach and segmented based on the lifestyle aspirations of buyers across the US. Mustangs were about prestige (P+). In the 1980s Iacocca moved to head up Chrysler after being fired from Ford. He repeated a similar approach to market re-segmentation.

After campaigning for a controversial $1.5 billion loan guarantee from the US government, Chrysler brought out efficient, reliable, front wheel drive cars – including subcompacts like the

*Dodge Omni and Plymouth Horizon, and later minivans like the Dodge Caravan and Plymouth Voyager. The Dodge Caravan was so popular it would remain the best-selling minivan in the US from 1983 (when it started the segment) to 2008 (when the Honda Odyssey outsold it 135,493 cars to 123,749 cars). Chrysler's $1.7 billion loss in 1980 rebounded into a $2.4 billion profit in 1984. Experts called it one of the most brilliant turnarounds in business history. The government-backed loans were repaid in four years, seven years early.*

*A key contributor to the Chrysler's success was re-segmentation. During the start of the 1980s the US economy was in recession. The new Chrysler subcompacts appealed to buyers wanting a smaller, cheaper car and wanting to buy American. At the time, Japanese car makers were gaining market share in the US. Iacocca became the TV face of Chrysler for a decade. Building on a theme of 'the pride is back,' Iacocca challenged Americans in the ads: 'If you can find a better car, buy it. I'm not asking you to buy any car on faith. I want you to compare.' Appealing to cost-conscious buyers and patriotic buyers allowed Chrysler to re-segment the market and target on these two key attitudes. These cheap, reliable new models were about certainty (C+) and national belonging (L+).*

Leaders like Iacocca are often presented as strategic geniuses. The Ford and Chrysler examples above are not remarkable because the market strategy involved was particularly brilliant, even though the subsequent success was significant. From a CX perspective, Iacocca's innovations seem obvious in hindsight. The key issue at Ford and Chrysler was the difficulty in redeploying resources away from business as usual into targeting new segments. It might only take 30 hours of labour to build a car after its 30,000 components are sourced, but getting to there can take years. Production lines in car manufacturing are typically set up around five years in advance for around $US 1 billion.[20] This makes it a vastly different proposition for a large car maker to pivot with a new car model compared to a start-up pivoting their launch offering. It may be the case that Iacocca was simply a brilliant change agent.

Faced with a choice of getting better at business as usual (exploitation), or learning how to succeed in an uncertain new market niche with an untried new product and/or unprecedented new business model, most firms choose to invest in an incrementally better version of business as usual. Perhaps one of the reasons opportunities exist for start-ups is because established firms are reticent to innovate more extensively.

In contrast to Ford and Chrysler, Tesla was designed from start-up to make electric cars and did not have to go through the problem of reorganising to pivot to a new product. Tesla also started out with shareholders with a different appetite for risk than the shareholders of Ford and Chrysler. Time and again companies like Tesla can enter mature markets and succeed. Without the baggage of a petrol engine legacy, sunk costs in established production lines, long term OEM channel partners, and a risk averse Board, Tesla was free to take on the challenge of electric vehicles.

The problem with this analysis is it ignores the inherent advantages of the incumbents. All large automakers theoretically could have pivoted into electric cars. Many had brand credibility, production assets, organisation capability, financial reserves, skilled people, and access to technology which could have been repurposed into targeting the electric segment. In some ways it would have been more cost effective and less risky for them to do so than it was for Tesla. The cost and risk of setting up Tesla from scratch were epic. In fact, history has shown established carmakers had tried electrics several times before.

> **C+ P+ F+ Tesla is the fourth try for US electric cars**
>
> Tesla was founded in July 2003 and received early funding from investors including Elon Musk. Musk envisioned Tesla Motors as an independent automaker, aimed at offering electric cars at prices affordable to the average consumer. In 2018, Tesla sold 245,240 cars. It was the number one manufacturer of plug-in electric vehicles with 12% share of the segment. US sales grew 280% from 48,000 in 2017 to 182,400 in 2018.[21] Just like Ford and Chrysler previously, Tesla has re-segmented the car market around attitudes by cashing in on consumer concerns over carbon emissions and climate change. Tesla also focused on demographics. The company's long-term strategy is to reduce prices to appeal to less affluent buyers over time. Tesla offers its customers fulfilment (F+) and status (P+) because its cars are perceived as environmentally better and they offer remarkable acceleration. However, previous versions of electric cars met quite different buyer needs.
>
> Electric cars have been tried several times by the US auto industry.[22] The first attempts at electric cars were in 1828–1835 as a replacement to horses and buggies. Between 1900 and 1912 the vehicles gained around one-third market share in the US. These cars were easy to drive, quiet, and didn't smell, offering a level of certainty (C+), particularly to women. The Model T Ford, electric starters, and cheap Texas oil meant the electrics were gone by 1935. They were reconsidered because of soaring petrol prices in 1973. Companies including General Motors (GM) began to experiment again with electric prototypes. Sebring-Vanguard sold more than 4400 electric CitiCars between 1974 and 1977 (it was the sixth largest US automaker in 1975). In 1996 GM brought out the EV1 in response to anti-pollution regulations, and in 1997 Toyota began to sell the mass-produced hybrid Prius. Electric cars in the late 1990s offered protection against rising fuel prices (C+) and a way to respond to air pollution fears (C+). By the time Tesla was selling cars in 2006, a segment of the market had moved beyond the fear of air pollution to certainty around the risks of man-made climate change. Buying an electric car was associated with an elitism (P+) around doing something important for future generations (F+).
>
> This history of the electric car industry shows how the US market has explored the possibility of electric cars multiple times. Even as individual carmakers struggled to pivot, preferring to exploit existing market niches, the market as a whole has continued to explore new opportunities just like many other markets in a wide range of industries.

## To Innovate or Increment?

Christensen's so-called 'Innovator's Dilemma' describes why traditionally well run companies tend to invest in incremental improvements over more innovative and market disrupting options. The Innovator's Dilemma is the problem of choosing between exploration (finding, creating, and sharing in new value) or exploitation (squeezing more value out of existing offerings). After factoring in the risk associated with achieving innovation success, most firms rationally decide to pass on disruptive initiatives. Incremental improvements are quicker to execute, easier to quantify, better understood, less effort to develop, less strange, less expensive, and less complex when compared to disruptive innovations. The problem is incremental improvement always fails in the long term. Incremental improvement is not a sustainable strategy.

Christensen's research was insightful because he was not highlighting poor innovation management. Christensen suggested the investment decisions managers were making made rational sense given a tactical orientation. In other words, incremental improvement looked like a lot safer bet than more significant innovation. This is the essence of the change problem lean CX overcomes.

Inside most large firms, pivoting away from a proven market opportunity and business model appears to be a suboptimal strategy. Continued exploitation seems to be lower cost and lower risk. But outside the company, the optimal strategy for a new entrant is exploring to find a new basis of competition. New entrants who succeed in finding this new basis of competition disrupt incumbents. They simultaneously devalue incumbents' differential assets and take market share, reducing the ability of the incumbents to respond.

The electric car case above shows how markets continue to explore, even as incumbents choose to switch to exploitation. The risk is not just an issue for car makers. More generally, companies in every industry must balance their need to exploit current business models and market opportunities in the short term versus insuring against obsolescence in the long term by exploring new options and innovating to capture value from them. Younger and smaller companies seem to be better at exploration, while older and larger companies seem to be better at exploitation.

Les McKeown describes why this difference exists.[23] Start-up companies are born around the vision of their founder. Start-up is a tough gig, where the founding team are searching to find a profitable sustainable market. This search is influenced by the founder's vision and occurs under time pressure, because funds inside the new venture are limited. Visionaries who contribute funds and attract seed investment operate with the hiss of a cash burning fuse. If the cash runs out before the start-up hits break-even, then the business normally blows up. McKeown calls this stage 'Early Struggle.' The chart below from GEM shows this is the single most common reason for start-up discontinuance reported by entrepreneurs (see Figure 2.4).

## Reasons Entrepreneurs Discontinue their Businesses

McKeown asserts that visionaries need to team up with a different type of start-up player he calls 'the operator.' Operators can take visionary ideas and translate them into reality. McKeown suggests the relationship between the visionary and the operator is symbiotic. Visionaries are good at designing and getting things started, while operators are good at executing and getting things finished. Successful visionary/

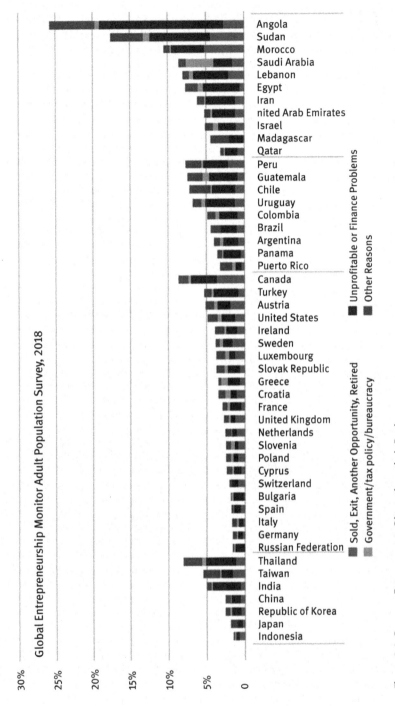

**Figure 2.4:** Reasons Entrepreneurs Discontinue their Businesses.

operator teams get their start-up from launch to a stage McKeown calls 'Fun' if they survive Early Struggle.

In Fun, the business is characterised as growing revenue fast, having turned the corner on the cash flow problem. McKeown suggests that firms become primarily sales focused as the single solution to most business problems. Fun is a good place to be, but it is not without risk. The Kauffman Foundation and *Inc.* magazine conducted a follow-up study of the 5000 fastest growing companies five to eight years on and found around two-thirds had failed.[24] This finding is echoed by a Start-up Genome study finding that more than 74% of 3200 high growth firms had failed due to growing too fast.[25] Ultimately growth (whether fast or not) increases complexity and other problems. McKeown calls this stage 'Whitewater.'

The Whitewater business stage requires the growing venture to add a third skill set to the team. McKeown's term for a player with these skills is 'processor.' Processors change the management approach of the visionary and operator team to a more controlled management approach designed to deal with complexity. It is at this stage that the business transforms from entrepreneurial to corporate management. In other words, the venture reduces it focus on exploration and switches to exploitation. McKeown is blunt about the challenge ventures have in introducing processors to change the way they work. In some cases the processor may not last. In other cases the visionary may exit. However, it seems it is not possible to scale to national or global significance without this change in management approach. Achieving this size is the stage McKeown calls 'Predictable Success.'

The irony of this evolution of the firm is that the very exploration strategy the firm was founded on becomes the threat to its survival at scale. McKeown also describes a further stage called the 'Treadmill' where firms overcorrect with bureaucracy and processes. In Treadmill firms are so determined to avoid risk they erode their capability for exploration in favour of exploitation. This loss of exploration function is ultimately the root cause of all companies' failures in the long run. McKeown asserts firms who remain in Treadmill too long eventually fall into a Rut. He cites common examples like Kodak.

*C- U+ Digital photography compels Kodak and Fuji to explore*
*Founded in 1880, the Eastman Kodak company was considered to be a marketing and technology innovator. By 1976, Kodak accounted for 90% of film and 85% of camera sales in America. Up to the 1990s it was regularly rated one of the world's five most valuable brands. In 1996, revenue peaked at $US 16B. Kodak filed for bankruptcy in 2012. Kodak's main rival prior to the digital photography era was Fuji Photo.*
*The Japanese firm had established a similar monopoly position to Kodak in its domestic market. Fuji took on Kodak in the US market in the early 1990s, growing from 10% to 17% share by 1997.[26] Then came digital photography and demand for film collapsed after a peak in 2000 (see Figure 2.5).[27]*

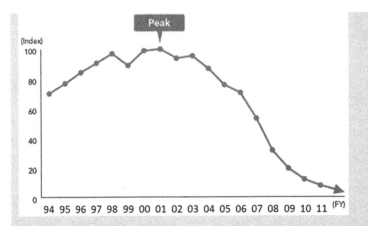

**Figure 2.5:** Colour Film Demand.

*Both Kodak and Fuji had seen the emergence of digital photography. Kodak itself built one of the first digital cameras in 1975. But both firms were reticent to move into digital photography due to the concerns over cannibalising their existing film businesses. They each tried to explore new markets instead. Fuji's strategy was to treat film as a cash cow, prepare for digital and develop other product lines. Kodak had similar intentions to diversify but pivoted more slowly and ultimately was not successful.*

*Kodak tried to repurpose some of its film chemicals into drugs but had to sell off its pharma operations in the 1990s. In contrast, Fuji was able to incorporate some of its 4000 antioxidant chemicals into a cosmetics line called Astalift. Starting in 2000, Fujifilm also invested $US 4B into making optical films for LCD flat-panel screens. Fuji achieved a monopoly position in one LCD film designed to expand the LCD viewing angle. Kodak tried to pivot into digital cameras and offered customers the ability to post and share pictures online. Kodak has been criticised for retaining production of cameras in-house instead of outsourcing. The business also struggled to find an alternative pricing strategy in digital to replace its original approach of cheap cameras/expensive film. Kodak's barely profitable digital camera business only lasted a few years before being disrupted by camera phones. Kodak also hoped the Chinese middle class would buy lots of film. Some Chinese did buy film, but later switched to digital cameras. Others simply went straight to digital photography without ever owning a conventional camera. In 2005, the Kodak business tried to pivot again to digital printing. Again it ultimately failed.*

The Kodak/Fuji case above is instructional because it shows two companies both trying to adjust to external market changes. Of the two firms, Fuji seemed to be better at balancing exploration and exploitation activities. This ability is called 'Organisational Ambidexterity.'[28] Rather than bet the company on a single new direction, like Ford and Chrysler, a better approach is to search for new opportunities before the current cash cow collapses. But our experience with large clients in Asia and the US is they implement CX initiatives largely as an incremental, defensive measure.

## Reversing Traditional CX to Be Agile

The traditional approach to CX in large firms involves seven different steps:
1. Hypothesise the stages of the customer journey to guide interviews
2. Undertake semi-structured customer interviews to collect data
3. Use affinity mapping to find pain points, moments of truth, and experience insights
4. Synthesise the research into a large customer journey map
5. Prioritise improvements around reducing pain points
6. Evolve delivery to be more consistent during moments of truth
7. Leverage experience insights to design CX innovations

One of the problems with this approach is the front-loaded costs in steps 1–4 before any possible returns can be created in steps 5–7. Many CX initiatives get stalled somewhere soon after step 4. As a result, few clients ever manage to drive a return from their CX investments. In a recent informal survey of around 30 clients, none of them had ever quantified a CX return. Figure 2.6 graphs orders of magnitude for accumulated cost and time for each of the steps based on years of working in the CX field as consultants. The costs only cover CX and no associated investments in new products or backend management information systems. If anything, these numbers are on the low side, based on some clients' implementation difficulties. Researching, designing, and executing CX improvements is less expensive than new product development or a full digital transformation, but it is still expensive and time consuming.

The process outlined above is a typical sequential waterfall process common in many large companies. It is how McKeown's processors deal with complexity. As Chapter 1 suggests, it typically results in CX fatigue.

CX managers respond to criticism around the lack of commercial returns by blaming a lack of support from the key executives in their organisations. They complain about inadequate budgets, conflicting KPIs across functional silos and impatience in the rest of the business for tangible results. There are reasons to take account of the perspectives from both sides of the argument. The alternative is to reverse the steps in the traditional CX process to get to potential returns faster and cheaper. This requires taking an agile approach. The result is a more entrepreneurial take on how to improve CX. It is more cyclic than the traditional waterfall project management used to date.

Lean CX involves many of the same steps as traditional CX, but the emphasis is on delaying large investments as much as a possible. Consistent delivery is considered secondary to finding what will cut-through for customers. Instead of hypothesising a customer journey to guide semi-structured interviews, lean CX operators start by considering what might matter most to customers in a purchase experience. Instead of affinity mapping to identify insights, moments of truth, and pain points,

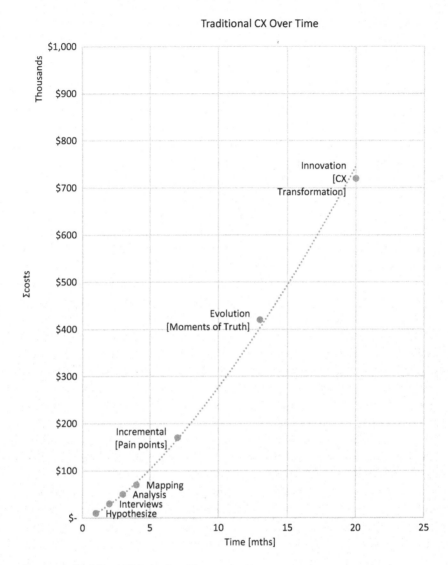

**Figure 2.6:** Traditional CX Costs Over Time.

lean CX operators simply generalise from their interactions with customers and from their own experiences. Instead of constructing a journey map and prioritising pain points to tackle, lean CX operators use acumen to prioritise CX improvement opportunities. Then they construct a minimum viable initiative (MVI) to market test. Most of the research required for good CX design is conducted during market testing. Iterative market tests improve the MVI over time until a scalable opportunity can be validated by small scale market feedback. The insights as to why something is scalable can come after the innovation is validated.

Results from Lean CX are achieved faster and cheaper because upfront research and design investment is reduced. Comparatively more effort and resources are invested in market testing and iterative improvement. This back-loading of the investment means comparatively more is spent executing, earlier and faster. Even though potential CX innovations may fail at the same rates with traditional and Lean CX approaches, Lean CX means failing faster and cheaper. The result is lean CX can be described more simply as four core steps:

1. *Use human-centred design techniques to design a change to a firm's current CX.* This change is based on what key staff believe could work better for customers they empathise with, not extensive customer research.
2. *Use rapid prototyping approaches to create the CX initiative analogue of the Minimum Viable Product, the MVI.* This allows the CX team to test options with customers fast, without needing to prosecute every initiative with a wider group of stakeholders in the firm.
3. *Execute live market testing on a small scale.* The purpose of market testing is to overcome the problem with intention to purchase research (notoriously unreliable). Customer feedback ensures lean operators learn what they need to know to fill their research gaps.
4. *Refine the CX prototype based on market feedback and quantify business costs and benefits.* This allows the data needed for subsequent scale investments to be validated cheaply.

These steps are analogous to the Ries lean start-up methodology already introduced. Perhaps the only difference is lean start-up is explicitly focused on getting to a profitable sustainable market, where Lean CX is about finding cut-though. The methods to get there and the potential business outcomes are often similar. The Votizen case below describes the process of searching for the right customer value proposition in a start-up, starting with a vision about what customers might want and then pivoting through various iterations of the business to confirm what worked.

**A+ Democracy for hire at Votizen**

*Votizen was a company founded by Dave Binetti and others in 2009.[29] The company was founded to reform the way the US government could use technology to be more accountable to voters. At the time (and perhaps still), social media was disrupting politics. Votizen has evolved to allow voters to aggregate their concerns and communicate in a more effective way to their elected representatives and candidates. A key problem Votizen set out to solve was to connect voters with officials directly at scale and increase civic participation. Low voter turnout is a chronic issue in the US because unlike most of Europe and Australia, voting is not compulsory there. The company used a lean approach to find a profitable business model leveraging social media to promote political advocacy.*

*Binetti asserts lean is 'not about small, not about cheap. It's about helping you avoid very expensive false positives.' His goal was to cycle through the four steps as fast and as cheaply as possible to find a business model to achieve his vision, earning revenues. Binetti is careful to define a pivot as being related to the business, not just the product. He also cautions against thinking small changes are pivots. He suggests pivots are about revisions of the assumptions the start-up is based on, rather than merely cosmetic changes. Consequently, pivots are vision driven and informed by learning. They are not merely responses to testing.*

*Votizen started out as Facebook for politics. The revenue model was based on clipping the ticket for donations made to candidates for specific political causes. Ideally, being a paid Votizen user would offer a stronger political voice. At the time, Binetti perceived the market to be hyper-fragmented with lots of local players and no dominant market leader. He set up metrics to track his progress based on McClure's Start-up Metrics for Pirates.[30] Binetti tracked Acquisition, Activation, Retention, Referral, and Revenue, quantifying the number of people at each stage of their customer journey:*

1. *Acquisition: created an account*
2. *Activation: validated registered voter status*
3. *Referrals: forwarded to friends*
4. *Retention: used the system three times or more*
5. *Revenue: donated to support a cause*

*Votizen 1.0 was built in 6 weeks for $US 1200. This was the start-up MVP. After making minor changes with AB testing, mostly related to making the registration flow faster and easier, the initial results were improved. Table 2.1 shows how the metrics changed across the different versions of Votizen. Version 1.1 was not considered a pivot by Binetti because the business model assumption remained the same as for version 1.0. Unable to improve on v1.1 results, Binetti decided to pivot. The inspiration for this was talking with customers and learning that they really wanted to get involved, but it had always been hard. He changed the product in Votizen 2.0 to be a simple messaging tool allowing voters to spam their officials. Still with no revenue, he pivoted again.*

**Table 2.1:** Votizen Pivots.

| Metric | 1.0 | 1.1 | 2.0 | 3.0 | 4.0 |
|---|---|---|---|---|---|
| *Acquisition* | *5%* | *17%* | *42%* | *43%* | *51%* |
| *Activation* | *17%* | *90%* | *83%* | *85%* | *92%* |
| *Referral* | *–* | *4%* | *54%* | *52%* | *64%* |
| *Retention* | *–* | *5%* | *21%* | *24%* | *28%* |
| *Revenue* | *–* | *–* | *1%* | *0%* | *11%* |

*Votizen 3.0 became about campaign management (making change at scale). Services included creating a custom website with tracking analytics and tools for specific campaigns. With positive feedback from customers voicing their intention to buy, the firm invested $US 120K to build the new platform. Disappointingly, customers who had expressed interest did not buy the new version. Votizen 4.0 pivoted again to improve the sales cycle, reduce the reliance on Twitter, and show immediate return on investment to potential customers. The interface was changed to look a lot more like Google AdWords and allowed clients to pay with a credit card immediately. Pricing was based on a*

*per-message basis. Version 4.0 delivered the proof the company needed to validate raising more capital. Votizen 1.0, 2.0, and 3.0 cost around $US 1K, $US 10K, and $US 100K, respectively. But the market validation achieved with version 4.0 allowed the company to attract $US 1M.*

*Ultimately, Votizen was acquired by Causes, an online civic engagement platform founded by Parker. Causes was subsequently rolled into another Parker company called Brigade. Brigade has since been broken up with the team going to Pinterest and the tech going to Countable.[31]*

The Votizen case study is supposedly about start-up, but also it is about CX. The firm had to explore different options to find a way to get cut-through. The lean start-up process used contrasts to the waterfall CX process above. But both processes start with a vision of what the customer might want but doesn't know to ask for. Lean start-up is simply the entrepreneurial approach to solve the problem. It has the advantage of being faster, cheaper, and lower risk than the traditional waterfall project management approach corporates have favoured.

Ries asserts entrepreneurship is actually a different type of management rather than just an alternative to traditional corporate management. The distinction matters because traditional managers must be open to exploration as much as exploitation if their business is to grow long term. Lean management provides a way to discover what innovations will cut-through.

Lean CX is not just lean start-up for established firms. Different constraints apply in mature firms compared to start-ups. Start-ups are typically resource constrained. This is more than just being strapped for cash. Sure, entrepreneurs inside start-ups are often focused on how to acquire more resources, particularly capital. However start-ups commonly lack other types of resources, too.

The Resource Based View of the firm (RBV)[32] considers firms as collections of six categories of resources. These categories are Physical, Reputation, Organisation, Financial, Individuals, and Technology.[33] The related acronym is PROFIT. Start-ups can be short in any of these resource categories. However, their stereotypical lack of Reputation, Organisation, and Individuals[34] resources allows them greater freedom to explore their markets compared to more established firms. But the ultimate goal of a start-up is 'not to be one.'[35]

A start-up transitions to an established firm when it finds a profitable, sustainable market and achieves better than break-even cash flow. At this point, it has probably acquired, developed, or established more than just cash reserves (F resources). The business may have a profitable location (P resource), growing brand recognition (R resources), effective routines around sales, fulfilment, and payment collection (O resources), a developing team (I resources), and be further down the learning curve (T resources). Some resource types can be acquired, developed, or established quickly, while others take longer.

Reputations, for example, are commonly established over time. Similarly, effective organisational routines are refined over time as the organisation gets better at exploiting their market opportunities and refining their business model. Individuals add to the firm's head count over time and their value increases as they learn more about how to contribute to the firm's mission and vision. This value takes time and suggests why established firms without forward contracts have 'goodwill value' over and above a start-up with the same business model, physical, financial, and technology resources.

## Overcoming Resistance to Innovation

Managers rationally act to protect the goodwill accumulated in their organisations. This means new initiatives are evaluated not only for their potential returns, but also for the possibility to impact or erode other resources. Is the new initiative brand-aligned? Does the initiative fit with corporate cultural values? How much does the initiative comply with established policies and procedures? Will the new initiative divert attention from the organisation's mission and current KPIs? Established firms struggle with innovation because (by definition) innovation is not core business and is therefore risky. Innovation can activate the 'corporate immune system.'[36]

Lean CX can help to overcome negative organisation reactions to innovation. It can be understood as a hybrid approach balanced between the resource-constrained start-up and the status quo-constrained large firm. In the same way lean start-up is a faster and cheaper way for new ventures to find a profitable, sustainable market, as Lean CX is cheaper and faster than traditional waterfall CX for established firms to find new growth options. Lean CX also helps avoid activating the corporate immune system.

Improving CX in an established firm is not normally considered as a risky move. Internal stakeholders see improving CX as supporting the firm's existing business model, rather than putting it at risk. As outlined in the opening chapter, corporate stakeholders will fund CX initiatives provided they can see a real return on investment. This means accountable CX improvement tends to be an acceptable form of innovation because it doesn't really seem like innovation. The challenge is identifying where to start. The case below describes some innovations related to secure online user authentication. The innovations described include both customer-centric initiatives designed to improve CX and potentially able to improve customer retention. Other examples in the case are not customer-centric and risk alienating customers.

*C- Security innovations impact customer retention*
*Keeping account log-in details secret is a common problem for many online consumers and service providers. Outside the banking sector, most account security is primarily implemented to protect service provider business models, rather than for direct customer benefit. The basic current solution for online security typically requires a password for user account access. But some passwords are better than others: Longer passwords are more secure; passwords with numbers, letters, mixed case, and special characters are also more secure. Providers encourage or constrain*

*users to create more secure passwords. Some go further to nudge users away from using passwords readily related to them like their date of birth, or common name. Ideally each login a user has is also unique, because if one password becomes compromised, any damage applies only to the relevant account. The user's other accounts remain secure if they use different passwords. The conflict is the more secure the password, typically the harder it is to remember.*

*When users are delayed or prevented from accessing their accounts because of security measures, they can become frustrated. In the worst cases, customers give up altogether and may churn to another service provider offering access with less effort – particularly if users don't see the security measures as necessary or relevant to them.*

*Various innovations have been implemented to help with password security. For example, ING bank rearranges the layout of PIN number pads with each online login to confound packet sniffing for keystrokes during logins to their banking portal. HSBC goes further by issuing their clients battery powered token generators. These small devices issue unique time varying codes in response to client password input. If the server doesn't calculate the same code as an attempted login, access is denied. Other service providers like Microsoft and Xero rely on a similar system implemented as an authenticator app on users' smart phones.*

*Most users have experienced the challenge of forgetting their password and having to go through a relatively onerous process to re-establish their credentials with an online service. Now state of the art password retrieval has become omni-channel. If you lose your password, you may be able to reset it with email, SMS, phone or online channels previously established as recovery pathways. The idea of omni-channel password recovery has evolved into multi-factor authentication (MFA). If more than one channel can be used to reset or retrieve your password, it makes sense to allow more than one channel for login authentication.*

*Additionally, MFA has been used for a different purpose by the online company Survey Monkey. Survey Monkey provides value-added web hosting services on a subscription basis for clients who want to implement online surveys. The company upgraded its log-in processes to require clients to use MFA. According to Survey Monkey, the reason for this was to ensure client data (including participant responses and contact details) were kept more secure. However, MFA also makes it much harder for Survey Monkey clients to share logins. This forces users to pay more. Unlike other providers offering MFA, Survey Monkey gave its clients no choice about switching to MFA. For many clients, the result was not an improvement in security, it was an unwelcome price hike. While Survey Monkey is quite within its rights to use MFA for this purpose, it is not customer-centric. Survey Monkey enjoys almost zero marginal cost per additional user in a client account, so compelling users to pay more is only about exploiting lock in.*

*A search for online survey alternatives to Survey Monkey reveals a range of results proving the company's market space has become very crowded. It is arguable that the sector is already commoditised, even though there are some variances between the feature sets of different platforms. For Survey Monkey, the longer-term customer-centric move to make logging in easier rather than harder would have likely improved customer engagement and loyalty. Working out how to add on optional value-added services for additional charges would have been a better way to grow revenue. Instead the company has taken a short-term approach to grab profits.*

In a start-up, the founder has an essentially unquestioned mandate to explore how to capitalise on an intuited or suspected opportunity derived from their vision. In established firms, innovation champions are often more critically scrutinised. Justification for where to search is demanded in the name of avoiding wasting resources going after pipe dreams. This may be why to date most traditional CX approaches have looked more like waterfall than agile project management: would-be CX innovators need to justify why they want to invest in new initiatives. They need to show how CX innovation will deliver cut-through. The idea of cut-through is the topic of the next chapter.

## Endnotes

**1** Womack, Jones, and Roos (1991). *The Machine That Changed the World*, Harper Perennial.
**2** Skhmot (2017). "The 8 Wastes of Lean," *The Lean Way*. https://theleanway.net/The-8-Wastes-of-Lean, accessed 1 September 2020.
**3** McLachlan (2017). *The Lean CX Score: How Does Your Business Measure Up?* Self-published.
**4** Schneider and Hall (2011). "Why Most Product Launches Fail," *Harvard Business Review*.
**5** Nobel (2011). "Clay Christensen's Milkshake Marketing," *Harvard Business School*. https://hbswk.hbs.edu/item/clay-christensens-milkshake-marketing.
**6** Dam (2019). "The MAYA Principle: Design for the Future, but Balance it with Your Users' Present," *Interaction Design Foundation*. https://www.interaction-design.org/literature/article/design-for-the-future-but-balance-it-with-your-users-present.
**7** Ries (2011). *The Lean Start-up*, Crown Publishing Group (USA).
**8** https://indicators.kauffman.org/indicator/start-up-early-survival-rate
**9** Survival rates of 3-year and 5-year-old enterprises, from *eurostat* https://ec.europa.eu/eurostat/web/structural-business-statistics/entrepreneurship/indicators.
**10** In this context, innovation and new product development (NPD) are used interchangeably. In practice NPD is only a subset of innovation.
**11** EY (2018). *Global banking outlook 2018: Pivoting toward an innovation-led strategy.* https://www.ey.com/en_gl/digital/banking-innovation.
**12** "Online Broker Comparison." https://brokerchooser.com/compare-brokerage (last accessed 3/12/19).
**13** Gallo 2016 'A Refresher on Marketing Myopia' *Harvard Business Review* [online] https://hbr.org/2016/08/a-refresher-on-marketing-myopia (accessed 5/8/20)
**14** From the customer's perspective these offerings are more often than not 'FAECES.'
**15** Puckette (2019) "The Oldest Winery in France is For Sale?!" *Wine Folly*. https://winefolly.com/update/the-oldest-winery-in-the-world-is-for-sale/
**16** Prial (1997). "Wine Talk: A New Wine and Other Tricks from an Old Loire Vintner," *New York Times*. https://www.nytimes.com/1997/11/05/dining/wine-talk-a-new-wine-and-other-tricks-from-an-old-loire-vintner.html
**17** See Rouse *Systems Thinking* (2005). https://searchcio.techtarget.com/definition/systems-thinking accessed 20/7/19. Apparently Systems Thinking was originated by Professor Jay Forrester in 1956 who founded the Systems Dynamic Group at the MIT Sloan School of Management.
**18** This seems to be an urban myth of sorts. See Vlaskovits (2011). "Henry Ford, Innovation, and That 'Faster Horse' Quote," *Harvard Business Review*. https://hbr.org/2011/08/henry-ford-never-said-the-fast, accessed 20/7/19.
**19** McFadden (2019). "Lee Iacocca, Visionary Automaker Who Led Both Ford and Chrysler, Is Dead at 94," *New York Times*. https://www.nytimes.com/2019/07/02/obituaries/lee-iacocca-dead.html.
**20** Caton (2019). "Automobile Design: How long does it take to develop a car design from scratch?" *Quora*. https://www.quora.com/Automobile-Design-How-long-does-it-take-to-develop-a-car-design-from-scratch. Caton is a former Engineer at General Motors. Here is his full quote: "5 years, from scratch. . . . Only posting b/c the other answers are too short and rely on input from media sources. Any of these 18–36 month Vehicle Development Plans leverage an existing architecture. If you're

genuinely starting fresh, figure 5 years from ideation to start of production. . . assuming you're as efficient as GM. Also plan to spend around $f1B."

**21** Wikipedia, "Tesla, Inc." https://en.wikipedia.org/wiki/Tesla,_Inc. (last accessed 27/11/19).

**22** US Dept of Energy (2015). "Timeline: History of the Electric Car." https://www.energy.gov/time line/timeline-history-electric-car

**23** McKeown (2009). *Predictable Success: Getting Your Organization on the Growth Track-And Keeping It There*, Greenleaf Book Group Press.

**24** Lidow (2016). "Why Two-Thirds of the Fastest-Growing Companies Fail," *Fortune*. https://fortune.com/2016/03/07/fast-growth-companies-fail/.

**25** Quoted in Jarvis (2019). *Company of One: Why Staying Small is the Next Big Thing for Business*, Penguin UK. Accessed from the preview https://books.google.com.au/books?id=gJZlDwAAQBAJ&pg=PT46&dq=kauffman+follow+up+study+on+high+growth+companies&hl=en&sa=X&ved=0ahUKEwiJg_bKz4nmAhWNXSsKHdyyA6AQ6AEIKDAA#v=onepage&q=kauffman%20follow%20up%20study%20on%20high%20growth%20companies&f=false (last accessed 27/11/19).

**26** Economist (2012). "The last Kodak moment?" *The Economist*. https://www.economist.com/business/2012/01/14/the-last-kodak-moment. Wikipedia, "Kodak." https://en.wikipedia.org/wiki/Kodak. Wikipedia, "Fujifilm." https://en.wikipedia.org/wiki/Fujifilm.

**27** Fujifilm Holdings Corporation (2017). "Integrated Report 2017."

**28** See March 1991, "Exploration and Exploitation in Organizational Learning," *Organization Science* Vol 2 No 1.

**29** Wikipedia, "Votizen." https://en.wikipedia.org/wiki/Votizen (last accessed 3/12/19).

**30** See Lehenchuk "AARRR Framework: The Best Startup Metrics for Pirates." https://producttribe.com/revenue-amp-growth/aarrr-framework-best-guide for a detailed introduction; and the video McClure (2007). "Startup Metrics for Pirates: AARRR!" https://www.youtube.com/watch?v=irjgfWOBIrw.

**31** Constine (2019). "Sean Parker's Brigade/Causes acquired by govtech app Countable," *techcrunch*. https://techcrunch.com/2019/05/01/brigade-countable/

**32** Barney (1991). "Firm Resources and Sustained Competitive Advantage," *Journal of Management* Vol 17 No 1.

**33** Conveniently, these categories form the acronym PROFIT. This was shared in a 1998 MBA class at the Queensland University of Technology by Professor Evan Douglas. He went on to describe how different resource classes can contribute to sustainable competitive advantage for firms [SCA]. Firms enjoy first mover advantages in three categories – Physical, Financial, and Technology. Acquiring the best location, winning a government grant, and discovering a patentable innovation are all examples of potential SCA. Together these spell 'PFT' – a sound indicating "hesitate and the opportunity is gone." Reputation, Organisation, and Individual resources spell ROI and tend to be build up over time.

**34** Ibid., footnote 70.

**35** See Les McKeown (2011). "Predictable Success Talks at Google," *YouTube* https://www.youtube.com/watch?v=AXXhxqHU5Fg (accessed 16/1/20).

**36** Pinchot and Pellman (1999). "Chapter 4, What an Intrapreneuring Program Looks Like," *Intrapreneuring in Action: A Handbook for Business Innovation*, Berrett-Koehler Publishers, for more on the corporate immune system.

# Chapter 3
# Creating Market Cut-Through

The business strategy problem can be considered from different perspectives. In 1987, partly as a way to codify the spread of strategic approaches, and partly as a way to introduce strategic business thinking, Henry Mintzberg suggested strategy was one of his 5P's: a plan, position, pattern, ploy, or perspective. These concepts make sense in environments where change is somewhat controllable and predictable. But just like the market, business strategy continues to evolve.

"During the 1990s, the highly dynamic business environment challenged the original assumptions of the Resource Based View (RBV), which are static and do not take account of market dynamism . . . Dynamic capabilities focus on the firm's ability to face rapidly changing environments, in order to create and renew resources, and change the resources mix."[1] Dynamic capabilities can be considered as the sensing, seizing, and transforming needed to design and implement a business model.

More recently the concept of dynamism has emerged in business strategy paradigms in response to the perception of modern markets as VUCA environments. VUCA means Volatile, Uncertain, Complex, and Ambiguous. Nathan Bennett and G. James Lemoine argue that the VUCA components each require a different strategic response. *Volatility* is managed by investing in slack resources to allow for flexibility. *Uncertainty* requires the collection of more and new information, possibly from a wider range of sources than traditionally used. *Complexity* can be tackled with restructuring to better match the internal organisation with the external environment. *Ambiguity* demands intelligent experimentation.[2]

VUCA is often used as a synonym for unpredictable or relentless change. The reality is deeper. A VUCA world is characterised by multiple challenges based around what is known and what remains unknowable (see Figure 3.1).

## Volatility

Volatility is driven by competition and information. Finding out about rivals' current features and prices is becoming cheaper, easier, and faster. Volatility occurs because of 'known knowns.' Market players research and react to their rivals' moves, and the rivals themselves are likely responding to changes by other market players. This creates a cycle where remaining active becomes its own validation.

Digital communications make it possible for marketers to adjust the information components of their offers far more frequently than ever before because of lower information management costs. This means intangibles like prices, warranty conditions, and delivery times are now less fixed.

https://doi.org/10.1515/9783110683929-003

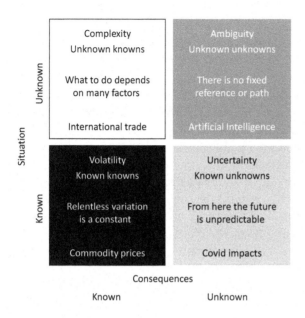

**Figure 3.1:** VUCA Quadrants.

Change becomes a constant in an attempt to cut-through competition. The price of hotel rooms, hire cars, and hedge funds changes with availability, perhaps hourly. The desirability of delivery, devices, and even debt can alter daily. Worries about product warranties; supply of utilities like water, energy, and internet; and concerns over welfare costs and benefits can change weekly. All of this creates and feeds volatility and activity volume.

Funds managers feel compelled to make trades to update their portfolios even when their current investments are sound. Marketers feel the need to continually tweak copy and messaging frequency. Developers add on new features instead of taking unnecessary ones out. All this volatility encourages customer churn.

Dealing with volatility requires slack resources. Spare capacity and reserves allow you to wait out the market until times turn around. Lean CX offers the potential to invest spare resources to take advantage of volatility far more efficiently than other waterfall CX processes. Lean CX is also useful for dealing with uncertainty.

## Uncertainty

The past no longer seems to determine our future. As China's growth slows, US foreign policy is revised, Europe's growth stalls, and the BRIC countries seek to expand, most of Africa and parts of South America struggle. The World War II marked a turning point for key nations on the global stage: Germany, Japan, and the UK are now at best secondary players in a world economy increasingly dominated by the US and China. Australia is an interesting example in this regard.

Over two generations, Australia has shifted exports from wool to beef to sugar to tourism to minerals to university education. Australia survived the 2009–2011 Global Financial Crisis better than most. However, mineral and oil price corrections and slower China growth hit Australian mining hard (particularly the state of Western Australia). Interest rates remain at record lows. Now Covid-19 directly harms the nation's tourism, education, and healthcare sectors. The pandemic has already decimated local capital markets.

After achieving a 10-year peak of 7289.7 in late February 2020, the S&P ASX All Ordinaries Index dropped to 4429.1 a month later. At the time of this writing, it has recovered almost half of the 40% drop from peak back up to 5608.8. Close to the end of May 2020 the index is at 77% of its former high-water mark from three months prior (see Figure 3.2).[3] Just like other current affairs, this volatility is almost disregarded because it is not really sensational.

Highly publicised media topics including royal commissions, floods, and fires are now all but forgotten with Covid-19 pandemic impacts. Previously all-consuming big picture issues are also passé. Few are commenting on Australia still having no carbon tax after the Kyoto and Paris Agreements, for example.[4] Against this backdrop, online commerce models are shifting consumer buying behaviours. Amazon and eBay continue to undermine traditional retail (with Covid-19 adding to their momentum). Uber has already devalued taxis and Airbnb has hit hotels. Hindsight may be 20-20 but what's coming next is hard to predict in 2020. It may be that 2020 marks the year or the decade of admitting any vision of the future is simply difficult to focus on.

Uncertainty exists when the current situation is known and the future is unclear. Market players take bets on how the field will pan out. Often their investments are biased to sustaining their current assets, exposing them to disruption. Dealing with uncertainty requires exploration. Lean CX offers a way to explore how to become the disruptor instead of waiting to be disrupted. Lean CX also provides a systemic response to complexity.

## Complexity

Complexity is growing exponentially in our world like an unchecked infection. Global population is approaching 10 billion. International trade is complicated by trade agreements, local regulations, and armed conflict. These increase with the emergence of each new nation state. Nearly 200 countries exist today versus only 107 in 1950s.

In this context, Australia is losing ground. Despite having the 10th highest GPD per capita, it has the export profile of Angola.[5] The nation's level of export sophistication fell to 93rd in 2017 because 70% of exports were minerals and energy. Food, alcohol, wool, tourism, and metal products made up 29% more. It may be that the

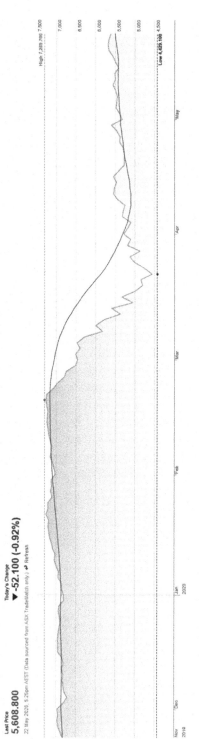

**Figure 3.2:** Recent ASX Performance.

governance and legal system is too cumbersome. The public service is more than 40% of GDP and 20% of all jobs.[6] The laws of Australia cover over 40,000 legal propositions. But it may also be local consumer markets. There are more than 2.3 million active businesses in Australia. Amazon alone sells more than 606 million products. eBay has 1.3 billion listings. Various estimates suggest first-world consumers are individually bombarded by 4,000–10,000 ads per day. Complexity is expanding relentlessly.

Complexity exists when we understand the cause and effect of choices, but just don't know where to start. Unravelling complexity requires focus, patience, and persistence. Lean CX offers a process to untangle complexity and reduce short-term ambiguity with market and split testing.

## Ambiguity

The worst aspects of complexity and uncertainty combine to create ambiguity. Ambiguity stems from unknown unknowns. Consider the problem of traffic congestion. Before the concept of induced demand was discovered, both the causes of and fixes for traffic congestion were unknown. Research now shows roads themselves cause traffic.[7] This may seem like tautology, but the reality is that building more roads to reduce congestion mostly fails because upgrading capacity motivates more people than before to use the new roads. Interesting cases include San Francisco, Paris, and Seoul. After the carrying capacity of major roads was reduced, traffic in these cities was no worse. What has worked to reduce traffic is congestion pricing. London, Stockholm, and Singapore have all introduced successful congestion charges to help manage traffic. It may be hard to convince commuters they should pay for roads previously usable for free, but ambiguity also offers opportunity.

*U+ Snapchat has profited from ambiguity*
*Snapchat has enjoyed exponential growth in its member base (most of whom are millennials). Despite its ubiquity, aspects of the app's value proposition are hard to understand in the context of how other social media platforms have evolved. For starters, Snapchat is designed for private one-on-one conversations. Social media is normally about public sharing. In Snapchat, so called 'Snaps' (texts, pictures, and videos) typically just disappear after being viewed by recipients. Collections of Snaps can be assembled into 'Stories' with a life of just one day. There is no manual for Snapchat because frequent upgrades mean its user interface is constantly changing. Every few days everything in the app can look and flow completely differently. Constant usage changes, temporary content, and lack of publicity seem to violate what makes social media social. However Snapchat's USP (unique selling proposition) is this very ephemeral nature of its content and interface. The short half-life allows users to share more indiscriminately than they might otherwise because they won't be haunted by anything they post. They can simply share whatever matters most in the moment. By letting users feel safe knowing they will be able to move, Snapchat offers a different sharing experience from other social media.*

## Defining Cut-Through

In marketing, cut-through is typically defined as the ability to get a message through to potential customers who take action as a result. In CX an expanded definition is more useful. Table 3.1 outlines five different levels of CX cut-through as an adaptation of McClure's Pirate Metrics.[8]

**Table 3.1:** Pirate Metrics.

| Level | Result | Impact[9] | | Example |
|-------|--------|-----------|---|---------|
| 1 | Acquisition | Attractive CX draws new customers | | ClassPass |
| 2 | Activation | Efficient CX speeds on-boarding | | Downtown Check in Hong Kong |
| 3 | Revenue | Effective CX increases spending | | Amazon One-Click |
| 4 | Repeat | Better CX enhances loyalty | | BMW |
| 5 | Referral | Remarkable CX prompts advocacy | | Rent the Runway |

Ideally the experience an organisation offers meets all five levels of potential cut-through. In practice many CX initiatives are designed with only a single objective in mind.

---

*C+ U+ ClassPass makes it easy to go to the gym[10]*

*ClassPass has partnerships with over 27,300 health clubs in 25 countries worldwide, making it one of the world's largest aggregators in the personal training market. Valued at $US 470M during the last round of funding in 2017, the company has succeeded using a Lean CX style approach. The original vision for ClassPass was a search engine and reservation system for fitness classes in New York.*

*The first version of the start-up, Classtivity, started out as a better registration system to fitness studios. Fewer than 100 classes were booked in the first year, but the company did learn something important. Users tried to hack Classtivity promotions to test out multiple different studios. The company pivoted to offering Groupon-like offers and changed its name to ClassPass. Customers paid $US 49 for 10 classes, usable over a year. After more customer feedback, the company switched to a 10 class $99 monthly subscription model. For the user, ClassPass stacked up: Memberships to a single yoga, Pilates, or spin studio can cost as much as $200 or $300 a month, or upward of $20 for an individual class. Like Uber, Didi, and Ola disrupting taxis, as the internet middleman ClassPass commands a volume discount and shares some of this benefit with users. For their side, the fitness clubs get more members. However in 2015, many New York partners were feeling the pinch after accepting ClassPass' low rates.*

*ClassPass pivoted again to introduce a credit system. Credits allowed differential pricing for different classes (reformer Pilates is substantially more expensive than Zumba classes, for example). Another pivot and the company had broadened its subscription levels. At the time of this writing, in Australia there are five levels ranging from $AUS 15 for 6 credits to book up to 1 class to $AUS 149 for 70 credits to book up to 22 classes. In London the range starts at £15 per*

> month for 9 credits/1 class. The top end is £149 per month for 125 credits/35 classes. The firm also charges cancellation fees for missing classes between $AUS 15–20 vs. £12–15 in London.
>
> The latest online ClassPass promotion seems targeted to acquisition. Unlike other gym memberships with discounted joining deals, ClassPass offers a first month free for mid-level Australian subscribers. Cancellation, downgrades, or upgrades are permitted any time. The London free period is only 7 days, but New York is 14 days. This suggests either the firm is still exploring the best acquisition model, or simply needs more users in Australia to get to scale fast and wants to exploit differential acquisition and pricing strategies. It has also added online video fitness classes. These can be purchased separately or bundled into a ClassPass subscription combining live streamed, recorded, and physical classes.
>
> ClassPass works because it solves the problem of gym membership usage. One survey of 5,300+ users found 22% stop going 6 months into their membership and 31% regret signing up. The same survey found 63% of memberships are unused.[11] It seems many people who sign up for the gym can't be certain they will keep going. By allowing them to try different fitness classes, ClassPass helps to keep it more interesting (U+) and improve the chances they will find something they can turn into a healthy habit (C+). By offering a free trial, ClassPass makes it easy to sign up. This improves and disrupts the traditional gym membership model. Little wonder the company has received Series A, B, and C funding rounds. Series C injected $US 70M into the company in 2017.

The ClassPass case example shows how a company applied lean start-up techniques to enhance its CX. ClassPass acquisition success is more than just a free gym trial. It leverages the prominent current internet aggregator business model. Like Uber and Airbnb, ClassPass succeeds not just by leveraging the internet to rent partners' physical and human assets, it succeeds by providing a more attractive CX.

> *C+ Downtown Check-in Hong Kong reduces luggage hassles[12]*
>
> In most cities, getting to the airport and dropping off bags involves time, stress, and constraints. By far the best CX created so far to manage this for economy class travellers is Hong Kong's downtown check-in. The value-added MTR service allows passengers to check their luggage and collect boarding passes on the day of their flight without leaving the CBD. Then they are free to spend more time in Hong Kong until it is time to take the Airport Express to aircraft boarding. The train journey is the fastest and cheapest way to the airport. The train is spacious, air conditioned, and offers free Wi-Fi, stopping right inside the airport terminals. The check-in service eliminates airport bag check queues and the need to store bags on the day of departure. The result is passengers can spend less time at the airport and more time enjoying Hong Kong, knowing they don't have to worry about their bags (C+). The service is free with an Airport Express ticket ($HK 100).

Hong Kong's MTR is one of the best-designed metro systems in the world. It is as extensive as the Tube in London or the Paris Metro, but far more modern. One of the other interesting aspects of the MTR is its Octopus card payment system. Like other mass public transit systems, the MTR has set up its own prepaid currency for fares. Normally these systems are a bane for travellers because they mandate account top-ups to travel (C-). There is virtually no advantage to users for these systems, but operators love them because they get prepayments (earning interest) and lost, abandoned, or forgotten cards result in revenue received for no service provided. Usually refunding card balances is impossible, locking users in. Proprietary fare systems also mean the operator reduces fees to third-party credit card platforms like Visa, Mastercard, and American Express. While users can normally top up using their third-party credit card, since this happens less frequently than for every ticket, the operator gets a savings. All of this inconveniences travellers however (C-). Hong Kong MTR has improved this prepayment pain point somewhat by opening up their Octopus card to shops in and around their stations. The Octopus card works just like a debit card and is cost effective for merchants and passengers alike. So in addition to helping make travelling around Hong Kong more efficient, MTR also helps provide greater revenue opportunities for businesses in the city.

Amazon has increased its revenue with a different CX improvement.

*C+ 1-CLICK® pivots drive revenue for Amazon[13]*
*Perhaps it is not surprising to learn that more than 67% of online shoppers abandon their shopping carts at the point of purchase.[14] This is the moment when fantasising about owning something switches to the reality of having to pay for it. Part of Amazon's amazing growth story is due to innovations around making it easier to shop. The company has expanded far beyond its original start as an online book retailer, by innovating a range of CX improvements for more revenue.*

*Amazon patented its 1-CLICK to Purchase button in 1999. The button allows online shopping transactions immediately, avoiding the shopping cart user experience. 1-CLICK allows impulse buying and avoids the tedious problem of re-entering credit card information for each purchase (C+). Combined with Kindle, 1-CLICK helped Amazon grow its online book sales. Since then, the firm has expanded to offer many more products online.*

*Amazon's Prime membership subscription bundles live video streaming, music streaming, free priority delivery, and regular member-only promotions. Prime users pay an annual fee to use the service, but generally this is less than delivery charges for even casual purchasers. Prime benefits prompt one-off purchasers to become repeat consumers and consume more.*

*The company has also experimented with other pivots away from online shopping. Dash is a physical Wi-Fi enabled refrigerator magnet. Push the Dash button and its matched product gets reordered via your Amazon account. Dash was targeted for repeat orders of staples like washing detergent, and each Dash only works for a specific SKU. Later a programmable version of the button was released, before ultimately Amazon discontinued them in 2019. Users were prompted to move to Echo.*

*Echo is another user shopping pivot for Amazon. The device provides a voice interface with Alexa (Amazon's audio chatbot) for internet searches, playing music, controlling home automation and making retail purchases. Echo is not bound by Google search policies and has been criticised for nudging customers to buy Amazon's preferred brand of product, even when other specific brands were requested. Even though they are physical devices, Dash and Echo are still based on online retailing.*

*Amazon's latest pivot has been away from clicks for orders to brick-and-mortar stores. Amazon Go is chain of convenience stores where customers simply pick up what they want from the shelves and walk out with having to queue to pay. Amazon Go uses the shopper's phone and*

> *some nifty recombination of tracking systems to work out what to bill to the user's Amazon account. The chain expanded to 18 stores between 2018 and 2019, another example of how Amazon is driving revenue with more effective CX. Next to come is Amazon 4-Star – a retail shop stocking only the highest rated online Amazon products.*

The meteoric growth of Amazon is not just due to CX innovations. The company also enjoys the advantage of having an investor base who do not demand the firm makes profits. The graph in Figure 3.3 shows how Amazon has reinvested prior to 2016 into growth. Yet its market cap of over $US 750B makes it one of the world's most valuable firms. Net income grew from $US 3 billion in 2017 to $10.1 billion in 2018 on the back of a 31% revenue increase. Not bad for a tech start-up 20 years on.[15]

**Amazon's Growth (1997–2018)**

Amazon's net sales and income trajectories, in billions

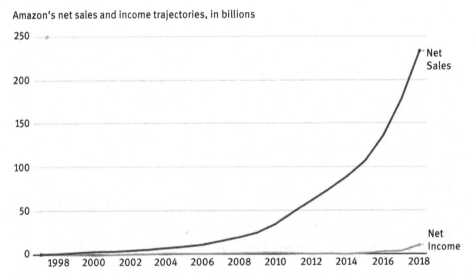

**Figure 3.3:** Exponential Revenue for 20 years.

> *C+ A+ P+ Buying a Beamer without the test drive*
> *In 2017, BMW Policaro dealership in Canada began offering customers a chance to test drive a new car from the comfort of their own homes[16] However, BMW in the US was enjoying even better CX engagement with customers. Around 30% of BMW purchasers bought their cars without taking a test drive.[17] Almost all these customers were repeat purchasers, certain their next BMW would meet or exceed their expectations (C+). BMW realised the reasons people buy a luxury car are different from why people buy just a car. Luxury vehicles satisfy needs for aspiration (A+) and status (P+). By meeting these needs at a high standard with excellent CX, BMW in the US has prompted many customers to have such faith in the BMW brand that they repurchase with ease.*

BMW's success in the US leverages the high-quality vehicles the German car maker is famous for. But repeat purchases without test drives are also due to a seamless end-to-end dealership experience characterised by customer centricity. BMW has developed a culture in its dealerships empowering customer-facing staff to consistently deliver on brand experiences with a personal touch. Customers feel special when they buy a BMW not just because of the car. They end up buying in to the belief BMW is simply and certainly better. It is arguable Mercedes or Lexus offers cars of similar luxury and quality, but somehow BMW's CX is distinctive and it drives repeat purchase and referrals.

---

*U+ A+ P+ C+ Rent the Runway referrals[18]*

*Rent the Runway (RTR) allows customers to rent and return designer dresses at a much lower price than purchasing outright. The online service, which provides designer clothing and accessory rentals, was launched in 2009 with the goal of allowing everyday women access to fashionable clothing. In 2019, the firm reached over 9 million members and more than 600 brand partners. RTR subscribers have access to everything from formal dresses and cocktail attire to work-appropriate clothing, shoes, bags, jewellery and more. In addition to making designer labels affordable (A+ P+), the company's business model means women can wear a wardrobe with more variety (U+) and without worrying about alterations if their size should change (C+). The concept has been so successful, RTR was recently able to raise $US 125 million in venture capital at a $1 billion valuation.*

*According to Jennifer Fleiss (cofounder), referral has been important for the growth of the business. "Word of mouth has been a key driver of brand awareness. Rent the Runway is an inherently social concept because when a woman is at an event and gets a compliment on her dress, she proudly starts talking about where she got it."*

*The business began offering 4-day outfit rentals from $US 30. Later pivots included subscriptions. Four pieces a month costs $US 69. Unlimited pieces 'on rotation, swap any time' costs $US 159 per month. Even though the business started out online, in 2014 it pivoted to open physical stores to improve CX. This provided customers with a high-touch experience they might not get at a traditional retailer, and difficult to impossible to get online. The full experience included working one-on-one with a stylist to discover new designers and trends. The company is still using lean methods to innovate CX. Fleiss confirmed the business was experimenting with 'practices that work best for us' after stores were opened. Part of the in-store CX includes customer dress selections and stylist notes being stored in a 'virtual closet' for later online access.*

*Recently the firm pivoted again, partnering with four W Hotels locations to offer a version of the in-store experience at the hotel. The firm also has drop-off boxes in certain WeWork and Nordstrom locations to make returning dresses easier. The CX evolution makes sense given the increasing competition in RTR's market. Rivals include One Kings Lane, Le Tote, Stitch Fix, Swap. com, thredUP, and Letgo.*

*The firm has recently expanded its range to include athletic apparel and ski attire. Perhaps the most courageous pivot is RTR kids. The firm is expanding the RTR range to include children's clothes rentable within parents' subscriptions. One reason the company believes this is good for customers is to help parents avoid the problem of children growing out of clothes too quickly. Time will tell if this drives word of mouth and keeps the company ahead of its rivals.*

---

The cases above validate the importance of exploring to find CX sweet spots for cut-through. They also suggest some patterns about where to look.

## Adjacent Positioning to Cut-Through

McKinsey was responsible for developing the H1/H2/H3 (Horizon Framework) innovation framework that Steve Blank favours (even if he thinks the timeframes suggested in the horizons are no longer valid).[19] The takeaway from the concept is that firms need to be considering all three innovation horizons:

- **Horizon 1** ideas provide continuous innovation to a company's existing business model and core capabilities in the short-term.
- **Horizon 2** ideas extend a company's existing business model and core capabilities to new customers, markets, or targets.
- **Horizon 3** is the creation of new capabilities and new business to take advantage of or respond to disruptive opportunities or to counter disruption.

In the framework, H3 includes big strategic bets and radical business model changes. Often these transformation-level initiatives are not as useful in CX because customers can be reticent to adopt them. This reduces their initial cut-through. In contrast, H1 initiatives are easy to adopt but often don't provide enough novelty or differentiation to motivate customers to switch. H2 is an interesting middle ground with greater impact than H1 and less risk than H3. Lean CX initiatives tend to test H2 innovations, even though the process can be relevant for any of the three innovation horizons.

Bansi Nagji and Geoff Tuff[20] extended the Three Horizons model outlined above. They added the detail overlaying product and segment extension dimensions shown in Figure 3.4. They classify innovations by the amount of change involved rather than the timeframe. Innovations comprise a portfolio considering core, adjacent, and transformational offerings. These classifications map directly onto H1/H2/H3 respectively.

- **Core:** The existing offering designed to serve current customers. The assets and capabilities used in the core could be extended to other customers with similar needs who have been just beyond the firm's focus up until now. This is what most effective businesses do month in, month out, sustaining their turnover and profits. The Core corresponds to H1 innovations. H1 innovations can be executed with no new investment. They leverage the organisation's existing capabilities inside one annual budget cycle. When McDonald's adds a new kind of burger to their menu, they are typically operating in their core.
- **Adjacent:** Organisations can stretch from a position of strength, both through exploiting customer relationships to offer a different value proposition to them, or by developing core capabilities and assets to access adjacent customer groups. Some firms will do both at the same time. The Adjacent zone corresponds to H2. H2 innovations require additional investment to be executed beyond a business-as-usual budget. They leverage the organisation's existing capabilities to exploit a new, nearby opportunity. The requirement for investment typically means these initiatives take more than one annual budget cycle to fund and implement.

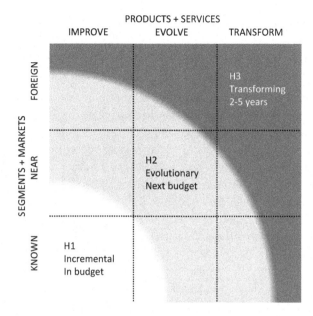

PRODUCTS + SERVICES

IMPROVE  EVOLVE  TRANSFORM

FOREIGN

SEGMENTS + MARKETS

NEAR

KNOWN

H3
Transforming
2-5 years

H2
Evolutionary
Next budget

H1
Incremental
In budget

**Figure 3.4:** Three Horizon Model.

When McDonald's added make-to-order and extended their menu items to include gourmet salads, they were pursuing adjacent opportunities.

- **Transformational**: Through the development of new assets and capital, firms should strive to discover new market needs before customers even know they have them. These moon shots include new-to-the-world offerings. H3 innovations cannot be completed merely with additional investment. They also require the firm to acquire or develop new capabilities. So these initiatives typically require several years at least of funding, development, and execution to mature. Ultimately they may not be successful at all. In 2019 McDonald's bought out a start-up with AI capability. The purpose of the acquisition was to create a customisable drive-thru experience responsive to weather, traffic, and popular items of the day.[21]

*C+ U+ McDonald's high tech bets*

*McDonald's is outperforming key rival Yum Foods (owner of Pizza Hut, Taco Bell, and KFC) but is losing ground to smaller, healthier fast food rivals like Five Guys and Guzman y Gomez. This is partly due to the trend toward healthier eating. In response, McDonald's is attempting to innovate around digital, delivery, and customer experience initiatives to retain its existing customers and acquire non-customers in adjacent segments.*

*The firm has recently acquired a stake in three companies to get access to new technology: Dynamic Yield for AI, Plexure for app development, and Apprente for voice technology. The innovation will happen in the McD Tech Labs located in Silicon Valley. This approach is not Lean CX. Instead McDonald's seems to be pursuing somewhat of an H3 moon shot through traditional front-loaded R&D.*

Nagji and Tuff found most established firms did not have a sure grip on where they spend their innovation resources. They lacked the systems to recognise how they invested funds and allocated staff across their Core/Adjacent/Transformational activities. All the companies involved in Nagji and Tuff's research vastly overestimated how much they were innovating beyond the core. More than 90% of innovation funding was focused on existing markets and customers. Unsurprisingly they found that the allocation of innovation resources was different across different industries and geographies. Technology companies allocated fewer resources to enhancing core offerings. These firms spent more on pursuing the next technology moon shot hit.

Nagji and Tuff also looked to see if there were any patterns relating share price performance to innovation investment allocations. They found that firms with a 70%/20%/10% resource allocation across Core/Adjacent/Transformational outperformed their competitors. This is consistent with 70/20/10 principle in place for many years at Google, encouraging all staff to spend 70% of their time on their core role, 20% as a member of another team, and 10% on blue sky projects. Nagji and Tuff's findings are supported by Innosight's 2019 report on the 'Transformation 20.'[22] The report showed the best performing firms adapting their core businesses through using digital technologies to create new types of digital experiences and offerings that create new value for customers, as well as pursuing growth beyond the core in adjacent and breakthrough arenas. The winners deployed new business models relying on the cloud, IoT, AI, and other technologies.

Growth beyond the core sees firms creating a higher-purpose mission that takes them into new territory such as sustainable business. To grow in new areas, firms must not be afraid to let go of the past but exploit core capabilities to enter new growth markets. They seize digital opportunities through new platforms and business models and operate in a way ensuring innovation is not isolated in a department or division. Innovation must become a strategic capability across the whole organisation – including core, adjacent, and transformational activities. Lean CX applies to all three horizons, but with the priority on H2. H2 is based on evolving products/services and shifting to near segments/markets. One of the main reasons for targeting Adjacent/H2 innovations is that they are easier for customers to take up.

Customers adopting innovations can be segmented into five groups based on their predisposition to switch to the new thing. Only 2.5% of the typical consumer market readily seeks out bleeding edge products and services. These 'Innovators' have a strong draw to novelty (U+) and like tinkering with new products and services to get them to work. The next fastest adoption group, 'Early Adopters,' comprise 13.5% of the market. They have a draw to being able to exploit the benefits of innovations first in their market (A+). Most of the time this puts them near the cutting edge, rather than at the bleeding edge because bleeding edge tech often still has teething problems. Public success with an innovation by Early Adopters prompts the 34% 'Early Majority' to get on board. This seems like a market-based herd effect (L+) because the Early Majority cannot purchase without tacit or explicit endorsement by another customer. The 34% 'Late Majority' are largely driven by a fear of missing out (FOMO) or simply being left behind (C+). The final segment, 'Laggards,' are the 16% of customers who only upgrade or update when compelled to (C-).

The most important customer group to target are the Early Adopters because this group is substantial and can act as a valid reference for the Early Majority if uptake is not a high involvement decision. This is typically the case for Adjacent/ H2 innovations. For high involvement decisions, Lean CX can also create innovations directly acceptable to the Early Majority. Adjacent/H2 innovations are more readily taken up than Core/H1 improvements or Transformational/H3 moon shots.

## Business Model Canvas and CX

The Business Model Canvas (BMC) describes the components of a firm's business model and can be used as a template for lean start-up innovation.[23]

Figure 3.5 adapts the BMC components to CX counterparts and plots them on the H1/H2/H3 innovation framework. For example, Revenue Streams in BMC

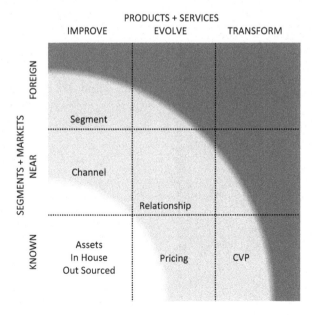

**Figure 3.5:** Business Model Canvas on Horizon Model.

translates to Pricing. Similarly, Key Activities and Partners translate to In House and Out Sourced, respectively.

The diagram shows how changes to the firm's internal operations tends to be limited to H1, where they apply to cost reduction. More externally/customer focused innovations are likely to result in H2 CX initiatives. H3 innovations do not necessarily lend themselves to CX improvement.

Not all CX innovations are equal. The case above outlining EY's perspective on digital maturity is an example of H1 changes with an H2 price tag. As previously suggested from a CX maturity standpoint, investing in digital maturity is more about cost reduction than differentiation. In contrast, the five cases above used to show different kinds of CX cut-through fit substantially in the H2 zone. This analysis suggests H2 may be the sweet spot for CX innovation.

Figure 3.6 shows how ClassPass pivots map onto the Horizon framework. The ClassPass 1.0 search engine and booking system was simply a channel innovation for fitness classes. Pivot to ClassPass 2.0 was discounted pricing similar to Groupon. The success of the business really happened with the pivot to ClassPass 3.0. This included a regular subscription payment. Even though the signup was similar to becoming a member of a gym, because ClassPass was many gyms and many different exercise experiences, customers were less likely to be stuck subscribed to something they couldn't sustain. ClassPass offered customers a key value proposition around trial to multiple providers without locking in to one.

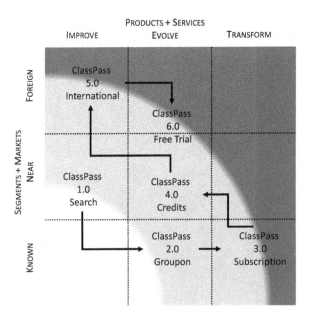

**Figure 3.6:** ClassPass Pivots.

Pivot 4.0 introduced credits to improve the relationship with suppliers by allowing differential pricing. Pivot 5.0 expanded the business internationally to foreign segments. Pivot 6.0 added free trials to international markets. This pricing strategy was designed to speed up penetration. The evolution of ClassPass from version 1.0 to version 6.0 has covered all of the H2 CX spaces in one way or another. The approach is indicative of how Lean CX should be applied.

A similar pattern plays out for pivots at Amazon (see Figure 3.7). Starting with a new channel, the retailer improved payments with 1-CLICK and introduced Kindle. This was the springboard for other products. Prime subscription came into its own as Amazon's product range grew, making it worthwhile for customers to subscribe for free delivery. Dash and Echo moved Amazon partially offline into people's homes with different interfaces. International expansion opened new markets. Finally, Go and 4-Star are Amazon innovating in the brick-and-mortar retail space. All the innovations are in the H2 CX space and this continues with Amazon Web Services in B2B.

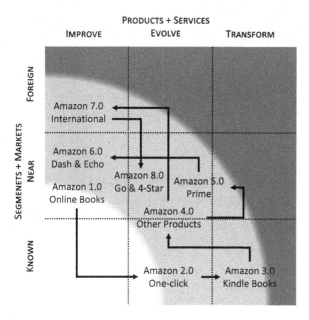

**Figure 3.7:** Amazon Pivots.

Rent the Runway has also limited its pivots to the H2 zone (see Figure 3.8). After changing from a piece by piece rental model to subscription, the company has expanded its range and footprint. RTR worked with partners like Nordstrom and WeWork so customers had more options to return items. This made using RTR more convenient. It also paved the way to add a store-based retail model for customers

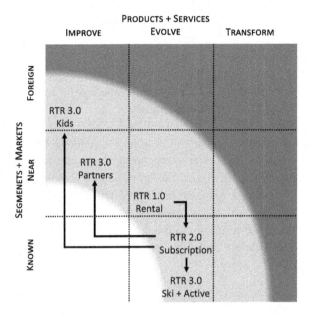

**Figure 3.8:** Rent the Runway Pivots.

wanting a more tactile experience than online shopping can offer. Stylists in store offer advice to further add value. The latest pivots are about expanding the range of clothes on offer beyond high-end fashion to include children, active wear, and ski clothes.

One possible reason H2 initiatives work better for CX innovation than H1 or H3 relates to adoption conflict. Innovations have an inherent liability of newness. At the same time, they are interesting because they are new. To achieve mass adoption, innovations need to be different enough to stand out but not so different they cannot be readily understood and used.[24] This is the essence of the MAYA design principle.

## MAYA – Most Advanced Yet Acceptable

Raymond Loewy, considered by many to be the father of industrial design, is the inventor of the MAYA design principle.[25] Loewy believed that consumers are torn between two opposing forces: neophilia and neophobia (curiosity about and fear of newness). Loewy advocated designing products bold enough to stand out, but instantly comprehensible. He said that to sell something surprising make it familiar; and to sell something familiar make it surprising. This is the essence of the MAYA principle and why it seems many Gazelles find the niche in the middle horizon of McKinsey's innovation chart.

*C+ U+ Alien cuts through for investors[26] and Plus60 cuts through for aged care*
*When the movie Alien was first pitched to Hollywood studios by writers Dan O'Bannon and Ronald Shusett as 'Jaws in Space.' The elegance of this tag line is that it is perfectly MAYA. It presents the plot as a new version of the familiar blockbuster Jaws. In doing so, it tells a would-be film investor everything they need to know to decide if they are interested: plot outline, budget, genre, distinctiveness, and potential sequel. The Alien and Jaws plots are centred on a monster attacking cast members one by one and getting away at the end, without killing the lead character. Both movies were big on budget and special effects. Jaws and Alien are both horror movies, but Alien is distinctive because it is also science fiction. Finally, the fact the monster gets away at the end lays the foundation for a sequel. In the end there were eight movies made in the Alien franchise.*
*Today entrepreneurs seeking investment funding for their start-ups are often coached to describe their business as a new version of a familiar business. For example, Pluss Communities is a social media platform designed to help aged care providers communicate with and involve their residents in social events. The app has been described as Facebook for aged care without the ads. At the time of this writing, the start-up has around 30% of the largest aged care providers as customers using or trialling the software to reinvent their customer communications.*

Cut-through requires solving the innovation/newness conflict. In CAPFUL terms, MAYA meets customer's needs for both certainty (C+) and novelty (U+) at the same time. The challenge is learning just how new something needs to be to get noticed, and at the same time ensuring it is familiar enough to be quickly and easily understood. It is about determining the right level of innovativeness.

Previously a three-factor construct for measuring Innovativeness[27] has been proposed for finding the innovation sweet spot. The Innovativeness level of an initiative is determined from how First, Useful, and Successful it is. Normally these factors are thought of as basic digital concepts – something is either first or not, useful or not, and ultimately successful or not. However, these variables can be expanded to cover a range when considering how innovative something is. For example, instead of thinking about First as a digital concept (as in "is this a world first?"). First considers the largest group of users as correlating with how first something is. For example, first in a particular country is not a world first, but still a first in some sense (see the left column of Table 3.1). Combining just two of the factors, First and Useful, offers an indication of cut-through.

Table 3.2 shows the how the ranges for both First and Useful are defined. First is related to the largest group for whom the innovation is considered new. Useful is related to the level of utility a user perceives the innovation offers. In the table, First and Useful are independent variables. The levels are also each inclusive of lower levels. This means a level 4 Useful innovation is not only suitable for a user's context, it offers an unprecedented benefit, is simple to use, and understood by users.

First and Useful need to be considered differently when trying to determine the ideal level of cut-through. This is exactly the principle Loewy hit upon with the

**Table 3.2:** Innovation Metrics.

| Level | First | Useful |
|---|---|---|
| 5 | A world first, never before seen | Trial is cheap and without switching costs |
| 4 | First time in this country or market | Take up fits in the user's context |
| 3 | New for a firm, following a market pioneer | Offers a benefit over previous solutions |
| 2 | First for a team/group/unit inside a firm | Simple/easy to use |
| 1 | Only individuals remain to adopt the idea | Essentially understood by users |

concept of MAYA. It is quite possible for an innovation to be too 'bleeding edge' to be acceptable to any but a small group of customers. Even merely 'cutting edge' innovations can be too radical for most customers in a market. Whether or not a specific customer is attracted or repelled by newness is defined as their *adoption profile*.

> **U+ C+ WeChat cuts through in China**
> WeChat is one of the largest messaging platforms in the world. It is essentially WhatsApp in China,[28] but with some more functionality. WeChat is obviously not a world first, but it is a first in China. This makes WeChat a level 4 First. WeChat can also be evaluated for its Useful level: As a messaging service it is simple and easy to use for anyone familiar with WhatsApp or Facebook Messenger. So it probably gets to at least level 2 for most potential users. WeChat also includes a payment platform, which increases its utility above a simple messaging service. Users can hail a ride share, buy rail or flight tickets, book a hotel, pay for utilities, and get a movie ticket. This potentially makes the app level 3 Useful because it does more than WhatsApp or Facebook Messenger. WeChat only works in China, however, and you have to have a Chinese bank account and understand some Chinese characters. For someone outside of China or visiting on holidays, the app is probably not a level 4 Useful because it doesn't fit with their situation. For a Chinese consumer, WeChat is likely to be level 4 Useful (if they own a phone). WeChat may even be level 5 Useful, because it doesn't lock users in. Unlike the Apple Product Ecosystem or Microsoft's attempts to link everything to a single login, it does seem like you could try WeChat and then just quit later if you didn't like it. However, you do lose contact information you have stored in the platform if you quit.

Everett M. Rogers defined five different segments of consumers based on their preference for taking up innovations (see Figure 3.9).[29]

Rogers found customers who took up innovations later tended to rely on the references, experiences, and endorsements of previous customers (whether implied or explicit). Moore discovered this didn't quite work the same in high tech markets, many of which are also B2B markets.[30] High tech purchases are typically more expensive and more involved than other purchases. This tends to amplify the differences between the needs of Early Adopter and Early Majority. The result is EAs fail

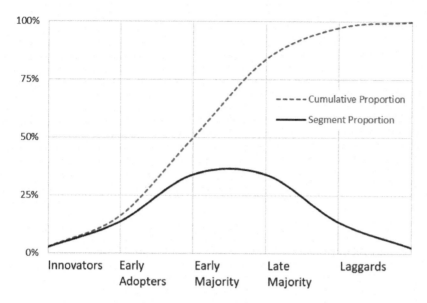

**Figure 3.9:** Innovation Adoption and Consumer Segments.

as credible references for EMs in high tech markets. Early Adopters purchase to get a strategic advantage by taking a risk. Early Majority customers prefer to purchase established quality to avoid taking a risk. This results in high tech products' sales stalling as they saturate penetration with EAs. EMs as a group tend to wait until other EMs have made a purchase before committing themselves. Moore called this phenomenon 'the chasm.' Crossing the chasm typically requires redesigning the high-tech product for the mass market. This involves reducing costs, simplifying operation, taking out some features and improving reliability. The product has to be adapted to reduce its liability of newness. Moore asserts increased levels of Useful (more benefits, better fit, and lower switching costs) are required to get the EMs to adopt. The finding is relevant for any highly involved innovation purchase even if it is not high-tech.

Rogers' and Moore's different findings fit neatly with the concept of MAYA and the H1/H2/H3 frame above. Rogers' adoption segments apply to H2 innovations. EAs like to adopt H2 innovations and will bet on H3 innovations. H2 innovations are often closer to what customers already understand and are more familiar with. EMs can adopt H2 innovations because the level of involvement with the purchase is much lower than most H3 innovations. Moore's caveats and the chasm apply specifically to H3 innovations. These tend to be more radical and a bigger jump for customers to accept. MAYA was Loewy's realisation H3 innovations needed to be scaled back and H1 innovations needed to be spiced up.

## Endnotes

**1** Landroguez et al. (2011). "Creating dynamic capabilities to increase customer value," *Management Decision.*

**2** Bennett and Lemoine (2014). "What a difference a word makes: Understanding threats to performance in a VUCA world," *Business Horizons.*

**3** Saved from author's Commsec share trading account. https://research.commsec.com.au/Chart/AdvancedChart?code=AFG (accessed 23/5/20).

**4** This may be a good thing because neither of the major parties are prepared to commit the carbon tax collection to climate change-related initiatives. Both sides would simply add the windfall gain into consolidated revenue and retard further private economic growth.

**5** Patrick (2019). "Australia is rich, dumb and getting dumber," *Australian Financial Review.* https://www.afr.com/policy/economy/australia-is-rich-dumb-and-getting-dumber-20191007-p52y8i (accessed 23/5/20).

**6** Trading Economics (2015) "Australia Government Spending to GDP," *Trading Economics* https://tradingeconomics.com/australia/government-spending-to-gdp (accessed 23/5/20).

**7** Mann (2014). "What's Up With That: Building Bigger Roads Actually Makes Traffic Worse," *Wired.* https://www.wired.com/2014/06/wuwt-traffic-induced-demand/ (accessed 23/5/20).

**8** Ibid., footnote 77.

**9** It was so hard to refrain from turning this into an acronym, it is now listed here: Cut-through CX gets you A BEER. Attractive, Better, Efficient, Effective, and Remarkable.

**10** This case was adapted from several sources: ClassPass website https://classpass.com; Wikipedia, "ClassPass" https://en.wikipedia.org/wiki/ClassPass (accessed 5/12/19); Wortham (2015). "ClassPass and the Joy and Guilt of the Digital Middleman Economy," *The New York Times Magazine.* https://www.nytimes.com/2015/03/05/magazine/classpass-and-the-joy-and-guilt-of-the-digital-middleman-economy.html; Shontell (2014). "How Getting Mugged and Maced Helped a World-Class Dancer Save Her Struggling Startup," *Business Insider.* https://www.businessinsider.com.au/how-payal-kadakia-found-success-with-classpass-2014-7?r=US&IR=T.

**11** Crockett (2019). "Are gym memberships worth the money?" *The Hustle.* https://thehustle.co/gym-membership-cost.

**12** Jaffe (2014). "Every City Needs Hong Kong's Brilliant Baggage-Check System," *Citylab.* https://www.citylab.com/solutions/2014/08/every-city-needs-hong-kongs-brilliant-baggage-check-system/378826/.

**13** Adapted from "T+ Instant satisfaction from One Click at Amazon," and "T+ E+ M+ Amazon Go evolves traditional shopping," in Dew (2018). *Customer Experience Innovation: How to Get a Lasting Market Edge,* Emerald Publishing Limited.

**14** See McLachlan (2017). *The Lean CX Score: How Does Your Business Measure Up?* pages 75–78.

**15** Frankenfield (2019). "How Amazon Makes Money," *Investopedia.* https://www.investopedia.com/how-amazon-makes-money-4587523.

**16** Greco (2017). "How to test drive a BMW without going into the dealership," *Policaro BMW.* https://www.policarobmw.ca/bmw-at-home-test-drive-lets-you-test-drive-a-bmw-without-going-into-a-dealership/.

**17** This was reported internally by consulting firm Strativity after they worked with BMW in the US to improve their CX.

**18** Goldberg (2014). "Rent the Runway Online Outlet Enhances Customer Experience with Offline Stores," *eMarketer.* https://www.emarketer.com/Article/Rent-Runway-Online-Outlet-Enhances-Customer-Experience-with-Offline-Stores/1011640.

**19** Blank (2019). "McKinsey's Three Horizons Model Defined Innovation for Years. Here's Why It No Longer Applies," *Harvard Business Review*. https://hbr.org/2019/02/mckinseys-three-horizons-model-defined-innovation-for-years-heres-why-it-no-longer-applies.

**20** Nagji and Tuff (2003). "Managing your innovation portfolio," *Harvard Business Review* Vol 90 no 5.

**21** Fleming (2019). "McDonald's turns to tech to build the future of fast food," *MarketingWeek*. https://www.marketingweek.com/mcdonalds-digital-transformation/ (accessed 14/7/20).

**22** Innosight (2019). "The Transformation 20: The Top Global Companies Leading Strategic Transformations." https://www.innosight.com/insight/the-transformation-20/ (accessed 5/8/20).

**23** Osterwalder et al. (2010). *Business Model Generation: A Handbook for Visionaries, Game Changers, and Challengers*, John Wiley & Sons.

**24** Another take on this is that technologies give rise to technologies, according to W. Brian Arthur in Arthur (2009). "Where Darwin doesn't fit . . . ." *New Scientist* Vol 203 Iss 2722. This 'piggy backing' to create composite technologies from what Arthur calls combinatorial evolution is another form of adjacent positioning.

**25** Thompson (2017). "The Four-Letter Code to Selling Just About Anything," *The Atlantic*. https://www.theatlantic.com/magazine/archive/2017/01/what-makes-things-cool/508772/

**26** Wikipedia, "Alien." https://en.wikipedia.org/wiki/Alien_(film) (accessed 28/12/19).

**27** Dew (2018). *Customer Experience Innovation: How to Get a Lasting Market Edge*, Emerald Publishing Limited.

**28** Kharpal (2019). "Everything you need to know about WeChat – China's billion-user messaging app," *CNBC*. https://www.cnbc.com/2019/02/04/what-is-wechat-china-biggest-messaging-app.html.

**29** Rogers (2003). *Diffusion of Innovations, 5th Edition*, Simon and Schuster.

**30** Moore (2014). *Crossing the Chasm, 3rd Edition*, HarperCollins.

# Chapter 4
# Where to Start

Creating MAYA CX is not straightforward. Many customers are at best only indirectly aware of what they really want. Most don't know how they come to realise what they think they want. Almost all are blissfully ignorant of what they might want in the future. The exception is that customers will say they want an extension of what they have now. This creates a challenge for designers involved in new product development and Lean CX alike – how to invent what customers want when designers cannot ask them directly what this might be. Ries intuited this as he was developing the Lean Start-up method within his own company. He asserted his team had to focus on what customers might want but without directly taking on board their expressed desires about how to deliver it.

> We really did have customers in those early days – true visionary early adopters – we often talked to them and asked for their feedback. But we emphatically did not do what they said. In fact, we were much more likely to run experiments on our customers than we were to cater to their whims . . . Traditional business thinking says that this approach shouldn't work, but it does . . . [1]

## Human-Centred Design

Ries was expressing the fundamental issue in human-centred design (HCD) when he shared his experiences about where to search for market traction. On the one hand, CX designers need to talk with customers to learn about what they do, think, and feel before, during, and after purchases. On the other hand, designers also need to intuit the underlying motivations for their clients' choices. They need to do this without being misled about what their customers may claim to be driving needs, imperative wants, and aspirational desires. This problem of how to empathise without being misdirected is an interesting part of the human condition. It is at the core of good HCD.

Empathy should be automatic for everyone. After all, we all share common drives to move away from pain and toward pleasure. The reality of the human condition is that getting along with others starts with ourselves and how we make meaning out of what other people say and do. Don Miguel Ruiz described an approach to dealing with the human condition as 'Four Agreements.'[2] The agreements are a useful starting point for how to think about the right attitude for HCD. Ruiz' agreements are:
1. Be impeccable with your word
2. Don't take anything personally
3. Don't make assumptions
4. Always do your best

https://doi.org/10.1515/9783110683929-004

The first agreement means to speak truthfully about the world as you would like it to be. More than simply being honest, this is about verbalising your preferred future. Designers are drawn to think about how the world can function better. This is the goal of good design. Design processes improve when designers go beyond merely describing their design problem to stating the ideal final result they want to achieve.[3] Many designers find making their aspirations explicit helps to evoke potential solutions. Inadvertently, customers do this when they describe how they would like things to be. Ironically, customers can obscure potential solutions when they discuss how problems can be solved. This is due to customers being anchored in the way things are now. Traditionally-managed organisations can be remarkably similar in this regard.

Organisations describe the future when they make promises about what they will deliver to customers. These promises can be explicit, like a written guarantee or an advertised promotion ("satisfaction guaranteed or your money back"). They can also be implicit, like the associations customers make about a firm's brand. When expressed or implied promises are broken, conflict can occur. This happens whether the promise is made by a company or a person. This is where the second agreement comes in.

The second agreement means understanding even a direct confrontation or pointed insult at you does not actually express anything about you. Instead the confrontation or insult is an indication of how your antagonist is thinking and/or feeling. Even if it seems intentionally and directly personal, the reality is simply that you happen to be proximate. You are the temporary focus of their tirade or tantrum. The same applies if someone is conciliatory or complimentary to you. Again, they are really communicating how they are thinking and feeling. They are not really conveying anything about how you really are. Gaining clarity of customer communications requires the CX designer to connect with customers and establish rapport, but at the same time not take anything they say to heart.

Applied psychology in Neuro-Linguistic Programming expands this idea. NLP suggests we judge ourselves based on our intentions. But we judge others based on the meanings we assign to their actions.[4] It is our assumptions about why others have done what they have done that is ultimately making us happy or unhappy. We all do this constantly. For the most part without realising we do it. This brings us to the third agreement.

The third agreement reminds us we can never truly know why someone else says or does anything, we only ever guess. There is a substantive body of research suggesting that we don't really know ourselves. Previous research relating to purchase intention and purchase behaviour suggests we are poor predictors of our future actions (see Table 4.1).[5]

This data shows how people can completely misreport their intention to purchase. The lamp, iron, and radio research results below show total disconnection between stated customer intention and action. The closest match between intention to buy and

**Table 4.1:** Purchase Intention Accuracy.

| Product | Year | Intenders not buying | Non-intenders buying |
| --- | --- | --- | --- |
| Cars | 1966 | 50.0% | 11% |
| Cars | 1974 | 62.5% | 8% |
| Toothpaste | 1989 | 48.0% | 17% |
| Diet drink mix | 1989 | 38.5% | 17% |
| Fruit sticks | 1989 | 56.5% | 16% |
| Milk | 1989 | 97.2% | 5% |
| Salad dressing | 1989 | 43.7% | 12% |
| Computer | 1989 | 57.1% | 4% |
| Phone | 1989 | 87.5% | 11% |
| Lamp | 1989 | 100.0% | 3% |
| Iron | 1989 | 100.0% | 0% |
| Radio | 1989 | 100.0% | 1% |
| Packaged goods | 1975 | 74.0% | 12% |
| Service option | 1986 | 65.5% | 10% |

actual purchase from the above studies was for diet drink mix. Even then, more than a third of those who stated they would buy, didn't. The table also shows how up to 16% of those involved in the studies went on to buy after stating they wouldn't!

**U+ A+ EdventureY highlights problems with intentions to purchase research[6]**
*One author's unsuccessful start-up was built on the idea of helping first-year students enjoy a gap year after high school while still going to university. Data on deferring first-year Australian students showed only around one in twenty ever made it to university if they chose not to take up an offered place in the year following high school. Analysis of semi-structured interviews suggested interesting motivational conflicts. Many of these students were not natural scholars. Despite this, they had worked hard for grades good enough to get them into university. They were driven largely by parental expectations, concerns about career prospects, and/or a worry of being left behind by their peers. Despite achieving the grades they needed to get in to university, almost all who chose to defer believed they would have been forced to drop out if they commenced their enrollments immediately after school. Most cited being unable to continue with the perceived stress and pressure of study. They believed university would be even more difficult than high school. They were either burned out or unable to force themselves to keep going without a break. When asked what they wanted to do, some related how a gap year overseas appealed to them.*

*EdventureY was designed so these students could get a needed break after the stress of high school and still commence their undergraduate degree. Students would travel from Australia to live and work in Europe at a pub for several months. The package included flight, accommodations, and meals, plus full wages for up to five days per week work. Also in the package was a learning experience designed as a game to be played during days off of work. The experience was created to be like the The Amazing Race TV show. In pairs, students would act like the contestants on the show, travelling from location to location, solving puzzles to get the clue to the next destination and challenge. The whole experience played out as a mobile tourist treasure hunt.*

*The locations and challenges meant players would learn about entrepreneurship through experiences instead of in lectures. Activities included going to London, Paris, and Amsterdam. In each city, students could compare and contrast how specific businesses operated differently compared to back home in Australia. The players learned step by step as they solved the puzzles in the game. Completing the program provided university credit without lectures or assessments.*

*The course was founded based on a survey of around 200 students. Students were presented with various destination, price, duration, and content combinations and asked if they would sign up. Conjoint analysis was used to identify the preferred bundle and pricing. The results indicated the most popular option should attract more than one in six enrollments. But when EdventureY was offered to 700 first-year students during their foundation business classes at university, not a single student took up the offer. Sadly, the project was abandoned a year later. This case shows the difference between intention to purchase and actual purchase.*

The mismatch between intention and action is why functionally or technologically sound innovations can still struggle to get market penetration. It is often better to invest resources asking customers to buy instead of surveying them about their intentions and motivations to buy. Real-life observation trumps theoretical interviews. Lean CX is about getting to real-life observation via market testing as quickly as possible. This makes it lower risk than traditional waterfall CX based on primary research studies.

Market testing as part of a lean process intrinsically involves learning from failure. This is where the fourth agreement comes in. Because the other three agreements are difficult to live by without lapsing, the final agreement admonishes for failure to be accepted. The idea is to try your best, learn from your experiences, and move on. The rhetoric in many corporates is that learning from failure is a core value in the organisation. In practice, employees often act to prevent being held accountable for getting things wrong. Process workers myopically run the process they have been taught because they fear being reprimanded or worse for using any of their own initiative. Organisational routines are established to prevent failures. Oversight is implemented to avoid mistakes. The reality is that organisations and their employees are not machines. Failures are inevitable when it comes to interacting with customers. HCD prompts the organisation to evolve to become more like a living system than a machine.

Classic HCD begins with creating a description of a typical customer's situation, cognition, and motivation. This provides design context. The form of a design context statement is "When I < . . . > I want to < . . . > so I can < . . . >." Inside each < . . . > is an observation, understanding, or intuition about what a typical customer

is doing, thinking, or feeling. For example, consider what it might be like for someone to travel overseas. Even if you have never travelled overseas, you can get a
sense of what it is like for some tourists as you read the following design context
statement: "When I <travel overseas> I want to <learn some local words> so I can
<feel like I am more part of it all>."

In combination, this sentence conveys an *experience insight* about international
travel in human terms (see Figure 4.1). Experience insights link how customers act
to their emotional state and cognition during a specific event. The linkage can be in
any order. For example, "When I <need to get away from it all> I want to <fly over-
seas> so I can <discover something new>" is ordered as feeling/doing/thinking in
contrast to doing/thinking/feeling for the first example.

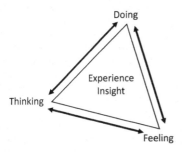

**Figure 4.1:** Experience Insight Components.

## Lizard, Labrador, and Leader Brains

The reason experience insights need to combine doing, thinking, and feeling is because of how the structure of the human brain dominates its function. The following description is not meant to be perfectly correct in a neurophysiological sense. It
is intended to help understand the practical complexities involved in the psychology of motivation.

Our brain can be divided into three different parts: a Lizard-like part, a Labrador-
like part, and a Leader part. Each of these parts arrived at different stages in our evolution. The younger parts got stacked on top of the older parts as we changed over
many generations from reptiles to mammals and then primates.

Our Lizard brain is the oldest part and includes the cerebellum, medulla, and
pons (see Figure 4.2). Our internal Lizards are constantly focused on our survival.
Much like reptile brains in other creatures, our Lizard brain is always on even when
we are asleep.

The Lizard is all about Doing. In any instant the Lizard can simply take over
and prompt us to act instantly.

It works in immediate mode. When we pick up a hot pan from the stove, the
Lizard causes us to drop it to avoid being burnt. If we knock a glass off the table, it

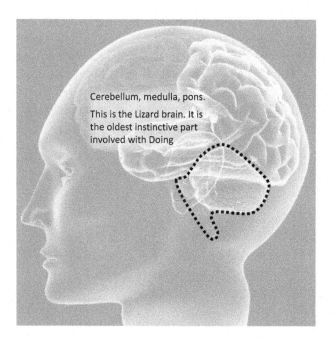

Cerebellum, medulla, pons.
This is the Lizard brain. It is
the oldest instinctive part
involved with Doing

**Figure 4.2:** Lizard Brain.

is our Lizard reflexes are used to reach out and catch it before it hits the floor and breaks. When we react without thinking, it is Lizard who is in control. As you are reading these words it is likely your Lizard who is speaking the words aloud in your head. You don't have to think to hear the words. You just read and it happens. Beyond automating some functions, your Lizard can make snap decisions.

Lizard decisions respond to the world in only two ways – toward or away. The Lizard wants more pleasure and less pain. In response to pleasure it moves us closer to get more. Pain creates the opposite response. For most people when pleasure and pain are in conflict, pain wins out in the short term.

The Lizard brain operates in a highly sophisticated way even though it only produces two outputs to decisions. Over time our Lizard learns and some of the things we learn become habits. Other things become unconscious competencies. Learning means cause-and-effect relationships are hard-wired into the Lizard brain over time as we accumulate experiences. This is called *operant conditioning*. Behavioural psychologists used to believe all motivation could be explained by this stimulus response. The famous experiments by Pavlov on his dog are all about training the dog's Lizard brain to associate food with the sound of a bell. When Pavlov rang the bell, the dog would salivate in anticipation of being fed. The ability for our Lizard to learn associations and then connect these to action enables our Lizard brain to work like our autopilot.

You can operate a car at a lower level of vigilance than when you were first learning when you know how to drive. If you a driving on a freeway at speed and the brake lights from the car in front come on, you don't need to think about slowing, you just automatically put your foot on the brake. It is your Lizard doing this. Much of our life is spent with our Lizard directing us on autopilot. If you have ever gotten part way to work while driving and couldn't remember the details of your trip, it was because your Lizard was doing the driving. Most likely your Leader brain was dealing with something else. This state is called Flow and it seems to be a condition where our Leader can access subconscious resources to solve problems.[7]

Our Leader brain is the youngest part of the brain in evolutionary terms. It is likely to be in the neocortex (see Figure 4.3). When people describe functions related to either the left brain

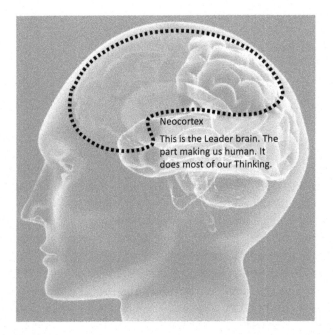

Neocortex
This is the Leader brain. The part making us human. It does most of our Thinking.

**Figure 4.3:** Leader Brain.

or the right brain, they are talking about the operations of the neocortex. The neocortex is the seat of our consciousness. This is where we do language, mathematics, strategy, and introspection.

Unlike the Lizard brain, our Leader brains are capable of varied and complex responses to the outside world. This part of the brain is a meaning-making machine. It is where we rationalise what happens to us and why. It enables us to consider right and wrong. It makes predictions about the future and deals with our past.

Surprisingly, for all its sophistication the Leader brain is the least powerful of the three brains. When we face internal conflict between an addictive habit and doing what is best for our long-term health, it is often the Lizard winning out over the Leader's more adult voice. Imagine being out late socialising and having a great time. Your Leader brain may remind you that tomorrow is a big day at work and you should retire to bed. But if your Lizard is having a fine time eating, drinking, and talking, it can be a challenge to leave the party early and do the responsible thing. Another example is the remarkable trouble most people have keeping their New Year's resolutions. According to one study, 29% of participants had failed to keep going by the end of their second week. Less than half were able to continue their resolution for six months.[8] Few of us have perfect Lizard control. Adding in the third key part of our brain complicates decisions even more. This brain part is our inner Labrador.

Brian Hare and Vanessa Woods described the research into the way dogs act.[9] Anyone who has kept a pet dog knows they express primary feelings including happiness, excitement, caring, fear, anger, and remorse. Having feelings allows dogs (and other mammals) to operate as social creatures. Mammals care for their young and live in packs, herds, and prides. This improves the chances for young animals to survive to breeding age. In contrast, reptiles are at best indifferent to their young. After laying eggs they typically leave them to fend for themselves. Occasionally reptilian parents rediscover their progeny after they hatch, fail to recognise them as their own children, and may eat them. Like us, mammals have both Lizard- and Labrador-like parts to their brains.

Also like us, mammals' feelings moderate the base selfishness of their Lizard brains. This makes mammalian brains more complex than reptilian brains. So dogs have a greater range of behaviour than skinks. Dogs will defend their young from other predators, for example. Realising that humans have an equivalent to the canine brain offers clues to unlocking how our motivations arise.

Our Labrador brain is younger than our Lizard brain and older than our Leader brain in evolutionary terms. It includes the limbic system and amygdala (see Figure 4.4). While pure pleasure and pain probably arise in our Lizard brain, other more differentiated feelings are likely due to our Labrador brain. This is where we enjoy love, rage furiously, drink in the thrill of the chase, jump at shadows, revel in triumph, drown our sorrows, and rue the bittersweet pang of parting. Our Labrador brain motivates us beyond the immediate toward more than just our selfish needs. It compels us to pursue more complex desires. This part of the brain is where emotion lies. It's more powerful and less clever than the Leader brain, but slower than our Lizard. And it does not plan.

We are complex creatures because our motivation arises from the interaction of our Lizard, Labrador, and Leader. After the Lizard reacts nearly instantly to move toward or away, then our Labrador gets us to feel. In the feeling we may suspend our instinctive Lizard or amplify its first impulse. It is only after that our Leader brain can catch up to become involved. The Leader somehow creates the story of meaning tying it all together while trying to provide a higher level of direction and control.

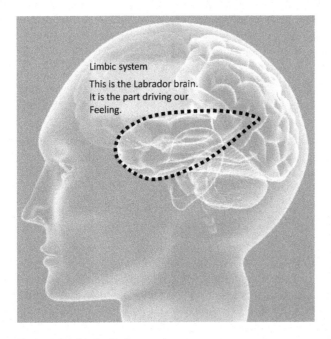

**Figure 4.4:** Labrador Brain.

Then the cycle repeats as the meaning made by the Leader brain becomes input for the Lizard and Labrador. Anyone who has ever tried to not think at all understands this cycle is remarkably persistent within our inner worlds. The three structures of the brain are why CX designers consider what customers are doing, feeling, and thinking as they interact with companies. It is the foundation for the three-pronged structure of experience insights.

Traditional CX research synthesises experience insights from semi-structured customer interviews. Researchers typically discuss with customers what they are thinking, feeling, and doing in steps before, during, and after specific purchases. Interviews can take up 90 minutes and ideally cover a representative sample of customers. Lean CX can utilise similar insights, however the alternative is to simply try to empathise with customers and propose potential insights. This shortcut tends to be effective only if the right employees are involved. The most appropriate are staff in customer-facing roles and have a more social personality type.

There are many personality frameworks useful for identifying personality types. The Myers-Briggs Type Indicator, for example, classifies people along four dimensions: Extraversion/Introversion, Sensing/Intuitive, Feeling/Thinking, and Judging/Perceiving. People with a Feeling orientation find empathy more natural than those with a Thinking orientation. Perceivers may find new possibilities easier to conceptualise than Judgers. Sensing types may be better at customer observation, but Intuitive types may be better at considering their motivations. Extraverts may be more attracted to customer-facing roles, yet Introverts may be better at learning what customers are thinking without influencing them. One simpler alternative to Myers-Briggs is the DISC framework. This classifies people as Dominants, Influencers, Supporters, or Conscientious. Of the four DISC types, Influencer and Supporter types may be more empathetic because they are more naturally people-oriented. Influencers are more extraverted. Supporters are more introverted.

Myers-Briggs, DISC, and other personality frameworks are useful for general personality classifications. CAPFUL is a more fundamental approach to psychology derived from Maslow's Hierarchy of Needs.[10]

## CAPFUL Customer Psychology

Previously we presented two possible experience insights related to travelling:
1. "When I <travel overseas> I want to <learn some local words> so I can <feel like I am more part of it all>."
2. "When I <need to get away from it all> I want to <fly overseas> so I can <discover something new>."

These insights are effective because they link directly with a CAPFUL need. The first example above is L+, relating to love and belonging needs. The second example above is U+ relating to the need for the uncommon and novelty. Considering additional CAPFUL needs can lead to other CX improvement opportunities for the same customers. Consider an international traveller with a certainty need (C+) rather than L+ or U+ needs. A relevant experience insight could be, "When I <am on holiday overseas> I want <to know what is best to wear> so I <feel comfortable all day>."

*C+ A+ P+ F+ U+ L+ Skiing CX in Campitello di Fassa*
*Dolomites Ski Tours [DST] is run by Mario Longitano, an entrepreneur with a flair for CX. Mario first skied the area around the Sella Ronda in 1982 and has now created a complete ski experience for beginners to experts in the mountains near Campitello di Fassa in Italy. What makes DST remarkable is the way the guest experience has been designed by skiers for skiers.*

*The company does the normal shuttle from the airport to guest hotels. The bus is driven by one of the ski guides. He explains over the two-hour run up to the town what to expect (C+). In addition to snow conditions and key runs to try, there are interesting stories about the history of the area and what makes skiing there different from other places around the world (U+). Mario has a core of regulars who know everything about the local scene. Guides are each responsible for a handful of guests and take care to escort them around and help with picking up rental skis and accessing lockers. One of the considered DST touches is ensuring every guest gets a locker in the closest location to the main gondola for the mountain. This minimises the amount of time and distance walking around in ski boots – a seriously good benefit after a long day on the slopes. But where the guides really excel is on the snow.*

*All DST guides have years of experience in the Dolomites around the Sella Ronda. They specialise in knowing the best run to ski next, the right lift to take, where to stop for lunch, the closest place for a comfort stop, and how long it will take to get back home (C+). They consider their charges' capabilities and confidence, plus the conditions and crowds at every choice throughout a day of skiing. More experienced skiers are shown the best off-piste trails to explore (U+) away from the crowds (P+). Guides are careful to ensure guests understand how to leave the lowest environmental footprint when skiing off-piste (F+). Less experienced skiers are matched to slopes they will enjoy and with the best locations for photo opportunities. The DST team are highly accomplished skiers and can help with lessons for skiers intending to level up (+A). They continue to care for guests after hours.*

*At the end of every day, it is customary for the DST group to meet in one of the local restaurants to share a drink before dinner. This gives everyone in the group more of a chance to get to know each other and ultimately eliminates any social distance between anyone in the group (L+). Guests are always free to go and do their own thing, and guides can help with recommendations about where to eat. However it is common for people to want to share stories about their day and something of their lives back home, so often there is a large group of guests happy to stay together (L+). Normally an evening finishes with agreed plans about who will ski with whom the next day and what time to meet (C+).*

*The reason the DST experience works is that it helps guests enjoy Campitello di Fassa as insiders instead of visitors. Somehow the various guides know how to make everyone feel part of it all, without being too close. They all share a passion for skiing. Part of their arrangement with Mario is to make sure they each get some time off during the tours to enjoy the mountain themselves. It may be this opportunity to recharge which helps them to keep it friendly and fresh with guests.*

There is a little more to the CAPFUL needs than first appearances. The needs can be sorted into conflicting pairs. For example, Certainty and Uncommon needs are opposed. Certainty needs include the desire to be safe and secure, have things happy automatically without effort, and quickly to avoid the potential for something to go wrong. Many of the customer-facing processes developed by banks are designed to be C+. In a world where everything is assured and predictable we can become bored. We also have a desire for the Uncommon in contrast to our need for Certainty. U+ includes seeking out novel experiences, looking for adventure, being curious, and playing creatively. It is our need for novelty and the uncommon driving industries with a high degree of aesthetic. These include fashion, movies, music, and high-end food. Whatever is on-trend in these industries cannot remain there forever due to our eventual need for something new.

The second pair of opposed needs are the needs for Love and Prestige. L+ includes creating connections, building relationships, being part of the team, and joining various tribes. Many of us do remarkably extreme things to show our support for our favourite sporting team and meet our L+ need to belong. We may wear our team's colours, paint our faces, and sing team songs while marching with other members of our sporting tribe. A moment of on-field success can have us standing and cheering. A questionable call against our side can have us booing the referee or umpire. Curiously, the act of becoming part of a larger group acts to erode our individual identity.

If you learn someone supports a team in a lower or upper socio-economic area, you are likely to associate them immediately with the stereotype of the team's supporters. Even the simple act of getting married carries with it the consequence of becoming another's spouse. Instead of being your own man or woman, you become somebody's husband or wife. Our need to form relationships conflicts with our need to establish our individual identities.

Prestige needs are essentially the social recognition of our individual identity. Driving a luxury car, wearing an expensive watch, drinking rare wine, and enjoying the perks of business class travel are all designed to appeal to our need to feel special. Meeting P+ needs can cause us to act in seemingly irrational ways. At work we may take on more responsibility to win a more prestigious title. PhD candidates aspire to add doctor to their name. Some people even buy a title.

---

*P+ F+ Becoming a Lord[11]*

*According to WikiHow there are several ways to become a Lord. The easiest way is to purchase a title from a website, which may or may not come with a token plot of land. At the time of this writing, the first ad appearing on Google for "become a lord" promoted becoming a Lord of Glencoe\* from just £30 was from www.highlandtitles.com. According to their website, "You obtain a personal right to a souvenir plot of land and our permission to use our registered trademarks, Laird, Lord and Lady of Glencoe" (P+). The funds go to The Highland Titles Charitable Trust for Scotland. The Trust ensures more than 400 acres it owns can only ever be used for the purposes of conservation. The trust is proud of its mission: "Simply put, we want to carry on what we're doing: Conserving Scotland, one square foot at a time" (F+).*

*Buying a Lordship does not make you legally a lord. The only way to become a lord in the full legal sense is to:*
1. *Buy an open estate that comes with the title of Lord*
2. *Marry into a noble family to receive the title upon inheritance*
3. *Be awarded the title by the House of Lords Appointments Commission*
4. *Be appointed to the House of Lords by the Queen of England*

---

Certainty, Uncommon, Love, and Prestige needs are so important (according to Robbins) [12] that people will even sacrifice their standards to meet these needs. The final two CAPFUL needs are less imperative. Like the others, they are somewhat opposed. Aspiration needs relate to growth, mastery, and achievement. Mastering how to paint, learning a musical instrument, beating a personal best time, climbing a mountain, getting a degree, or working to becoming financially independent are all possible examples of A+ pursuits. The range of aspirations we have is limited only by human imagination. In most Western cultures, we venerate overcoming the odds to persist and achieve. However going after personal goals like these is fundamentally self-centred. The alternative is to seek a greater purpose leading to fulfilment.

Fulfilment needs are met by giving back to others or the greater society somehow. Doing something for the environment, coaching a children's sporting team, helping in a soup kitchen, volunteering for a charity, and mucking in after a natural disaster to help with clean-up are all things done to meet F+ needs. The orientation for these activities is other-centred, potentially putting them in conflict with A+ needs.

Everyone desires to meet their CAPFUL needs to some degree. It is usual for different people to prioritise one or two CAPFUL needs above others. Table 4.2 maps the typical priority of CAPFUL needs as primary [1], secondary [2], or tertiary [3] for each DISC[13] personality type.

Table 4.2: DISC and CAPFUL.

| DISC Type | C | A | P | F | U | L |
|---|---|---|---|---|---|---|
| Dominant | 2 | 1 | 2 | 3 | 3 | 3 |
| Influencer | 3 | 3 | 1 | 3 | 2 | 2 |
| Supporter | 2 | 3 | 3 | 1 | 3 | 2 |
| Conscientious | 1 | 3 | 2 | 2 | 3 | 3 |

Identifying the most important CAPFUL needs of different customer cohorts and linking them into experience insights is foundational for Lean CX. Instead of investing in extensive primary research interviewing a representative sample of customers, Lean CX designers can use inductive reasoning. Designers can either start with a familiar customer's experience, or their own experience. Either way, their objective is to try and generalise to how others relate to similar situations. There is always a risk of missing the mark. Lean CX manages this with market testing and pivots. There are also other design tools useful for intuiting customer needs and experience insights. The next section introduces one of these tools called TERMS.

## Customer TERMS

The TERMS[14] transaction framework is a simple design tool useful for identifying CX improvements for customer value propositions. TERMS is an acronym for time, emotion, risk, money, and situation. Sometimes it is useful for the last letter to also stand for sensation in CX design applications. Each letter is a prompt to redirect attention to an aspect of the customer's experience related to value. The designer considers how to improve the CX with both more and less of each TERMS aspect across the customer's imagined journey.

*C- A- P- TERMS of engagement*
*For some, buying an engagement ring is an enjoyable event. For other people, aspects of the experience can be difficult and/or uncomfortable. Imagine some of the difficulties for a would-be groom trying to find the right ring for his partner. Our hero may find his only chance to look for a ring is during his lunch hour. Opening hours for jewellery stores are like most other retailers. If he works far from a retail shopping district, his time may be strictly limited. Particularly if*

*parking is limited. Arriving at the jewellery store he could be confounded by the array of choice on offer. All these concerns relate to time aspects.*

*Looking at the rings, he may find that they are displayed without prices. This forces him to go inside and deal with the jeweller. It can be an anxious moment if you are unsure whether you can afford a ring. It is uncomfortable for some men to ask for help in this situation. Not being able to afford the ring you want is potentially embarrassing. Buying an engagement ring is a high-involvement purchase and it is important to get it right. Most people hope to only complete this purchase once in their lifetime. It can be emotionally risky to go through the process.*

*Our hero also faces more material risks. He must pick a ring his partner will love for years to come and such a ring may be beyond his budget. If he is with his partner and they cannot agree on a specific ring, then their engagement is potentially at risk. If he is operating alone (perhaps hoping to keep his proposal a surprise) he may not get the ring his partner had their heart set on. Especially if they have not really discussed getting engaged previously. Couples can be reticent to discuss formal marriage plans if their de facto relationship is mutually satisfying. Particularly if they have concerns about the costs of getting married.*

*Engagement rings are expensive items. In 2019, the average price paid by US consumers was close to $US 6000.[15] For many customers, it will be their third most expensive purchase after a house and car. For some millennials it may be their second most expensive purchase if they choose not to buy a house. The price of the ring is mostly based on the stone in the setting. Cut, colour, clarity, and carats impact the price. The jeweller commonly is more knowledgeable than the groom-to-be about such matters. This puts our hero at a significant disadvantage in price discussions. On top of this, our hero needs to consider whether to bear additional costs to insure the ring. Assuming our hero gets past these money aspects and purchases a ring, he has a final hurdle to overcome.*

*If he wants to surprise his partner with his marriage proposal, the ring may not be the right size for his partner's finger. They will have to go through the additional effort of returning the ring to their jeweller to have it resized. The ring's setting or the material may limit how much the size can be altered.*

*All these CX aspects can be improved. The time aspects can be improved with extended opening hours, designated parking, and/or a mobile jeweller service. Considerate jewellers can offer how-to guides in hard copy or online to make the process easier. Some couples are purchasing engagement rings online to bypass their time-related issues. Perhaps the easiest solution is to encourage customers to bring a friend or family member who has done it all before. Having someone you trust who knows what to expect can make everything feel easier and safer. Good retailers can help a groom de-risk the purchase by advising him to talk with his partner about their aspirations and expectations. Sharing product catalogues can help to select the right style of ring. Agreeing a realistic budget in advance may not be romantic, but part of a successful marriage is learning when to be pragmatic. Ideally, jewellers are transparent about their pricing and try to learn tactfully about budget constraints before presenting unrealistic options. Finally, there must be a way to help a groom-to-be learn the size of his partner's finger without giving away the surprise. A clever jeweller would help him enlist another family member or friend to try on some rings 'just for fun.' In doing so, the partner's size could be determined without alerting them to the real reason for visit to the jewellery store.*

Each DISC personality type prioritises a different aspect of TERMS. Dominant types are focused on achieving their mission or goal as fast as possible (A+ in CAPFUL). The Time operator in TERMS is most relevant to them. They act quickly to attack challenges head-on with power and intention. Dominants are driven to be the boss in their world to ensure everything remains under control (P+ C+ in CAPFUL). Their goal orientation and sheer drive can cause them to seem somewhat callous (L- in CAPFUL).

Influencer types, in contrast, are the consummate socialisers. They crave the centre of attention and want to be the star of the show (A+ in CAPFUL). They love to share news and gossip (U+ in CAPFUL). They are the people who can somehow strike up a conversation with a stranger in an instant (L+ in CAPFUL). The Emotion operator in TERMS is most relevant to them. Influencers love of new things means sometimes the Sensation operator in TERMS is also relevant to them. Their social nature and predisposition to jump on the new thing means they can come across as shallow (F- in CAPFUL). The other personality types in DISC are more inwardly focused.

Conscientious types yearn for their world to be as perfect as they imagine it could be. They tend to create detailed plans and processes. The imperfect world we live in often leaves these types disappointed (C- in CAPFUL). More than any other DISC cohort, these people are primarily motivated by a move away from pain, rather than a move toward pleasure. Many of them learn to become vigilant in identifying and avoiding risks. They tend to be experts in their field and prefer third-party accreditation or endorsements of capability (P+ in CAPFUL). At their core, they yearn for harmony in a discordant and chaotic world (F+ in CAPFUL). Unlike Dominant types, they do not want things to happen too fast, as this is when things go wrong. The Risk operator in TERMS is the most relevant to them.

Supporter types want the simple life and adapt with their circumstances to flow like water around life's obstacles. They are naturally better than the other types at remaining in harmony with others in the world (F+ in CAPFUL). Of all the types, this one has the strongest sense of personal identity. This causes them not to need to achieve to feel better about themselves (A- in CAPFUL). Supporters tend to meet people where they are at. This enables them to avoid conflict (L+ in CAPFUL). They prefer the status quo simply because it often requires less energy on their part to deal with (C+ in CAPFUL). The Situation operator in TERMS is the most relevant to them.

The descriptions above have omitted the Money operator in TERMS. This is because for all customers money considerations are generally at least a hygiene factor in purchase situations. Both Economics and Accounting disciplines tend to try and relate everything back to money somehow. In some situations, money concerns rise above being mere baseline considerations and can become the most important focus for each DISC type. Dominants may push hard to win the best deal. Influencers will wheedle and charm to try get a discount. Supporters secretly hope to avoid the stress of running out of cash. Conscientious types can become fastidious over specifications and how these relate to value. Conscientious types are often the most price sensitive.

Daniel H. Pink describes some of how money works as an employee motivator.[16] Most managers assume money is a simple cause-and-effect motivator. However, research shows money incentives work only for simple mechanical tasks. When conceptual or creative thinking is required, inadequate money can be a distractor. Worse is how performance incentives tend to have the opposite of their intended effects. Higher incentives often lead to lower performance for any task beyond purely mechanical. Pink asserts we are more motivated at work by the potential to be self-directed (C+ in CAPFUL); to develop our skills and capabilities (A+); and when working toward a higher purpose we believe in (F+). Pink's summary of the research suggests thinking about money in a broader way is more useful for CX designers.

The economic, engineering, and accounting approach to money is often limited to *how much*. Paying less for the same quality good increases value. However in the TERMS framework it is often more useful to consider linking money with one of the other operators to develop an improved value proposition. Table 4.3 provides some generic examples.

**Table 4.3:** TERMS Examples.

| Money and | + | − |
|-----------|---|---|
| Time | Payment over time/credit terms<br>Annuity versus lump sum | Investment returns paid earlier<br>Discount for cash |
| Emotion | Payment on satisfaction/tip<br>Donation in lieu of fixed charge | Refund if unsatisfied<br>Discount if unsatisfied |
| Risk | Share savings/performance<br>Capped maximum price | Fixed price for work done on rates<br>Liquidated damages clauses |
| Situation | Contingent payment<br>Payment amount decided by client | Offset account reduces interest<br>Eliminating roaming fees |

## Design and the Matrix

The Lean CX designer has many options to cut-through if the three frameworks above are combined with generic purchase stages into a design matrix.[17] The matrix is a design space with many possible CVPs to be explored. The matrix is shown in Table 4.4.

Design with the matrix by choosing at least one option from each column and relating it to your CX to create a CVP. You can choose more than one option in a column. For example, choosing Dominants and Influencers in the DISC column would prompt for CX designs relevant to extraverts.

**Table 4.4:** Generic CX Design Matrix.

| DISC | CAPFUL | TERMS | STAGE |
|---|---|---|---|
| Dominant | Certainty | Time | Discover |
| Influencer | Aspiration | Emotion | Buy |
| Supporter | Prestige | Risk | Use |
| Conscientious | Fulfilment | Money | Share |
| All | Uncommon | Situation | |
| | Love | Senses | |

## IKEA vs. Amazon Go and Time

Historically, IKEA's retail CX has been based around customers winding their way through carefully staged display rooms. This is well-suited for Influencer customers who enjoy the creative inspiration and the opportunity to discuss interior design possibilities with shoppers (see Table 4.5).

**Table 4.5:** IKEA Retail CX.

| DISC | CAPFUL | TERMS | STAGE |
|---|---|---|---|
| ~~Dominant~~ | Certainty | Time | Discover |
| Influencer | Aspiration | Emotion | Buy |
| Supporter | Prestige | Risk | Use |
| Conscientious | Fulfilment | Money | Share |
| | Uncommon | Situation | |
| | Love | Senses | |

IKEA affords these shoppers a leisurely stroll around the store with many different things to look at. Many contemporary consumers aspire to improve their home's appeal and IKEA offers this (A+). IKEA aims to help customers get a sense of how they can improve their homes (Senses). It is set up to help them Discover interior furnishing they may not have realised they needed. It is also set up to help them buy staple homeware accessories for living areas, bedrooms, kitchens, and bathrooms. The logic of this CX is the longer IKEA can keep shoppers engaged in the store, the more they are likely to spend. The experience insight could be "when I am shopping I want to take my time, have fun, and be inspired by new possibilities." IKEA's customer value proposition is based on being entertaining.

This CX design is very frustrating to Dominant types who simply want to buy what they came for and get out as fast as possible. Their experience insight is closer to "when I shop I already know what I want so I get frustrated when things get in my way and slow me down." IKEA has tried to address this by providing shortcuts through the store. Tellingly, its staple items are not located to allow Dominants to pick them up without a journey through the store. Online shopping is IKEA's preferred option for Dominants. But the customer still has the problem of the delay for delivery. IKEA does not offer same- or next-day delivery. Amazon Prime does. Amazon Go is designed for Dominants (see Table 4.6).

**Table 4.6:** Amazon Retail.

| DISC | CAPFUL | TERMS | STAGE |
|---|---|---|---|
| Dominant | Certainty | Time | Discover |
| Influencer | Aspiration | Emotion | Buy |
| Supporter | Prestige | Risk | Use |
| Conscientious | Fulfilment | Money | Share |
| All | Uncommon | Situation | |
| | Love | Senses | |

Amazon has continued to evolve its retail offerings from online to offline. Amazon Go allows shoppers to simply select what they want and walk out without dealing with a cashier. Clever technology simply charges whatever customers take directly to their Amazon accounts. Since Amazon is selling mostly staple grocery items, they have less incentive to try and slow shoppers down to entice them to make unsought purchases. This ability to get in, grab what you want, and get out fast is a very appealing value proposition for Dominants. To attract this group of customers, IKEA needs to change their current CX and CVP.

A possible Lean CX initiative for IKEA could be IKEA *Express*. Express stores could be set up to offer only a limited range of staple accessories. This store would be much smaller than a traditional IKEA warehouse because it would not have any furniture. Traditionally, IKEA warehouses are located away from major retail shopping areas. Express stores would ideally be in major retail shopping centres. The concept could be tested as a pop-up to limit lease costs while getting the CVP right.

### Public Transport and Emotion

CX customer value considerations are not limited to the private sector. Public transport around the world ranges from terrible to excellent depending on the city you are in. The quality of public transport CX is grounded in how frequently services run, their speed, range of coverage, and cost to use. These aspects are linked directly to the economics of the network and are difficult to change. One area where a Lean CX might be useful relates to some aspects of public transport that are much cheaper and easier to change.

Public transport throughout the world is passively hostile due to the dictatorial signs displayed in passenger areas. There are signs prohibiting food, drink, smoking, talking, sitting, standing, changing carriages, using phones, chewing gum, graffiti, and travelling without a valid ticket. There are signs for various emergency related items including exits, lighting, stop buttons, alarms, intercoms, glass breaking, fire extinguishers, and procedures.

Many of these signs also include information related to the fines applicable for misuse. It is as if the public transport administrators felt the need to go into extreme detail about all the potential risks they could identify.

The biggest systematic risk seems to be the potential bad behaviour of the passengers themselves. Signs are designed to compel compliance by highlighting the penalties for stepping out of line. It seems public transport managers across the world are either Conscientious or Dominant personalities. Conscientious types love to set up detailed rules in systems where they get to impose penalties for transgressions. Dominants love the opportunity to exert their authority and reject any attempts to dilute or temper their power. Public transport is often anti-customer-centric in this way. This lack of empathy in the system lowers the customer value proposition (see Table 4.7).

**Table 4.7:** Public Transport CX.

| DISC | CAPFUL | TERMS | STAGE |
|---|---|---|---|
| Dominant | Certainty | Time | Discover |
| ~~Influencer~~ | Aspiration | Emotion | Buy |
| ~~Supporter~~ | Prestige | Risk | Use |
| Conscientious | Fulfilment | Money | Share |
| | Uncommon | Situation | |
| | Love | Senses | |

The irony is that this approach doesn't work as well as some other more human-centred alternatives. Passengers who intend to violate the rules are unlikely to be dissuaded because of some signs. Much more useful is to try and get them to buy in to wanting to act sensibly and safely. Sutherland describes how speed cameras with light up smiley and frowny faces are far more effective and cheaper to operate than traditional speed enforcement cameras.[18] Influencer and Supporter type managers are far more comfortable with encouragement regimes. Dominant and Conscientious managers want enforcement. The amount spent removing graffiti from public transport every year suggests enforcement is ineffective as a deterrent.

Matt Mason described a theory of the psychology behind graffiti.[19] He asserted that street art (or vandalism, depending on your perspective) protested advertising. Advertising is a widespread form of visual pollution in many public spaces. Public transport advertising is designed to get attention. It is often intrusive rather than aesthetically pleasing. The ugliest public transport spaces are commonly plastered with both warning signs and commercial ads.

Mason suggested graffiti and public advertising were essentially similar. Property owners generally don't like graffiti. Similarly, few members of the public would assert they enjoy commercial advertising on public transport. Graffiti is rarely commissioned or welcomed by property owners (with the notable exception of famous artist Banksy). Ads in public spaces are even less requested or welcomed by the public. Both ads and graffiti are considered ugly by most people (other than their creators). Perhaps there is a Lean CX approach worth investigating to improve the aesthetics of public transport in the hopes of reducing graffiti vandalism. The cost to trial in a few public transport services would be low.

This example also shows how CX improvement initiatives can be validated in the public sector. Good CX lowers costs. At the time of this writing, the coast of the Mediterranean near Barcelona has just recovered from one of the worst storms in decades. After the storm, crowds of people organised themselves to clean up the debris washed up on the beaches near their town. They didn't need direction or funding from the municipality, they just wanted their local beach to be back to normal. This suggests signs and fines for littering on the same beaches are not needed.

## Dell vs. Samsung Warranty Risk

Customers take a risk every time they buy a product or service because the outcome may not be as they expected. To counter this, many companies offer warranties with their products. It is now common for retailers and manufacturers to offer extended warranties for an additional price. This has changed the value of a warranty to customers. In the past, well-made products were offered with longer warranties at no charge. This signalled to customers the manufacturer's preparedness to stand behind their products. The length of the warranty was related to how likely the product was to operate without a failure. The problem with the current extended warranty option is it is simply an insurance play. Customers can commonly purchase the same warranty extension regardless of the brand of appliance they are purchasing. This warranty is not backed by the manufacturer, it is covered by a third party. This means the warranty no longer signals anything about the quality or reliability of the product. Instead it signals something about the average price of a repair or replacement. This destroys part of the value of seeking a warranty. Customers don't get an emotional reassurance their purchase is any more reliable than any other brand in the category. It also destroys the potential for differentiation around building more reliable products.

Purchasing extended warranties is financially irrational. A scaled up third-party warranty provider takes no risk in their business model because the price of the extended warranty is calculated to add a margin on top of the average cost of a warranty claim. The warranty provider is guaranteed to make a profit if they have a large enough book, understand the incidence of claims, and the average cost to rectify. But for a rational customer this is a bad deal.

Such a customer should rationally choose to self-insure against product failure because in the long run it will likely be cheaper than purchasing extra product protection. Over the customer's lifetime they will suffer their share of product failures. With a warranty, the cost of rectification is covered; without a warranty, they must cover the repairs themselves. If they can afford the fix they are always better off in the long run not having paid a third party for the warranty. This is because covering rectification themselves saves the additional mark-up a warranty provider needs for their overhead and profit. The customer also avoids the risk of whether the warranty will be honoured.

*C- U+ Dell doesn't deliver on warranty but Samsung is serious about support*

*Dell has traditionally offered different levels of warranties like many other computer manufacturers. There is a base level included with product purchase. The second most expensive option extends the term of the warranty. The highest level of warranty includes a 1-2-day response for onsite rectification. Sadly, even though I purchased this highest level of warranty (irrationally), Dell failed to live up to its end of the deal.*

*Soon after I took delivery of the laptop, the screen started to fail. All manufacturers have improved their reliability around this issue. The root cause of the problem is that the connection between the screen and the main board needs to cross the hinge between the device's cover and base. This connection is prone to problems because the hinge has to move. I hadn't even had my new Dell machine for a week when the screen started acting up. It would display for a while and then pixilate into nonsense after each reboot.*

*I called Dell to raise a repair ticket and get the machine repaired before travelling overseas with it. The plan was to use it to deliver my lectures at a business school in the Netherlands. But Dell Australia was out of the part required to complete the repair. Dell's support tech explained I only needed to contact Dell in Singapore when I arrived during a stopover and they could help. He assured me that being there overnight would be enough time to arrange and complete the repair. Dell's Singapore support branch also was out of stock and suggested I take up the issue with Dell in the Netherlands when I arrived.*

*Dell in the Netherlands was very reticent to honour my warranty claim. They claimed the ticket number I had was not in their system because they were a contractor to Dell, not Dell themselves. They initially refused to honour my warranty. After some back and forth with Dell Australia, Dell Netherlands finally agreed to help. When they arrived on site, their tech had not bothered to take account of the diagnostic already done and did not bring the necessary part. He could not return for several days and ended up repairing my machine at 8PM on the Friday night before I was to leave to fly back to Australia. The repair should have happened in 48 hours. In the end it was closer to three weeks. Angry and disappointed, I took up the issue with Dell Australia when I was back home. I wanted a refund for the extended warranty which had not been honoured. I was unsuccessful. I have never bought another Dell machine since. They have not even been in my consideration set.*

*In contrast to Dell's poor warranty service, Samsung Appliances was recently excellent. I had bought a Samsung refrigerator with only the included manufacturer's warranty several years ago. A little over six months out of warranty the fridge failed. I called the retailer I bought the appliance from to arrange repairs since they typically arrange repairs for warranty claims on behalf of their suppliers. The retailer was able to book a repair for me but could not diagnose the fault or quote a likely call out cost. They did put me in touch with Samsung directly. After getting enough information to diagnose the likely fault, including my model number, the support staffer (unprompted) offered to complete the repair at Samsung's cost. This was a surprising and welcome turn of events. Perhaps this was a holdover from having to deal with failing Note 3 phone batteries on planes. Maybe they had done the research and worked out the numbers on referral would more than offset the repair cost. It's possible they knew of a problem with my particular model of fridge and this was simply a cost effective way to avoid a country-wide recall. Whatever the reason, it was quite remarkable to get the solution I really wanted without even having to negotiate.*

Warranties are the primary method of reducing customers' purchase risks. If CX matters at all, then the basic message is to honour any warranty you have made. This applies even if technically your company did not offer the protection the client thought they were buying. The insurance industry has a long history of selling the perception of coverage only to use their fine print to in some cases avoid paying out on a claim. The problem isn't the agreement with the customer, it's the customer's perception of what they were agreeing to. Trust is broken when this expectation is not met.

Third-party warranties should be used carefully. As globalisation has increased competition, many manufacturers have shifted from building more reliable products to products with short mean time to failures to increase the potential market for repeat purchases. Third-party warranties have accelerated this tendency because more reliable manufacturers are no longer able to enjoy a differentiation. A cheaper alternative with an extended third-party warranty seems directly comparable. Third-party warranties shift risk perception to price perceptions.

### Patreon and Prime Pricing

One of the most challenging aspects for many companies to understand is that their business is only sustainable if their customers are happy about paying for their products and services. Sadly, many utilities, government agencies, and some software companies (see the Survey Monkey case in Chapter 2) seem to operate under the assumption they have a right to impose charges on their users, regardless of what the users think. Two organisations with a more customer centric approach to pricing are Patreon and Amazon Prime (see Figure 4.5 for some statistics on Prime).

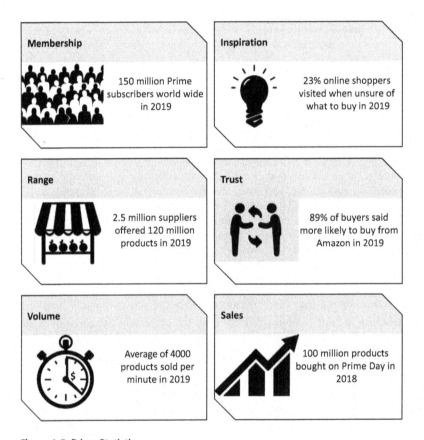

**Membership** — 150 million Prime subscribers world wide in 2019

**Inspiration** — 23% online shoppers visited when unsure of what to buy in 2019

**Range** — 2.5 million suppliers offered 120 million products in 2019

**Trust** — 89% of buyers said more likely to buy from Amazon in 2019

**Volume** — Average of 4000 products sold per minute in 2019

**Sales** — 100 million products bought on Prime Day in 2018

**Figure 4.5:** Prime Statistics.

Prime is a membership service designed to convert infrequent Amazon customers into regular purchasers. A Prime subscription is essentially a bundled and capped delivery fee – by paying around $100 per year, users get free delivery on a large range of Amazon products. However, the membership also includes free video and music streaming services, free prime books on Kindle, and faster delivery. The faster delivery service on most products is next day in the US and parts of Europe. Some products are delivered in just two hours in some locations. In Australia, expedited delivery is normally ranges from a couple of days for locally stocked products to up to two weeks for goods from international suppliers.

Prime members also get access to special Prime Days where sellers offer remarkable savings. The psychology behind Prime is compelling: Users who sign up for the delivery benefits are pre-committing to purchase at some level. Robert B. Cialdini found consistency was one of seven powerful influencing factors.[20] Users who sign up for the streaming benefits have free and fast delivery should they choose to buy a physical product on Prime. This contrasts with the normal drag of having to pay extra for delivery with online purchases. Cialdini also found contrast was a powerful influencing factor. At the time of writing, Prime now has 150 million users worldwide.[21] All of these people have subscribed to Prime because they want to be there. Perhaps the most interesting statistic about these customers is 28% of shoppers go on Amazon first for inspiration when they don't have a specific product purchase in mind.[22]

Prime's benefits appeal to all personality types. Dominants get fast delivery, Influencers enjoy inspiration, Conscientious types get to compare prices and get access to remarkable savings on Prime Days, Supporters get to stream content at the click of a button, without having to worry about paying each time. Prime is an exemplar in the 'retail therapy' space offering superior product range and inspiration (A+ U+). It is an example of a subscription service with a well-designed CVP more focused on retaining customers through choice rather than simply the inertia of forgetting to cancel their subscription (see Table 4.8).

**Table 4.8:** Prime CX.

| DISC | CAPFUL | TERMS | STAGE |
|---|---|---|---|
| Dominant | Certainty | Time | Discover |
| Influencer | Aspiration | Emotion | Buy |
| Supporter | Prestige | Risk | Use |
| Conscientious | Fulfilment | Money | Share |
| | Uncommon | Situation | |
| | Love | Senses | |

Patreon uses a different psychology to get customers to be happy to pay. The website was set up in 2013 to help online content producers collect subscriptions from their fans, instead of presenting advertising. Creators who have sizeable followings tend to make more money than they would with ads. Most of the creators on Patreon allow their consumers to decide if they want to subscribe. This means contributions to creators are generally voluntary (F+ L+). Patreon collects around 5% of the donated subscriptions for its 'lite' service. It collects 12% for its 'premium' service. The more expensive service includes coaching and support for creators.

Patreon[23] discovered an unmet need in the online content marketplace. More than 125,000 patrons signed up to pay regularly for subscriptions in the first 18 months, sending over $1,000,000 per month to creators. By early 2016, the site had raised $US 47.1 million across three rounds of venture capital raising. By the start of 2017, Patreon had sent more than $US 100 million to creators since launching. In the middle of that year, 50,000 creators were receiving support from more than one million patrons. But the site has had several controversies and some failed pivots.

In 2015, Patreon was hacked for password data, donation records, and source code. More than 2.3 million email addresses were published and some patrons received extortion emails to keep their personal information protected. In late 2017, the site tried to add on an extra service fee to be covered by patrons instead of creators. The fee added 38 cents to a $US 1 pledge and 50 cents to a $US 5 pledge. It was abandoned after some creators protested when they found their low-end patrons withdrawing support. At the time, the average pledge on Patreon was around $US 12. In 2018, the site expanded its publication guidelines after banning a handful of different creators. This triggered a protest petition from 1800 creators who perceived the bans as censorship. Jordan Peterson and Dave Rubin chose to delete their Patreon accounts at the start of 2019 citing censorship. At the time Peterson was giving up almost $US 1 million per year in revenue on principle.[24] Rubin gave up more than 60% of his income.[25]

Patreon seems to be in danger of diluting its customer value proposition because the new investors are focused on corporatising the site. If patrons were more conservative consumers, the security leak would have killed Patreon. It didn't even slow down growth because patrons care most about supporting their creators. At its core, the decision to donate to a creator on a monthly basis is emotional, not rational, because patrons can get most of the content for free anyway. The last round of 2017 investors missed this. They seemed to be more focused on extracting more of a clip than growing the membership base when they tried to increase fees. That put their business model at risk because it shifted the focus off supporting creators and onto the friction in the transaction. It's likely many patrons hadn't previously considered there would be a clip (see Table 4.9).

Now it seems Patreon wants to become more inside the mainstream to broaden its base. Part of this strategy seems to be about constraining creators from posting some types of controversial content. This risks alienating the people already prepared to pay. Right now these patrons feel special by supporting their preferred content creators because it's not something everyone would do. They identify with the producers they support – some only because they feel like their more extreme opinions are given a public forum online. The cash is in the fringe not the

**Table 4.9:** Patreon CX.

| DISC | CAPFUL | TERMS | STAGE |
|---|---|---|---|
| Dominant | Certainty | Time | Discover |
| Influencer | Aspiration | Emotion | Buy |
| Supporter | Prestige | Risk | Use |
| Conscientious | Fulfilment | Money | Share |
| | Uncommon | Situation | |
| | Love | Senses | |

mainstream. Time will tell if Patreon survives or gets replaced by the new platform Peterson and Rubin are planning to set up.

### Porto vs. Marrakesh Alcohol Appropriate Situations

One of the best events in Porto is the Festa de São João do Porto. This is the festival of Saint John of Porto celebrated on June 24. During the 19th century, this day became the city's most important festival. The celebrations include decorations, street concerts, popular dancing parties, jumping over flames, eating barbecued sardines, caldo verde, and meat, drinking wine, and launching lit candle-propelled balloons into the sky.

One of the stranger traditions is people hitting each other with soft plastic hammers. Apparently this has something to do with the festival's 14th century pagan origins before it was made into a Christian celebration. The party continues until dawn, fuelled by the many impromptu vendors who offer the masses alcoholic drinks. What makes the festival special is that despite the potential for public disorder due all the alcohol, it is actually a family friendly crowd. There are no fights, public drunkenness and other disorderly conduct is exceedingly rare. This is despite an absence of laws to control or restrict the consumption of alcohol. Somehow people in Porto can act responsibly (see Table 4.10).

In contrast to Porto, Marrakesh in Morocco has wide ranging limitations around the availability of alcohol. Similar to most European countries, alcohol can be bought and consumed in licensed establishments. It is also for sale in most large supermarkets. However, despite the formal laws, there many additional cultural constraints around alcohol due to the country's dominant Islam religion.

In supermarkets, alcohol is often held in a separate room to the main supermarket. Outside of tourist areas, many venues will not offer alcohol if they are in sight of a mosque. Moroccans may drink alcohol indoors only. Most bars don't have

**Table 4.10:** Festa de São João do Porto CX.

| DISC | CAPFUL | TERMS | STAGE |
|---|---|---|---|
| Dominant | Certainty | Time | Discover |
| Influencer | Aspiration | Emotion | Buy |
| Supporter | Prestige | Risk | Use |
| Conscientious | Fulfilment | Money | Share |
| | Uncommon | Situation | |
| | Love | Senses | |

windows because being seen by those outside is not permitted. There are a few establishments allowing outside drinking for tourists only. Passing locals tend to look down on the tourists who do drink outside. Some bars will not permit women. Other bars will only permit women in the company of a man. Many venues also choose to suspend the sale of alcohol around Ramadan. Few venues publish their policies relating to alcohol online, so it can be an unwelcome surprise to turn up at a steak restaurant and learn you cannot have a glass of wine or beer with your meal. Apparently the people of Marrakesh don't have faith alcohol can be consumed entirely responsibly.

The cultural taboos associated with alcohol in Marrakesh add to how exotic the city feels (U+). This is part of what makes it appealing to travellers. Influencers are attracted to Marrakesh because it is different. Conscientious types may be attracted to Marrakesh because it is culturally conservative – this is particularly true for Conscientious types who are very immersed in religion or existentialism and sympathetic to Islam. It is unusual to find a CVP attractive to both Influencers and the Conscientious because in some sense they are opposites: Influencers tend to be more extraverted, shallow, big picture, creative, social, optimistic, risk-tolerant, and interested in novelty. The Conscientious tend to be more introverted, deep, detail-focused, analytical, solitary, pessimistic, risk-averse, and interested in certainty. Travellers come in all types.

### Flexitarians, Impossible Burgers and Cauliflower Pizza Sensations

One of the most pleasurable things about travelling is the possibility to experience different foods. At the time of this writing, there are some interesting current food trends.[26] One of the most compelling trends to build a CVP around is the idea of casual veganism/vegetarianism. One pundit has named this being 'flexitarian.'

Apparently flexitarians are vegans who occasionally eat animal protein either because it avoids the polarising conflicts possible when dining in a group of carnivores or because being completely vegan or vegetarian is too hard to sustain. Around 37% of the people who buy meat alternatives are flexitarian.

The Impossible Burger is designed to appeal directly to this group. Its CVP is not to be a meat substitute. This burger is "meat" manufactured entirely from plant-based materials. The key ingredient is heme. Heme is produced from genetically modified yeast and makes the Impossible Burger taste like meat. The US FDA approved heme in 2019, paving the way for Impossible Burger products to be sold in US supermarkets and fast food chains. By October the same year, the burgers were available at 10,000 fast food restaurants across the United States, Hong Kong, Singapore, and Macau.[27] Europe may be harder to get into because of strict restrictions on genetically modified foods.

Impossible Burgers have spread because they mimic the experience of eating meat. It's not just the taste – most people who try the product say it tastes good but not exactly the same as real meat. The manufacturer (Impossible Foods) has gone to great lengths to make the whole experience of storing, cooking, and eating the product as close to the real thing as possible. The burgers look like meat, smell like meat, have the same texture to bite into, sizzle and drip fat when cooking, get a browned crust when grilled, and store in the freezer just like normal meat patties. According to some they are also unhealthy, just like real burgers, and the only valid reasons to eat them are environmental and moral.[28]

> The point of a plant-based diet isn't to live a healthy life, though of course you can live healthily as a vegan. The point is to reduce your impact on the environment, to fight the overuse of antibiotics in livestock raising, and to promote animal welfare more generally . . .
>
> I've hung out with enough Silicon Valley start-up vegantrepreneurs to know that their overarching goal is to convert more people to plant-based lifestyles for animal rights and tenuously environmental purposes. They think that the way to do this is to recreate whatever people are already eating, often with a weird stereotype of a guy in a pickup truck from Alabama in mind as their target audience. I'm not sure if it actually works for converting people to alternative burgers.
>
> . . . I personally have started to try out a vegetarian lifestyle (again, for animal rights and tenuously environmental reasons), and sometimes I just want to shove a greasy, salty, tomato sauce-slathered disk-on-a-bun into my pie hole and feel like a piece of crap all night. The Impossible and Beyond burgers let me do that.[29]

Dedicated carnivores may read the first paragraph of the quote above and believe their suspicions about vegans are now confirmed: the diet restriction is more about feeling morally superior than it is for any nutrition concerns. Perhaps flexitarians are influenced by animal welfare and environmental considerations, perhaps they don't go all the way vegan to avoid conflict, perhaps they really like meat and find it too hard to give it up for good. Life is an act of consumption after all. Whatever their reasons, the Impossible Burger (and competing products like the Beyond Burger) meets these needs.

The design matrix for this CVP is quite complicated (see Table 4.11). Like Marrakesh above, Impossible Burgers appeal to different DISC types. Influencers can feel part of the moral elite by being flexitarians. They also have the advantage of not having hard-and-fast diet rules should they want to try something new. The Conscientious can feel like they are doing the right thing for the environment and animal welfare, though some are likely to have issues with the fact heme is from genetically modified yeast. It's likely Supporters will be happy Impossible Burgers allow them to dine with friends who are anti-meat consumption with less conflict.

**Table 4.11:** Impossible Burger CX.

| DISC | CAPFUL | TERMS | STAGE |
|---|---|---|---|
| Dominant | Certainty | Time | Discover |
| Influencer | Aspiration | Emotion | Buy |
| Supporter | Prestige | Risk | Use |
| Conscientious | Fulfilment | Money | Share |
| | Uncommon | Situation | |
| | Love | Senses | |

The Impossible Burger is one product growing because of being on-trend with changing consumer diet preferences. At first glance, pre-made cauliflower pizza bases would seem to offer a similar CVP to the Impossible Burger (see Table 4.12). The idea of a pre-made cauliflower pizza base appeals to dieters on a range of different

**Table 4.12:** Pre-made Cauliflower Pizza bases CX.

| DISC | CAPFUL | TERMS | STAGE |
|---|---|---|---|
| Dominant | Certainty | Time | Discover |
| Influencer | Aspiration | Emotion | Buy |
| Supporter | Prestige | Risk | Use |
| Conscientious | Fulfilment | Money | Share |
| | Uncommon | Situation | |
| | Love | Senses | |

popular food elimination regimes. Just like the Impossible Burger, cauliflower is a suitable inclusion for many of the most popular diets including keto, paleo, 4-hour Body, Atkins, low carb, low fat, whole food, Mediterranean, South Beach, vegan, and gluten-free diets. They are fast (Time CVP), vegetarian (Emotion CVP), and fans say they taste good (Sensation CVP). The disconnect is that they are not anywhere near as popular, and the reason is pre-made cauliflower pizza bases fail to deliver on the emotional and sensation CVP parts.

The pre-made cauliflower pizza bases available in supermarkets contain wheat flour to help with their texture and shelf life. Flour as an ingredient means the product is no longer suitable for any of the popular elimination diets listed except straight vegetarian and vegan. This is more of an issue than genetically modified foods (GMFs).

People prefer to avoid GMFs, but they can rationalise why some compromises are necessary for their diet choices. They absolutely cannot manage the same justification for wheat flour. Flour is specifically excluded from most of the diets above. Not consuming flour is almost the definition of what defines those diets as different and effective. This means consumers cannot get the feeling of elitism (P+) they associate with being on a diet if they eat products with flour in the ingredient list. Perceptually it's like trying to say you are on a diet while eating bread or cakes. No diet from the list includes those things, except vegetarian and vegan. This is not the major issue however. The real problem is sensation.

Unlike the Impossible Burger, a cauliflower pizza base does not smell, feel, or taste like a real pizza even though it looks close to a real pizza. Few people other than vegans or vegetarians enjoy the difference between a real pizza and a cauliflower one, so the product has stalled. Impossible Burgers appeal to flexitarians, it seems cauliflower pizzas do not. It may be because they contain flour and put the dieters off. It may be because they don't taste good to non-vegetarians and non-vegans. This reduces the coverage of the value proposition from flexitarians to just vegetarians and vegans. The Conscientious may still go for the product, but it will remain in the category of a product like bran – something you eat because it's the right thing to do rather than because you enjoy it. This case shows the hedonistic aspects of food consumption are critical (C+ U+) to new food adoption rates. It also shows how hedonism moderates the effects of higher order needs like saving the planet and animal welfare (F+). Personality-based segmentation using DISC may not be appropriate for some products and services like new foods. Designing effective CVPs for new foods is often easier using behaviours or benefits sought for segmentation. The next section provides an alternative for CVP design less prone to segmentation complications.

## Kano Quality Framework

During the 1980s, the business world became consumed with the concept of quality as the key to successful business. Quality was defined by experts including Joseph Juran and William Deming as 'fitness for use.' A quality product was one where the customer's specified need was met. A defective product failed to achieve this. For quality engineers, quality means just-good-enough functionality. This interpretation falls short of what most customers think about when they consider the definition of a quality product. For customers, quality often means something more than the minimum and relates to satisfaction. The synthesis of function and satisfaction perspectives produced Kano diagrams (Figure 4.6).[30]

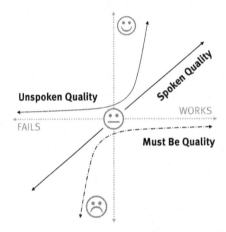

**Figure 4.6:** Kano Diagram.

A comprehensive Kano diagram includes five different quality elements:
1. Must be/hygiene factors customers expect
2. Spoken elements customers openly value
3. Unspoken elements are unknown value
4. Unimportant features don't matter to customers
5. Undesired features drive customer dissatisfaction

Each element inherently defines a relationship between customer satisfaction and functionality. Lean CX reduces these to just three as shown in Figure 4.6. These are must-be, spoken, and unspoken quality elements. Each element can offer opportunities to develop superior CVPs. Most CVPs include more than one type of Kano element.

Kano is easier to understand when applied to an example. For a business traveller who wants to take a plane flight, must-be quality elements include:
– Destination suitable to where they want to travel
– Date of the flight matches their schedule
– Safety
– Check-in times are efficient
– Luggage allowance is adequate
– Cabin baggage allowance is adequate

If any of these things are not up to standard, the traveller will become dissatisfied. In the case of a flight to the wrong destination or outside of the traveller's schedule, the flight will just be rejected out of hand at the booking stage. An assistant booking the wrong flight in error can have very bad flow-on effects. Similarly, long check-in times, inadequate luggage allowance, or limits on cabin baggage can become quite frustrating. Generally travellers would not pay more to get these things right because they are expected. Few people will pay more to travel on an airline they consider offering superior safety. Instead travellers simply reject travelling on any airline they feel is unsafe. Offering a discount to entice travellers to fly with an airline perceived as unsafe just doesn't work. Malaysian Airlines was renationalised in 2015 after losing two flights (Flight 370 and Flight 17) in 2014. The losses damaged consumer confidence in the carrier.[31] The airlines financial problems were only due to a loss in consumer confidence over safety as the case below shows. They were also due to poor CX focused on maximising short-term pricing instead of customer retention and referral.

*P- Malaysia Airlines doesn't get must-be quality[32]*
*Five years on from the two tragic losses of aircraft in 2014, Malaysia Airlines [MAB] is still struggling. The airline has apparently not turned a profit since 2010 due to increased competition, cost problems, and the aftermath of the 2014 tragedies. MH370 disappeared in 2014 less than an hour after take-off from Kuala Lumpur International Airport. Four months later, MH17 was shot down over the Ukraine killing all on board. The tragedies amplified the airline's decade of ongoing financial woes. Having just travelled with them this month, we learned some other reasons why the national carrier is continuing to fail. The 12,000-employee airline delivers an average to remarkably negative customer experience. Our particular experience suggests dental surgery would have been faster, cheaper, and less upsetting.*
*The company extracted an extra $500 from us when we missed our connecting flight due to the airline itself – remarkably short sighted for an airline needing all the positive word of mouth it can get. It is worse when you realise helping us out would have cost them nothing. Our story is not happy, but it is instructive. We had bought tickets to get from Brisbane to Bangkok, changing planes in KL. Our first plane ran late, but we were still able to make the connection because the second plane was delayed for a tyre change. You could see the work happening from the gate lounge as we arrived. Unfortunately we ended up missing that plane because of some bad advice from ground staff. Our challenges started as we got through security into the gate lounge.*

*We experienced a minor medical emergency. The details are not worth sharing, but basically we needed to get to a pharmacy to still be OK to fly. So we approached gate attendants for help. They shared directions to the pharmacy in KL airport. This meant taking an internal airport train to a different terminal and back. The gate staff assured us we had time and this seemed to be confirmed by a public announcement about when the boarding information for our flight would be made available.*

*After getting to the train, waiting to board, traveling to the other terminal, finding the pharmacy, queuing to pay, and then retracing our steps, we arrived back at the gate. The gate lounge was empty and we could see our bags being wheeled across the tarmac outside. Boarding must have started almost the moment we left. Upset at this turn of events, we set off to try and get another plane. Things went downhill further.*

*At the service desk for Malaysia Airlines, we learned we could not fix the problem from the transit side of the airport. The service staff had no ability to issue new tickets. They advised we had to pass customs into Malaysia, get our bags back, and then get tickets from level 5 of the terminal. It took hours to get through customs and retrieve our luggage before setting off for the airline ticket counter.*

*At the ticket counter we explained what had happened to the staffer and asked her to issue tickets for the next flight. She advised that she had seats, but we would have to pay $800 in penalties for missing our connection. After extensive negotiations, being accused of lying, not being backed up by the ground staff, and finally escalating to a manager, we managed to get nowhere. End to end, we endured four hours of stress, disappointment, and frustration just to be extorted.*

*It would have cost MAB nothing to put us on the next flight with spare seats. Instead, they lost any chance of future business with us and suffered reputation damage with all the friends we talked with, plus anyone who reads this or the social media posts I made at the time. MAB's CX issues appear to be systemic. I followed up with customer service and complained in writing as directed. It took them weeks to get back to us with their verdict. They basically said we lied and they were completely within their rights to charge us penalties when we missed the flight. When a customer feels upset about how they have been treated, it does not improve their mood to state your company has followed its own rules. Especially if it is those rules which caused the customer to be upset. Given the head of CX for MAB has a Six Sigma background (good for cost reduction but poor for customer satisfaction), it's no surprise MAB is only still running because of the government bailout in 2015. Their CX in this situation is up there with the worst I have ever experienced.*

Airlines who levy additional charges on must-be quality elements destroy customer goodwill. A common example is luggage allowance. The standard allowance for luggage on most international economy flights is 23 kg. Some airlines offer 30 kg. While this is a benefit, it is unlikely passengers consider this at the booking stage. Other airlines only offer 15 kg included with a ticket. These carriers seem to have set this policy in the hope of extracting additional fees out of customers at check in. While they are careful to include the limited weight in the fine print of the ticket terms and conditions, the low allowance is often not mentioned at booking. These carriers generally set the price of additional luggage to be far higher if purchased at the airport than online.

This approach to luggage allowance might seem efficient from the airline's perspective: Customers only pay for a small luggage allowance in their ticket as standard and if they need more they can purchase it as an extra. The rest of the plane's cargo capacity can be used for air freight to keep ticket prices low. The problem comes because as a must-be quality factor – adequate luggage allowance – is expected. When it is missing, customers get upset. Sure the airline can fix the issue for a price. When they do, it doesn't seem like they are helping, it seems like they are taking advantage – especially if the airport price for extra luggage is higher than at online booking. It's not as if a traveller checking in at the airport has much choice but to pay whatever extra is demanded. For customers this can feel like booking a hotel room and then being charged extra if you take more than one shower. Customers are quickly dissatisfied with expected product or service components being left out and then charged as extras.

Customers don't feel the same way about spoken quality elements. These are *extra things* customers might want. They may not choose to pay extra for them, but they accept that if they do then there is an extra charge. For most customers the legroom they enjoy on the plane is a spoken quality element. Everyone would prefer to travel business or first class, but not everyone is prepared to pay the extra to get a better seat. Some parts of in-flight entertainment and catering can be considered spoken quality and other aspects are must-be. Having the ability to watch movies on long flights is must-be quality for many travellers, however a business traveller may prefer to work on a laptop for the duration of the flight. Internet access, phone calls, and a power socket for their device is most welcome but unexpected in economy class. Some airlines are starting to include power in economy in their newer planes. Others are offering in-flight internet and charging roaming fees for the data used. A useful business traveller CVP might include a 'business pack for economy.' This would be an economy seat set up to allow work on a laptop with power, in-flight internet, and the ability to receive phone calls included in the upgrade pack.

A focus on regulatory compliance and yield management has prevented airlines from effectively differentiating their CX in significant ways. Few airlines have been able to identify and implement unspoken quality elements in their CVPs. KLM tried to introduce 'Meet and Seat' as a way to leverage social media platforms to help with seat selection beside a stranger. The initiative failed to take off.[33] This highlights how offering unspoken quality elements can be risky. But now a focus on improved CX is starting to help other innovations get traction in the industry.

Promising CX options are in the wings from Air New Zealand and Collins Aerospace.[34] Air New Zealand has worked out how to offer lie-flat beds in economy class, cost effectively. They have applied for patents and permits with a view to roll this out in the next year. Collins Aerospace wants to offer a 'self-serve social zone.' The concept is to use aircraft doorways as bars with self-serve drinks and snacks. Passengers can socialise in these areas mid-flight. This may pose a problem for US flights where regulations restrict passengers congregating as a response to the 911 terrorist event. Ryanair is going in a completely different direction. The budget carrier is considering implementing 'standing' Skyrider seats to cram 20% more people onto a plane. The seats look a bit like a horse saddle, are closer together, higher off the ground and don't recline. For budget-focussed travellers the savings may be worth the reduction in comfort on short European flights.

Lie-flat economy, a self-serve bar, and standing flights are all examples of unsought CVP elements. These are not things customers might ordinarily ask for without being prompted. Their appeal only becomes obvious after they are offered. Because of this, unspoken quality elements are not always the best place to find CVP improvement opportunities with Kano.

The most commonly overlooked opportunity when developing a CVP is to reduce over-serviced must-be quality elements. An over-serviced element is anything a customer doesn't want or need, especially if they would give up functionality to save money. The opportunity inherent in identifying over-servicing is to cut back the functionality and invest the savings somewhere else. Ironically for airlines, luggage allowance can be an over-served must-be quality element for business travellers on short flights. Some business passengers will fly a few hours to a city for meetings only to return the same evening. These travellers do not need *any* luggage allowance other than carry on. It can be the same for overnight return travellers as well. If travellers confirmed no checked luggage during booking then the airline could use the space for freight. It would make sense to ask travellers who are returning the same or next day if this was the case. Travellers who opted in could be offered bonus points, lounge access, a free drink or some other perk in return for allowing their checked luggage allowance to be used for another purpose. Spoken quality elements present different opportunities.

Spoken quality elements are things customers expect to pay extra for if they want them. The main opportunity here is based on setting price points correctly. Spoken quality elements are best offered at three points – budget, value, and premium. Airlines have this covered with economy, premium economy, and business class seats. Many other industries fail to cover the spread. In healthcare and aged care, providers generally don't offer different levels of service at the same establishment. Often this is complicated by service level agreement obligations complicated by government funding eligibility requirements. Yet it is these industries who most need to expand their service offerings beyond the minimum to earn extra revenue outside their government funding. The same thing applies to schools.

State run schools tend offer budget education. Privately run schools may offer value or premium education and charge accordingly. What does not exist is the schools offering budget, value, and premium education on the same campus. This may not seem feasible at first consideration. Questions include how a budget, value, or premium level of education is different to the basic service a school offers now. Perhaps the biggest concern is how parents would feel knowing they paid a different price than another family for their children to attend a school. The airlines have been pioneers in this space. No one is concerned they may have paid more for their seat than the person sitting beside them. Price pointing is not the only CVP differentiation available from Kano spoken quality elements.

Low cost quality elements can be offered to clients for free. Brussels Airlines has run flights bound for Tomorrowland with a music DJ, costumed cabin staff, and free glow sticks for passengers during the flight. The Tomorrowland festival is a kind of modern day Woodstock – it is a massive music festival. Changing the atmosphere inside the aircraft cabin starts the party before passengers even arrive at the festival. It makes for a remarkable CVP some passengers have recorded on their smart phones and posted online. This adds to the hype around Tomorrowland and confirmed Brussels Airlines as the preferred airline to get there.

Kano quality elements are useful for evaluating CVPs in comparison to key rivals. This concept was first proposed as value curves by researchers who went on to write Blue Ocean Strategy.[35] Figure 4.7 shows comparative value propositions for Xero and rival accounting packages in the market at the time.[36] Xero's main feature difference at the time was using cloud architecture. Rivals like MYOB and Quicken were based on

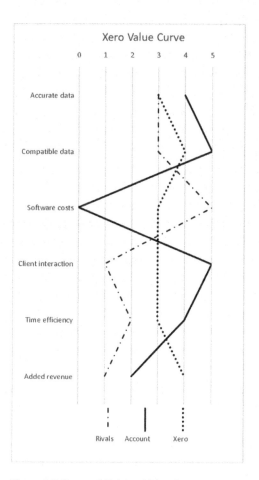

**Figure 4.7:** Xero and Quicken Value Curves.

individual machine software installations. This meant tax accountants often had data compatibility issues between the version of MYOB or Quicken they were running and version many of their clients were using.

In some cases the accountant needed to run multiple versions to be backward compatible with their client's data. There was also the frustrating issue around pricing. Xero, MYOB, and Quicken all ran subscription models. The difference however had to do with taxation rate changes. Accountants were forced pay for upgrades they didn't necessarily want just to keep current tax rates in their software. To allow their account-ants access to their books, clients were forced to do the same. So the upgrade cost be-came a grudge purchase for clients their accountant had to push them into. This took a time, money, and emotional toll on the tax accountants. The cost was not there with Xero because the cloud deployment eliminated upgrade issues on the both the accoun-tant and client sides. Xero also gave accountants another reason to migrate their clients away from MYOB and Quicken. Xero opened an additional revenue opportunity.

Accountants with a Xero log in were able to access their clients' books and cor-rect general ledger entries a bookkeeper may have made incorrectly. This is a com-mon issue when depreciation schedules are involved. Bookkeepers may expense items needing to be depreciated and vice versa. They may also get the depreciation term of capital items wrong. The Xero functionality meant some accountants were able to expand their services from tax-only to more advisory work. Some of the most entrepreneurial were able to become part-time financial controllers for their clients. This replaced the need for smaller clients to employ another staffer and en-sured the tax accountant had ongoing income through the whole tax year.

The chart (see Figure 4.7) shows how the value curve for Xero is superior to rivals across the board. Compatible and accurate data are key must-be quality factors for tax accountants. Xero meets the first requirement and is on par with rivals for the second. Cost, client interaction, and time are all spoken quality elements. Xero goes closer than rivals to meeting tax accountant preferences. Note that ideally accountants would like to have the software for free. Xero is superior to rivals because it avoided the problems related to upgrade costs. Finally, Xero offers an unsought benefit in terms of opening up advisory opportunities and part-time financial control services. Prior to that, addi-tional work coming out of tax work was because of the software platform.

So far this chapter has covered approaches to innovate CVPs. This included both product or service improvements and experience improvements. This ap-proach to innovation ensures adjacent positioning because it starts with existing customer needs and the current business model. The next section covers how to de-sign other types of adjacent positioning.

## Value Stream Maps

Previously we showed how the business model canvas corresponds to CX innovation (see Figure 3.5). This diagram shows where to look for potential CX growth initiatives. This chapter has covered the areas related to customers (CPV, Pricing, and Relationship). Here we introduce value stream maps (VSMs).[37] VSMs provide a visual representation of the value chain relevant to a firm's delivery. The map can be used to identify new segment options, channel strategies, and vertical integration issues. An organisation's vertical integration relates to what they insource and outsource to deliver their CVP.

VSMs are two-dimensional representations of the organisation's adjacent market environment. The horizontal axis relates to the value chain. On this axis, left represents closer to the customer and more visible to the customer. Right represents further away. The vertical axis of a VSM represents the level of market maturity. It is split into six stages:

1. *Introduction.* This is where R&D is first commercialised or where a new to market product is first brought to market. For example, VisiCalc was the first spreadsheet program for personal computers introduced in 1979 and went on to sell a million copies.[38]

2. *Customised.* As markets mature, copycat products enter and market competition becomes based on differences in feature sets. During the 1980s Lotus 1-2-3 emerged as the standard for IBM PCs, and VisiCalc for Apple machines.

3. *Mass Market.* Eventually the market gets to a point where it offers standardised products and has high market penetration. Microsoft Excel replaced Lotus 1-2-3 as the market leader in spreadsheets in the late 1980s. It was the first spreadsheet program to offer a drop-down graphical user interface in 1984. Originally released for 512K Apple Macintosh, Excel was also one of the first application programs released for Windows in 1987 and is still the market standard for spreadsheets today.

4. *Servitised.* During the servitised market stage, competition becomes more price competitive and brands become similar on feature sets. Augmenting the core offering with services (servitisation) becomes significant. This includes offering rental, subscription, maintenance, and upgrade services. Market leaders emerge and some competitors exit. By 1995, other spreadsheet products TWIN and VP planner had come and gone. Office 365 (the subscription service containing Excel) was not offered until 2013.

5. *Commodity.* Servitised markets without network effects tend to ultimately become commodities. Commodity markets are characterised by price competition and high levels of standardisation and/or regulation. These markets have the lowest levels of volatility, innovation, and profitability. Normally, commodity markets have gone through a shakeout and fewer, larger players remain the only significant players. The spreadsheet market has not reached this stage yet. However the level

of free support online for building Excel formulas and coding VBA macros suggests the ability to use a spreadsheet is becoming a commodity.

6. *Decline.* The final stage of the market is where it goes into decline because its product offering becomes obsolete. In this stage, small niches may survive, but the mass market heydays of the product are over. Some products never seem to reach this stage. Instead they seem to fragment into many niches and then re-emerge into the customised stage. Craft beer in Europe,[39] US,[40] and Australia[41] is experiencing a resurgence around the western world even as traditional volume brands are in decline. Vinyl record sales grew 25% in the 12 months ending June 30, 2019, however they are only 4% of music industry revenues with 62% coming from paid streaming services.[42]

The vertical axis of a VSM is drawn with market maturity increasing down because, like gravity, all markets tend to move down the curve over time. An example VSM is shown below for part of the Residential Aged Care (RAC) value chain (see Figure 4.8).

At the highest level, the diagram splits RAC into clinical care, emotional support, room & board, and domestic help components. The map then outlines the value chain for the food component in more detail. It is apparent from the map that room & board is poised to become servitised. This means it is expected that RAC providers

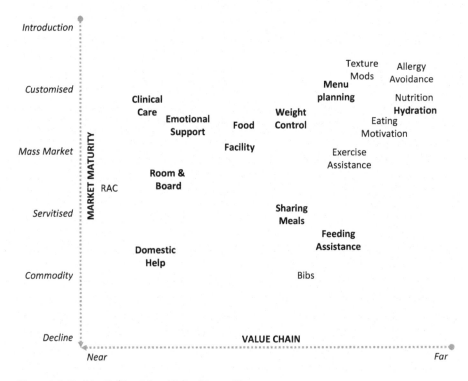

**Figure 4.8:** Residential Aged Care Value Stream Map.

will switch to offering rental agreements and begin to differentiate around the quality of infrastructure offered. Business class aged care is likely to be introduced along with a range of additional upgraded services. Despite RAC currently being a mass market, a number of lower level components of the food service in RAC are still substantially customised. Other aspects have been close to commoditised.

Historically, RAC has been almost entirely funded by government. Now the sector is subject to severe 'irregulation' because of concerns over care quality. Irregulation occurs when regulators rewrite the rule book. Two main forms are deregulation to promote competition, or increased enforcement to raise standards. Policy makers may act to drive outcomes, without understanding the causes of the current situation. Aged care is reeling in response to government policies to increase competition and enforce higher care standards in the wake of a Royal Commission. However, government seems oblivious to how their past funding and compliance policies caused the sector's problems. They simply trust the strong will survive somehow. A Royal Commission investigating aged care began in January 2019 and is due to present its final report in November 2020. According to the National Seniors Australia website:[43]

> The Royal Commission into Aged Care Quality and Safety is a landmark inquiry for Australian residential and in-home aged care. Its establishment followed media investigations and more than 70 reviews by successive governments over the past 10 years.
>
> Despite ongoing reform, systematic failures leading to poor quality of care for older Australians continue. Statistics show the number of serious risk notices issued to aged care providers jumped 170 per cent in the past year and significant non-compliance leapt 292%.

On July 1, 2019, the Australian government implemented a new Quality Standard for Aged Care and since then has increased scrutiny of providers. Figure 4.9 shows the increase in non-compliances to 2020.[44] Note the apparent reduction in the period to January 2020 is because the data only covers a six-month period rather than the whole year. The increased scrutiny is not the only worry for RAC providers.

The reality is the government cannot continue to fund the sector to the same degree over the next decade and beyond. In 2017, 15% of Australians were aged 65 and over. By 2057 this group will be 22% of the population. Increasing the overall funding to the sector by 50% as the proportion of taxpayers reduces is not sustainable. The government is in the process of overhauling the main funding instrument, ACFI (Aged Care Funding Instrument), as part of a strategy to reduce costs in real terms over time. This is despite 44% of RAC providers reporting a loss in 2017–2018.[45] In 6,600 reviews of ACFI cases through 2018/2019 the government downgraded more than 43.2% and upgraded 0.3%.[46]

> Leading Aged Services Association (LASA) conducted an aged care financial risk survey and found 80 percent of providers who participated in the survey are facing challenges. According to LASA, 15% may have to withdraw services, 41% may have to reduce direct care staff, and 62% may have to reduce investment.[47]

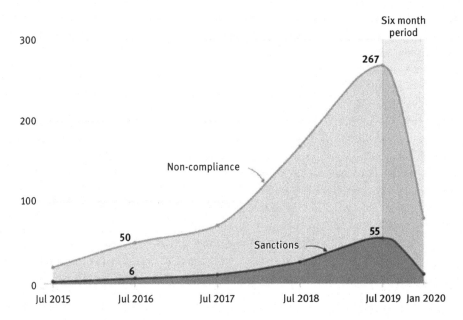

**Figure 4.9:** Residential Aged Care Non-compliance.

The government is also testing consumer directed care (CDC). Under CDC arrangements, RAC providers are not block-funded to provide a set number of beds. Instead the funding goes to residents who can choose their provider. This change dramatically increases the level of competition in the sector. The combined challenge of higher quality standards and tighter funding means RAC providers need to access other revenue sources. The VSM above is an instructive example for where they might look to improve their CX with adjacent positioning to increase profitability. The key to using VSM is to consider how the map will change over time and position your organisation to exploit or influence changes.

There are six basic approaches to use a VSM to find adjacent positioning opportunities for lean CX. These are:
1. Specialisation
2. Integration
3. Segment expansion
4. New channels
5. Mass customisation
6. Servitisation

Each of these is explained in turn below and an example related to the RAC case above is outlined. Not all the opportunities presented by the VSM are equally feasible. This is not critical, for the RAC sector now the challenge is to cover enough opportunities to identify how to find more sustainable funding. The basic strategy is to change from government as the sole source of funding to providing value adds residents and their families are happy to fund. This is possible because like many other government funded sectors, innovations around quality have been hindered by past funding policies. Funding arrangements were established to pay only the minimum service level the government deemed to be required.

## Specialisation

The first opportunity in the VSM is to consider how to reduce coverage in the value chain. Not all parts of the value chain are equally profitable. Generally customised parts of the value chain have the highest margins. A 2016 study on the economics of the aged care sector showed four sectors captured more than 70% of the flow-on demand from the sector.[48] RAC providers could specialise by outsourcing their property ownership and domestic staffing to just provide the clinical care part of their current service portfolio (see Figure 4.10). This eliminates the most capital in-tensive and low margin parts of their business (room & board, domestic help).

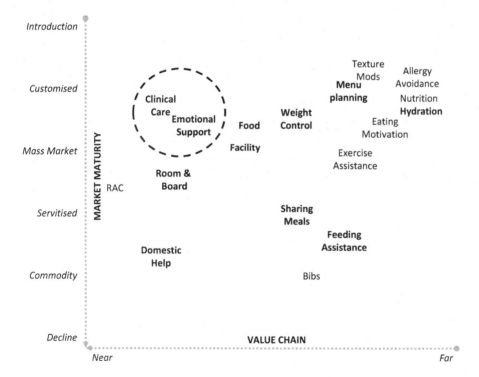

**Figure 4.10:** RAC Specialisation Opportunity.

## Integration

The second opportunity in the VSM is to consider how to increase delivery across more parts of the value chain. Insourcing customised services can increase differentiation and scale advantages to improve perceived quality and lower costs. The key is to find economies of scale for currently outsourced parts of the value chain. In RAC, the non-bold specialist services selected (see Figure 4.11) are sourced from contractors, even if the provider has adequate scale to offer full-time employment. The opportunity is to switch from contractors to employees to reduce costs.

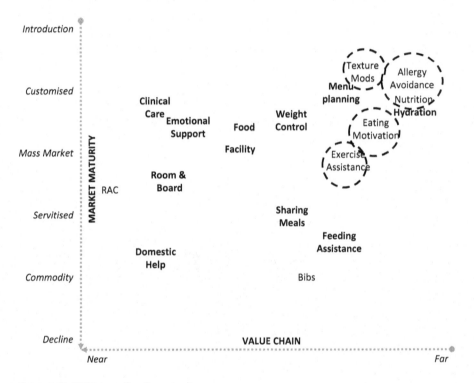

**Figure 4.11:** RAC Integration Opportunity.

## Expand Segments

Mass market services may be able to be expanded to other segments in the market. RAC providers mostly service the consumer market. However, there is an opportunity to provide transition beds to hospitals for private patients in recovery after hospital treatment. In many cases the RAC service offer is equivalent to the services provided by hospitals to recovering patients, but more cost effective (see Figure 4.12). Providing transition beds could increase profitability for both hospitals and providers.

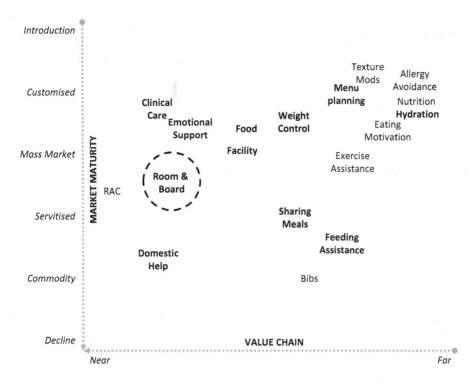

**Figure 4.12:** RAC Segment Expansion.

## New Channels

Any of the outsourced items on a VSM can provide options for new channel part-ners. For RAC providers, a partnership with a gym specialising in senior members makes sense (see Figure 4.13). The gym could increase its revenue by providing services to RAC customers and in return recommend partner providers to members as their health declined to the point where they needed care. Right now most RAC providers receive referrals only from other clinical care providers. Most of these are primary care providers with no incentive to fully partner.

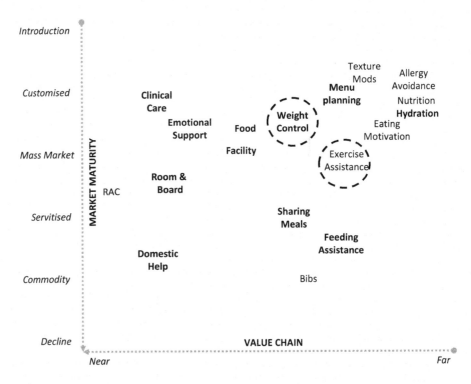

**Figure 4.13:** RAC New Channels.

## Mass Customisation

Value chain elements still in the customised stage may offer an opportunity for more of a mass market approach. Typically this involves technology. In RAC there are opportunities to use software for customisation related to clinical care, weight control, menu planning, and nutrition. There are also opportunities to implement market maker business models similar to Airbnb or Uber for parts of the value chain. One example would be a network of part-time carers available to provide short interval companionship to help with emotional support and reduce isolation concerns (see Figure 4.14). This model could apply for both RAC clients and other elderly services recipients utilising in-home care. For clinical care this looks more like locum placement services.

## Servitisation

Any value chain elements in the mass market stage can be potentially servitised. In RAC there are providers who are offering spare rooms on a rental basis rather than

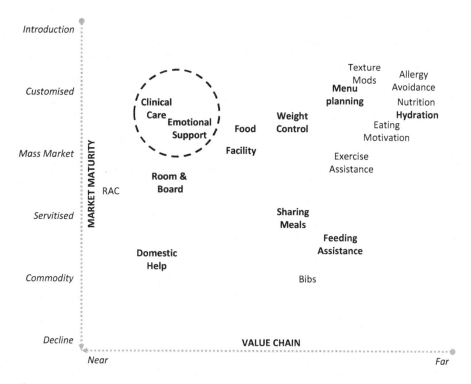

**Figure 4.14:** RAC Mass Customisation.

the current approach involving returnable accommodation deposits (RADs). RADs cost hundreds of thousands of dollars and are more like buying a bed from a provider than renting. There is also a model based on a subscription service for aged care appropriate meals. Providers like YouFoods and HelloFresh have targeted younger demographics and proven the home delivery of menu plans and ingredients on subscription can be a profitable business. RAC providers have the expertise to deliver a similar service end to end or partner with existing providers to solve the logistics challenges. This would ensure spare kitchen capacity at residential facilities could be better utilised to add on additional revenue by serving non-residents (see Figure 4.15).

The opportunities above are not the only possibilities identifiable within a VSM, however along with the other methods in this chapter, they provide attention directing tools for where to look for Lean CX improvement opportunities. The next chapter covers how to market test the potential to identify the best minimum viable initiatives (MVIs) to scale.

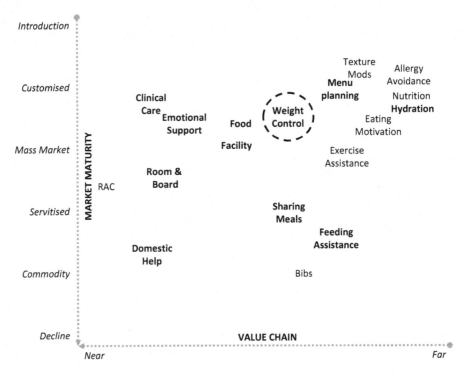

**Figure 4.15:** RAC Servitisation.

## Endnotes

**1** Ibid., footnote 55 (location 134 in the Kindle edition).

**2** Ruiz (1997). *The Four Agreements: A Practical Guide to Personal Freedom*, Amber-Allen Publishing, Inc.

**3** Norman (2013). *The Design of Everyday Things*, Basic Books.

**4** Ramsey (2019). "NLP Practitioner Certificate Course (Beginner to Advanced)," *Udemy* https://www.udemy.com/course/nlp-practitioner-neuro-linguistic-programming-online-course/.

**5** Young et al. (1998). "The Stochastic Modeling of Purchase Intentions and Behavior," *Management Science* Vol 44 No 2.

**6** Adapted from "S- Intention to purchase research" in Dew (2018). *Customer Experience Innovation: How to Get a Lasting Market Edge*, Emerald Publishing Limited.

**7** Czikszentmihalyi (2008). *Flow: The Psychology of Optimal Experience*, Harper Perennial Modern Classics.

**8** Norcross et al. (2002). "Auld lang syne: Success predictors, change processes, and self-reported outcomes of New Year's resolvers and non-resolvers," *Journal of Clinical Psychology* Vol 58 no 4.

**9** Hare and Woods (2013). *The Genius of Dogs: How Dogs Are Smarter than You Think*, Plume.

**10** Ibid., footnote 16.

**11** WikiHow Staff (2019). "How to Become a Lord," *WikiHow*. https://www.wikihow.com/Become-a-Lord (accessed 4/2/20).

**12** Ibid., footnote 16.

**13** See https://www.DISCprofile.com/what-is-DISC/overview/ for an introduction of the DISC framework developed by Wiley and retained under their copyright. The original DISC types were presented by Marston (1928) *Emotions of Normal People,* Routledge. The book was last revised and reprinted in 2012 with Bill J. Bonnstetter and Ron Bonnstetter adding some additional content. According to Google Books, "This work has been selected by scholars as being culturally important and is part of the knowledge base of civilization as we know it."

**14** TERMS was described previously in Dew (2018) *Customer Experience Innovation: How to Get a Lasting Market Edge,* Emerald Publishing Limited. The concept was first published in Dew and Robinson (2004) "Terms – Creating Disruptive Entrepreneurial Strategy." In Murray Gillin, L (Ed.) *Regional Frontiers of Entrepreneurship Research 2004. Proceedings of the First Annual Regional Entrepreneurship Research Exchange.* The Australian Graduate School of Entrepreneurship, Hawthorn, Victoria, pp. 588–603.

**15** Guzman and Perry (2019). "Here's How Much to Spend on an Engagement Ring," *The Knot.* https://www.theknot.com/content/how-much-to-spend-on-engagement-ring (last accessed 6/2/20).

**16** Pink (2009). *Drive: The Surprising Truth About What Motivates Us,* Riverhead Books. Also see the 2010 video "RSA ANIMATE: Drive: The Surprising Truth About What Motivates Us," *YouTube* https://www.youtube.com/watch?v=u6XAPnuFjJc (accessed 6/2/20).

**17** The Design Matrix was adapted from "The Idea Box" p. 117 in the Kindle edition of Michalko (2006). *Thinkertoys: A Handbook of Creative-Thinking Techniques, 2nd Edition,* Ten Speed Press. For CX specific applications see "A Design Matrix can revolutionise your product or service" in Dew (2018). *Customer Experience Innovation: How to Get a Lasting Market Edge,* Emerald Publishing Limited.

**18** Sutherland (2009). "Life Lessons from an Ad Man," *TED Talks.* https://www.ted.com/talks/rory_sutherland_life_lessons_from_an_ad_man (accessed 2018).

**19** Mason (2009). *The Pirate's Dilemma: How Youth Culture Is Reinventing Capitalism,* Free Press.

**20** Cialdini (2009). *Influence: The Psychology of Persuasion,* HarperCollins e-books. The other factors are scarcity, reciprocity, consensus, contrast, expertise, and liking.

**21** Easton (2020). "Amazon Prime hits 150 million users," *DigitalTV Europe.* https://www.digitaltveurope.com/2020/01/31/amazon-prime-hits-150-million-users/ accessed 16/3/20.

**22** Moshin (2019). "10 Amazon Statistics You Need to Know in 2020," *Oberlo.* https://au.oberlo.com/blog/amazon-statistics accessed 16/3/20. The infographic shown above is adapted from the same source.

**23** Wikipedia (2020). "Patreon," *Wikipedia.* https://en.wikipedia.org/wiki/Patreon accessed 16/3/20.

**24** Hearn (2018). "The rise of Patreon – the website that makes Jordan Peterson $80k a month," *The Guardian.* https://www.theguardian.com/technology/2018/may/14/patreon-rise-jordan-peterson-online-membership accessed 16/3/20.

**25** Huillet (2019). "Dave Rubin Turns to Bitcoin for Crowdfunding After Alleged Patreon Censorship," *Cointelegraph.* https://cointelegraph.com/news/dave-rubin-turns-to-bitcoin-for-crowdfunding-after-alleged-patreon-censorship accessed 16/3/20.

**26** McDowell (2019). "20 foods expected to be on the rise in 2020, from Impossible Burgers to oat milk," *Business Insider.* https://www.businessinsider.com/popular-foods-everyone-will-be-eating-in-2020?r=AU&IR=T (accessed 18/3/20). Weinberg (2020). "The 12 Food Trends You're Going to See Everywhere in 2020," *Delish.* https://www.delish.com/food/a30431915/food-trends-2020/ (accessed 18/3/20). Thorn (2019). "25 Interesting Food Trends to Follow In 2020," *Big 7 Travel.* https://bigseventravel.com/2019/12/food-trends-in-2020/ (accessed 18/3/20).

**27** Vegconomist (2019). "Impossible Foods Requests Permission to Enter European Market." https://vegconomist.com/companies-and-portraits/impossible-foods-requests-permission-to-enter-european-market/ (accessed 18/3/20).

**28** Mandelbaum (2020). "Impossible Burgers Aren't Healthy, And That's the Whole Point," *Gizmodo*. https://gizmodo.com/impossible-burgers-aren-t-healthy-and-that-s-the-whole-1838263145.

**29** Ibid., footnote 142.

**30** Kano et al. (1984). "Attractive quality and must-be quality," *Hinshitsu (Japanese Journal for Quality Control)* Vol 14.

**31** Hamzah et al. (2014). "Malaysia Airlines to Go Private With A$435 Million Government Investment," *Business Insider*. https://www.businessinsider.com/malaysia-airlines-overhaul-2014-8?r=AU&IR=T (accessed 20/3/20).

**32** Adapted from Dew (2019). "Another reason not to fly Malaysia Airlines," *LinkedIn*. https://www.linkedin.com/pulse/another-reason-fly-malaysia-airlines-robert-dew/ accessed 20/3/20.

**33** Cohen (2018). "Has Meet & Seat by KLM Royal Dutch Airlines Failed?" *The Gate*. https://thegate.boardingarea.com/has-meet-seat-by-klm-royal-dutch-airlines-failed/ accessed 20/3/20.

**34** Taylor and Blackall (2020). "Lie-flat beds in economy class: Air New Zealand unveils bunks for budget travellers," *The Guardian*. https://www.theguardian.com/world/2020/feb/26/lie-flat-beds-in-economy-class-air-new-zealand-skynest-bunks-budget-travellers accessed 20/3/20.

**35** Kim and Maugborne (2004). "Value Innovation: The Strategic Logic of High Growth Companies," *Harvard Business Review*. https://hbr.org/2004/07/value-innovation-the-strategic-logic-of-high-growth accessed 20/3/20.

**36** This is based on an interview in 2020 with Wayne Schmidt, the first sales manager at Xero during its start-up phase. He was responsible for developing and communicating Xero's CVP to the market to drive sales. The interview had to do with what actually made Xero different to other accounting packages out there at time. Schmidt had to work out how to make a cloud installation something his client cared about.

**37** This concept was adapted from Wardley Maps. See Wardley (2018) "Wardley maps – Topographical intelligence in business," blog chapters 1–19, https://medium.com/wardleymaps accessed 20/3/20 for a complete primer on Wardley Maps. Also see Wardley (2015). "An introduction to Wardley (Value Chain) Mapping," *Bits or Pieces?* https://blog.gardeviance.org/2015/02/an-introduction-to-wardley-value-chain.html accessed 20/3/20.

**38** Inarda (2018). "The history of spreadsheets," *Sheetgo Blog*. https://blog.sheetgo.com/spreadsheets-tips/history-of-spreadsheets/ accessed 21/3/20.

**39** Arthur (2018). "Unprecedented boom in microbreweries helps boost European beer volumes and variety," *BeverageDaily.com*. https://www.beveragedaily.com/Article/2018/12/06/EU-beer-statistics-Microbreweries-and-craft-beer-provide-big-boost accessed 21/3/20.

**40** Jones (2019). "Craft Beer Boom: The Numbers Behind the Industry's Explosive Growth," *Visual Capitalist*. https://www.visualcapitalist.com/numbers-craft-beer-industry-u-s/ accessed 21/3/20.

**41** Wynne (2020). "Craft beer – Bucking the trend in Australia," *Deloitte Perspectives*. https://www2.deloitte.com/au/en/pages/consumer-business/articles/craft-beer-bucking-the-trend-in-australia.html# accessed 21/3/20.

**42** Leight (2019). "Vinyl Is Poised to Outsell CDs For The First Time Since 1986," *Rolling Stone*. https://www.rollingstone.com/music/music-news/vinyl-cds-revenue-growth-riaa-880959/ accessed 21/3/20.

**43** National Seniors Australia (2020). "Royal Commission into Aged Care Quality and Safety." https://nationalseniors.com.au/advocacy/royal-commission-into-aged-care-quality-and-safety/ accessed 21/3/20.

**44** Low (2020). "Which aged care services near you weren't up to scratch in 2019?" *The Conversation*. http://theconversation.com/which-aged-care-services-near-you-werent-up-to-scratch-in-2019-131449 accessed 21/3/20.

**45** Martin (2019). "Australia's aged care sector may not be financially sustainable, Senate committee hears," *The Guardian*. https://www.theguardian.com/australia-news/2019/oct/23/australias-aged-care-sector-may-not-be-financially-sustainable-senate-committee-hears accessed 21/3/20.

**46** Egan (2019). "ACFI downgrades, sanctions increase," *Australian Ageing Agenda*. https://www.aus tralianageingagenda.com.au/2019/11/29/acfi-downgrades-sanctions-increase/ accessed 21/3/20.

**47** Alderslade (2019). "LASA review finds nearly 200 aged care services are in financial distress," *Aged Care Guide*. https://www.agedcareguide.com.au/talking-aged-care/lasa-review-finds-nearly -200-aged-care-services-are-in-financial-distress accessed 21/3/20.

**48** Deloitte Access Economics (2016). "Australia's aged care sector: economic contribution and future directions," *Deloitte*. https://www2.deloitte.com/au/en/pages/economics/articles/australias-aged-care-sector-economic-contribution.html accessed 22/3/20.

# Chapter 5
# Managing the Cycle

So which kind of animal is your organisation? Is it a Monkey trapped by its own initial success, with your CX practice focused mainly on better fur lining for the mouse trap? Or is it a Gazelle bounding across the savanna in pursuit of the next delicious market opportunity? Well, unless you are working for one of the few organisations that has worked out how to turn CX into a productive innovation and value creation function for the organisation you might be feeling a little lost right now.

The good news is that Monkeys can morph into Gazelles. It will take some work, but by adopting and applying the Lean CX approach, your organisation will start to realise benefits more quickly than before. Over time Lean CX will become an accepted part of your organisation's operating rhythm.

As you discovered earlier, learning is at the heart of the Lean CX philosophy. You should strive to learn as much as possible as quickly as possible, leveraging the MAYA principle – searching for the Most Advanced Yet Acceptable CX innovation that will yield value. There are two key elements to developing a MAYA concept:
1. Exploring to find potential MAYA concepts
2. Testing and iterating the concepts

You are searching for the 'Goldilocks' combination of features and benefits in your concept. The concept needs to be right in the zone of consideration. It needs to go beyond the familiar to be interesting for your target audience. This is advanced enough to be different and interesting, but not so advanced as to be seen as 'blue sky.'

In the early stages of the process, the focus is on learning about your customers, the competitive and contextual environments to help identify and shape up potential CX innovation concepts. In the latter part of the process, it is about learning what elements of your MAYA concept work. Some elements will align with what is important to your target audience. Other elements will not. The point of Lean CX is doing this quickly. You want to get to real-life observations via market testing as quickly as possible. What follows is the 'how to' of Lean CX.

## Four Phases of Lean CX

There are four key phases to creating real value through CX innovation using the Lean CX approach (see Figure 5.1):
1. Prepare & Align: Getting the business ready for the process
2. Find an Adjacent Market Opportunity: Doing the work to uncover the adjacent market position and to define the MAYA that will achieve cut-through in that position

https://doi.org/10.1515/9783110683929-005

3. Design your Minimal Viable Initiative: Develop and test your MAYA concept with real customers to see if it achieves the cut-through hoped for
4. Refine & Validate: Use feedback to refine and improve your MAYA concept and prove the value opportunity

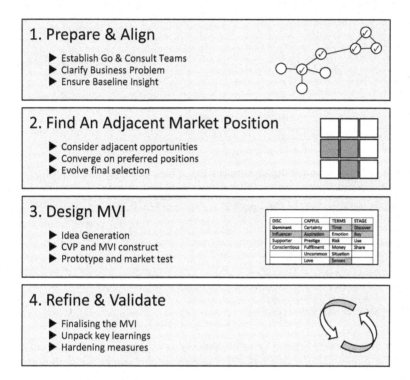

**1. Prepare & Align**
- ▶ Establish Go & Consult Teams
- ▶ Clarify Business Problem
- ▶ Ensure Baseline Insight

**2. Find An Adjacent Market Position**
- ▶ Consider adjacent opportunities
- ▶ Converge on preferred positions
- ▶ Evolve final selection

**3. Design MVI**
- ▶ Idea Generation
- ▶ CVP and MVI construct
- ▶ Prototype and market test

| DISC | CAPFUL | TERMS | STAGE |
|---|---|---|---|
| Dominant | Certainty | Time | Discover |
| Influencer | Aspiration | Emotion | Buy |
| Supporter | Prestige | Risk | Use |
| Conscientious | Fulfilment | Money | Share |
| | Uncommon | Situation | |
| | Love | Senses | |

**4. Refine & Validate**
- ▶ Finalising the MVI
- ▶ Unpack key learnings
- ▶ Hardening measures

**Figure 5.1:** Lean CX Phases.

Each phase contains specific steps and utilises the techniques and concepts presented in Lean CX to quickly create cut-through CX innovations.

Astute readers may already have seen a pattern analogous to the widely understood 'Design Double Diamond' framework (DDD) used extensively in design practice around the world.[1] DDD involves four key phases of discovery, definition, development, and delivery. Two divergence-convergence cycles lead to clarity around the problem being solved for and a solution to that problem. Figure 5.2 shows how this framework is adapted to Lean CX. The focus is on finding the right market position to attack and the right minimum viable initiative to scale.

It is useful to compare and contrast DDD and Lean CX approaches. Designers using DDD look for the right problem to solve in the first divergence-convergence phase, where the design double-diamond model looks for a problem to solve, Lean CX

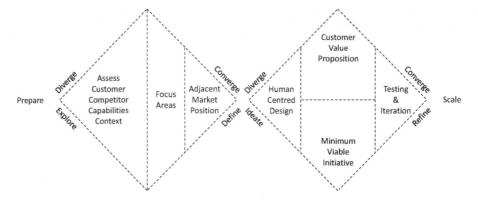

**Figure 5.2:** Lean CX Double Diamond.

looks for an adjacent market position opportunity to exploit. In the second divergence-convergence phase the models are more similar: each involves ideating around potential solutions and then using rapid iterative testing to refine and adjust the solution to achieve a scalable outcome. Lean CX also specifically includes the definition of the CVP in this phase to ensure the customer value exchange is clearly articulated and used to guide the evolving MVI.

## Phase I: Prepare & Align

Preparing your organisation for the Lean CX process is critical to ensure the right level of buy-in, resource access, and action at the end of the process. After all, Lean CX is about creating value through action. It is about the implementation of CX innovations – not just the design of them. In the Prepare & Align phase there are three key steps:
1. Establish the Go and Consult teams
2. Clarify the business problem (opportunity)
3. Ensure you are starting with the right level of baseline insight

### Structure

Lean CX leverages two specific teams. The Go Team and the Consult Group. The Go Team is the team that gets stuff done. The Consult Group are the collection of external stakeholders who help the Go Team avoid triggering the corporate immune system to attack the innovation.[2] It is easy to understand the roles of the Go Team and Consult Group with the RACI framework.

RACI[3] is a construct with four key role types related to the participation in project delivery. RACI stands for Responsible, Accountable, Consulted, Informed. RACI is often used to clarify roles and responsibilities in cross-functional projects. In Lean CX, the Go Team is responsible and accountable. The Consult Group is consulted with and informed.

The Go Team should be comprised of specialists across the organisation who can contribute to the design and test process. Operatives can come from CX, marketing, operations, contact centres, finance, sales, or technology. You may also consider someone from legal as a valuable resource for the Go Team. Many organisations automatically accept the status quo regarding regulation and compliance. This generally makes customers' lives miserable because the primary focus on risk and compliance is at odds with customer value and ease. A Go Team legal expert can help discover ways to deliver on an improved customer value proposition and still stay inside compliance requirements. Importantly, the Go Team needs to work as a team. The whole Go Team is collectively responsible for getting stuff done (R in RACI).

In this structure, the Go Team leader has a critical role akin to the product owner in traditional agile methodology. This person is accountable for the planning, direction, and management of the Lean CX process. Successful leaders can come from any part of the business. They may typically be a senior CX operative or marketer. Sometimes firms need an external consultant to lead their Go Team to add horsepower, additional intellect, or cover skill gaps. The leader's business speciality is not important, it is their ability to work with other players from across the organisation to elicit the best ideas, develop and test them, and ready concepts for scaled deployment. The leader is accountable for coordinating the Go Team to ensure they can meet their responsibilities (A in RACI).

The Go Team are responsible for the work to uncover an adjacent market position, to work up the draft CVP that responds to the AMP, to identify ideate and design Minimum Viable Initiatives, and run the design sprints to develop those into a strong MAYA concept. Lastly, the Go Team takes the learnings from the design and test phase to polish and complete the MAYA concept ready for hand off to the business to scale. They are also responsible for getting value from the Consult Group.

Consult Group members are typically senior leaders from across the organisation who can lend their expertise, perspective, and influence to help drive the project. An important difference between this group and typical senior governance teams is that they are not given the ability to actively change the process or the emerging design. The way the Consult Group functions is also different to the Go Team. They do not need to come together to ensure alignment on their perspectives because they are not a team. Instead they are a collection of individual stakeholders with uniquely valuable and valid perspectives. One important aspect of how Lean CX works is to avoid trying to homogenise or align the members of the Consult Group. It is more valuable to understand the differences in their perspectives. Lean CX ultimately uses market results as the motivation for alignment when an initiative is ready to scale. Instead of requiring satisfaction from the Go Team, the Consult Group are required to act more as servant leaders.

The Consult Group provides two key benefits to the Lean CX process. First, this team provides an external cross-functional sounding board for the Go Team. The Consult Group helps with responses to key questions, ideas, and opportunities as they arise through the process. Second, the Consult Team serves as the entry wedge for wider organisational adoption of the resulting MAYA concept. This is a critical success factor in Lean CX, since without wider adoption, CX innovations rarely succeed (this is both C and I in RACI).

### Clarity

A central tenet to Lean CX is acting because there is a problem or opportunity suspected to have large value attached. There are many possible drivers to invest in a Lean CX process. It could be that your organisation is struggling with differentiation in a competitive market. There may be an imperative to find new ways to grow and/ or add on additional revenue streams. Part of your customer experience may be causing customers grief and making them consider competitors. Whatever the problem or opportunity is, a critical step in the Lean CX process is ensuring clarity and alignment around the problem you are trying to solve.

There is plenty written about developing clarity around problem definition. At its most simple, it is about creating a one sentence or single paragraph statement about the problem in focus and the value attached to that problem. This is one of the first uses of the Go Team/Consult Group dynamic. As a unit they develop and reflect on the business problem to ensure that the project is clear about their intent and the potential for it to fit with the rest of the business.

### Baseline

The last step in Phase I of Lean CX is to ensure that your project team has access to a useful level of baseline insight. Lean CX is faster than traditional CX because it starts with ideation based on existing insight, rather than extensive primary research. We respect the in-built understanding of customer needs and market context key players have built up through successful years of operations. The Lean CX process operates to leverage this organisational acumen together with existing research and insights as quickly as possible. Lean CX is about finding new sources of value for your organisation by improving your customers' experiences. It is not useful to keep fine-tuning customer insights instead of acting. Spending too much time and resources trying to get the perfect level of insight delays creating the value your organisation needs. This does not mean abandoning research altogether.

Primary research is valued as a way of developing insight to support innovation and decision making. The problem is that many organisations are observed to stall at the research phase. This conclusion comes from more than a decade of advisory and consulting experience. Organisations can spend too much time and money trying to develop the perfect set of insights instead of moving to action. Many end up missing the boat on CX innovation. There is a simple frame to determine the right level of research your organisation should undertake (see Figure 5.3).

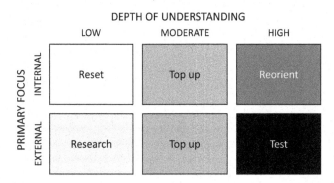

**Figure 5.3:** Preparation Research Required.

The framework classifies three levels of customer understanding (low, moderate, and high) on the horizontal axis and two levels of focus on the vertical axis (internal, directed toward company processes; and external, directed toward the market). Few firms are so out of touch with contemporary needs, wants, and drivers of customer behaviour they need to perform extensive foundational research. These are the firms in the left column of Figure 5.3.

Firms in the bottom left position of Figure 5.3 have a market orientation but don't know much about their customers. The optimal approach for this cohort is to invest in customer research to maximise their ability to get cut-through. A typical example would be a start-up trying to commercialise a technology breakthrough or medical research innovation. Many of these firms exhibit a technology push bias. They have data on the size of their target market and a customer value proposition based on a rationalisation of what they think their target customers will buy. They are victims of the Dunning-Krueger Effect.[4] They think they understand what their target customers want, when in practice they often miss many key aspects impacting customer take-up. These include emotional considerations, technical skills, price performance, switching costs, stakeholder influence, operational competency, evaluation reticence, and risk aversion. These firms survive only by learning more about what their customers truly value during their early struggle stage. It is different for organisations insulated from early struggle by time or fiat.

Firms in the top left position of Figure 5.3 tend to not really care about customers because their monopoly or oligopoly status means they do not have to. There are long-established parts of the public service and utility providers who operate without much consideration for customers because they do not perceive a need to. This perception persists because there is a disconnect between the source of funds for the organisation and the consumers who must interact with it. Many government organisations with an enforcement role as part of their remit exhibit this arrogance.

*P- L- Core mindset underpinning law enforcement*
*One of the most confrontational CX projects we are aware of relates to law enforcement operatives trying to design target state experiences for criminals. The enforcement operatives involved strongly believe in the deterrent and retributive theories of punishment. As a group they wanted greater powers to compel adherence to the law. Some were negatively biased by their experiences in law enforcement and others retained a low opinion of other people in general. The group stereotype was a Dominant Conscientious personality who want to force everyone to have to obey the rules. They advocate for offenders to be punished and shamed to reduce reoffending. It was apparent some in the group were attracted to the idea harming offenders as a payback for their crimes. They tended to ignore the situational drivers of criminality (low socioeconomic status, poor ethical and moral role models, and substance dependency issues) and their own ethnic and racial biases. They also reject the rehabilitation and protection theories of punishment, asserting the inappropriateness of 'bleeding hearts' who hold more liberal views. It seems some take their self-image from achieving a position of power over others. Sadly, the target state experience they designed was not informed by a full understanding of what offenders were typically feeling, thinking, and doing when they committed crimes.*

There is not much point in these companies conducting customer research as a starting point because they are not ready for CX innovation. Instead a reset is required to change the way they value their citizens or customers before they have any possibility of positive CX change. Fortunately, both types of organisations characterised in the left column of Figure 5.3 tend to be rare. In our experience, perhaps 5% or less of organisations are on the far left of this spectrum. Perhaps another 20% require a significant 'top up' before they can confidently commence a Lean CX approach.

Most firms have conducted some level of market and customer research. They often have a reasonable suite of market and customer insights useful for designing a Lean CX innovation. The proof of this is their ability to survive in a competitive market or operate as a government monopoly without a high volume of complaints. Some of these firms fit in the middle column of Figure 5.3. They may only require a 'top up' in the form of a market scan, competitive benchmarking, or interviews with a convenient sample of key customers to fill in some gaps before continuing with Lean CX. They do not need to invest in extensive research.

The rest are ready and primed and just need the right approach and mindset to achieving scaled value quickly. It is important to note that Lean CX treats employee insights and acumen as a valuable part of the firm's overall level of customer understanding. Unlike other approaches to CX design, the deep well of insight and understanding that can be tapped from across the organisation is not discounted. It is the baseline insight required to pursue a Lean CX approach.

So this last step in Phase I is about finding out what level of customer and market insight your organisation has and assembling it for easy use by the team. This will be in the form of market studies, primary research reports on buying behaviour, usage attitudes, and need states. You should also consider the acumen that each of the team members brings to the table. Often, they will have years of experience in certain areas that provides sufficient insight for the Lean CX process to run.

Now, what if your organisation is one of the 5% who have an exceptionally low understanding of customers and market? If that is the case, we would recommend performing some foundational research to properly update and inform your teams and the wider organisation as to what is driving customer interest, behaviour, and motivations. You will want to do at least a basic market scan and competitor analysis. There are a range techniques and methods using primary and secondary research methods that you can use to build this foundational insight.[5] The next phase of Lean CX assumes you have access to the right level of insight.

## Phase II: Find an Adjacent Market Position

Chapter 3 introduced the idea of gaining cut-through by finding and exploiting an adjacent market position. To refresh your memory, this is about considering those possible segments or markets, products, or services that are 'next' to your current position, but not too 'far out' that they are either way too risky or costly to attempt. This is the matrix on the left in Figure 5.4 below. The matrix on the right is what the Three Horizon model looks like when you start to translate the "CX" elements of the business model canvas on it. Naturally, your organisation's mapping will probably look quite different from the example below.

Critically, in undertaking exploration for an adjacent market position opportunity, there is no one defined starting point. This might confuse some readers who are used to a strictly prescribed step-by-step process. But it is a more useful approach as our starting position is not constrained by one specific tool or technique. In other words, where to start and which tool to use depends on your organisation's context, current circumstances, what you know, what competitors are doing, and what customer behaviours you are observing. It is more important to simply start with a learning orientation using an action research philosophy. This is where what you learn determines how you proceed next.

One of the principles Lean CX utilises extensively is fluidity. This means not being locked in too early to either a process stage or an emergent idea. Therefore, another critical point when it comes to finding an adjacent market position is that you might actually find it in the third phase of the Lean CX approach!

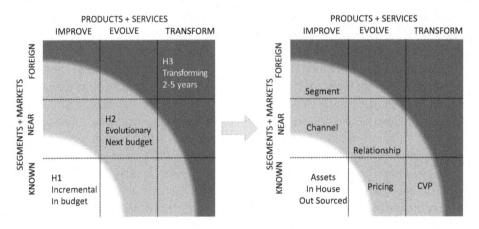

**Figure 5.4:** Exploring for an Adjacent Market Position.

***C+ P+ Providoor – Add A Chef initiative creates an adjacent market position to UberEats***
*Providoor[6] is an Australian company making big waves in the growing food delivery market through an innovative adjacent market position. Like many other restaurants, they are in the business of making and delivering meals to people at home. However, they differ in that instead of delivering cooked meals ready to eat, they deliver meals that have been mostly cooked then cooled and packaged for final heating in your home. The key benefit is that meals are tabled fresh without the sogginess that sometimes accompanies hot food that is delivered to your door. By partnering with some of Melbourne's leading restaurants, Providoor is providing an upmarket, table-fresh alternative in the crowded home delivery market.*

*How is this an adjacent market position? Well, Providoor examined the food delivery landscape and discovered that an important segment was being underserved by the incumbent providers like UberEats. This segment is defined by people with a higher than average ability to spend and a desire for much more upmarket and exclusive foods that they would otherwise have enjoyed at their favourite expensive restaurants. From a CAPFUL perspective, they desired Prestige (P) and Uniqueness (U) but were getting neither.*

*Providoor created a CX that met those needs and ensured they delivered on the requisite quality level by adjusting the cooking process to include two steps – the cooking, and then the subsequent controlled cooling and packaging for reheating in the customer's kitchen. This 'position' is different enough from incumbent providers to stand out yet is close enough in conceptual understanding for people to 'get it.' In other words, it is a MAYA concept that is achieving cut-through.*

*Now, Providoor is not standing still and has created another adjacent market position building on the CAPFUL elements of Certainty (C) and Prestige (P). Providoor customers will be able to 'add a chef' to their meal delivery, guaranteeing the food quality and presentation will be exactly as it is in a restaurant (C+) while adding a large touch of panache to their dinner party (P+) – because who wouldn't be impressed by having a chef preparing and serving dinner at their friend's home?*

Phases II and III of the Lean CX process are about finding an adjacent market position (AMP) to exploit and designing a solution to scale for value. The earlier chapters introduced a range of techniques to uncover new market opportunities. Armed with a range of insights, ideas, and opportunity areas you now need to make choices and home in on an AMP. Do this by harnessing the acumen of stakeholders to identify small signals that can guide to a suspected AMP. This is where you can again leverage the Go & Consult Team dynamic and add other participants into the process. The best results come from ensuring a diversity of perspective and experience at the table. This is the cornerstone of an effective cross-functional group. This group should span different levels of the organisation from executive to front-line staff. It may include key customers where feasible.

Plan a series of workshops where the various elements of Customer, Competitor, Capability, and Context are used as primes to elicit ideas for a potential adjacent market position. Importantly, design your facilitation approach to avoid brainstorming leading to groupthink. This is where one or two dominant voices (typically the more senior voices) tend to influence others' thinking, reducing objectivity and creativity.

### Using Nominal Groups

One of the most pervasive issues in organisational decision making is how to harness the collective acumen and information available to a decision-making group. Humans are social creatures who naturally establish hierarchies to collectively solve problems. Dominant leaders can push groups to solve problems faster at the expense of narrowing the range of options they can reasonably consider. There is a structuring solution to improve the effectiveness of a decision-making group.

Most decision-making groups operate as an interactive group. They use a process a bit like brainstorming. The problem is that brainstorming was developed to help with option generation not decision-making. The basic brainstorming process involves one person sharing an idea with the rest of their group for consideration. Ideally ideas presented will trigger other ideas. In practice, this triggering effect is rare. Even after directing members to suspend judgment of others' ideas, brainstorming is just not that effective in helping groups be creative. Brainstorming groups have issues with production blocking and social loafing. It is inherently inefficient to have the whole group stop thinking about the problem for one member to present their idea (production blocking). This also leads to some group members not contributing very much at all because other members are taking up all the airtime for idea sharing (social loafing). When brainstorming groups shift from option generation to decision-making, they often end up continuing with one person speaking at a time. Only this time group members are sharing their judgments about options. Interactive groups like this work even less for decision-making than brainstorming works for creativity.

Generally, the first opinion voiced will have a disproportional impact on the opinions of the rest of the group. This can lead to groupthink. The other bias inherent in interactive group decision-making relates to hierarchy. The opinion of the most powerful person in the room has more weight than any other point of view.

This means interactive groups end up more about achieving apparent alignment than making the best decision from the available information. Interactive groups tend to operate in a flawed way to achieve a suboptimal consensus.

There are better approaches to decision making than brainstorming-style groups. Nominal Group Technique (NGT) and Delphi are basic alternatives[7] to interactive groups for decision making. In practice it is apparent the core requirements for convening an effective Delphi panel are more difficult and slower than NGT for adjacent market position selection.

NGT works by having group members work individually on a problem for a defined period before sharing their views sequentially with the rest of the group. The group process is group in name only (nominal) because the members do not initially interact. There are two ways to use this in decision making. Each member can choose the best option from the set under consideration. Alternatively, each member can evaluate all options independently.

The level up from NGT is to arrange group members into pairs. Nominal pairs works similarly to NGT. Each pair operates independently of the others to evaluate options. The difference is the nominal pair approach allows the members of each pair to discuss their ideas with their counterpart prior to presenting to the rest of the group. This approach is still highly efficient and has the advantage of including the potential for triggering effects.[8] Applying nominal pairs or NGT is simple for adjacent market position selection. As a group, the various AMP options are listed. Each individual or pair decides on the best AMP in their opinion according to an agreed set of criteria arranged in a simple table or matrix. This approach to multivariate decision making is called Decision Criteria Matrix (DCM).

### Decision Criteria Matrix

DCMs are widely known and used across a range of disciplines. They include a range of criteria used to score different AMPs and derive a focus through a linear 'side-by-side' comparison of already-stated potential AMPs. DCMs can be simple as shown in Figure 5.5. In this simple DCM, each AMP is evaluated in terms of six criteria. The example shows potential AMPs are assessed according to:
1. Potential for revenue
2. Ability to deliver ongoing revenue
3. Cost to implement
4. Speed of execution
5. Difficulty to test and scale
6. Fit with organisational values

A more complex DCM (Figure 5.6) includes a range of considerations and is useful for gaining higher fidelity in the decision-making process. This example has the same

| Team Member A | Team Member B | Team Member C | Team Member D | Idea | Revenue Potential | Ongoing Revenue | Low Cost | Fast | Easy | Value Fit |
|---|---|---|---|---|---|---|---|---|---|---|
| | | | x | AMP 1 | | x | | | | |
| | x | | x | AMP 2 | x | | | | | x |
| x | | | | AMP 3 | | | x | x | | |
| | | x | | AMP 4 | | x | | | x | x |
| | | | x | AMP 5 | x | x | | | | |
| | x | x | | AMP 6 | | x | | | x | |
| x | x | | | AMP 7 | | | | x | x | |

**Figure 5.5:** Decision Criteria Matrix.

approach to listing potential AMPs, though they are called CX innovations. The difference is that this model expands criteria to help select an AMP based on relevance, opportunity for scale, likely value, and innovation potential. This example has been modified from the original used to help a suburban rail operator improve the CX for commuters.

The Opportunity Areas evaluation helps decision makers understand how relevant an AMP is in terms of coverage of the key customer opportunities uncovered. More relevant AMPs work to improve CX across more opportunity areas. The criteria also include application to different commuter Journey Stages. Innovations useful for improving CX across more of the customers' journeys are of higher utility.

The Kano Drivers evaluation gives us a signal of the likely value of an AMP. The more Kano Drivers an AMP positively impacts the more valuable it is likely to be. And lastly, an evaluation against different Segments gives a signal for how scalable the AMP will be.

These are also used in this model which provide an indication of how innovative your AMP is. In this client example the funding context for the CX improvement made innovation a key consideration. The three innovation criteria (first/useful/successful) are detailed in a previous book by two of the authors of this book called *CX Innovation: How to Get a Lasting Market Edge.*[9]

The greater complexity of the second DCM still works the same way with NGT or nominal pairs to provide a basis for selection of the preferred AMP to develop into a minimum viable initiative for testing. For many Lean CX applications, this is sufficient. DCMs can become unwieldy when lots of AMP options are under consideration or when team members struggle to rank CX innovations in a consistent way due to definitional uncertainty or scale issues. The solution is to use an evolutionary algorithm.

| Category | Attribute | CX Innovation 1 | CX Innovation 2 | CX Innovation 3 | CX Innovation 4 | CX Innovation 5 | CX Innovation 6 | CX Innovation 7 |
|---|---|---|---|---|---|---|---|---|
| | 5+ | × | × | × | | × | × | × |
| | 3+ | × | × | × | × | | × | × |
| | 0+ | × | × | × | × | | × | × |
| | Successful | Leverage | Repeated | Repeated | Leverage | Leverage | Leverage | Repeated |
| | Useful | Staged | Staged | Fits | Staged | Staged | Fits | Fits |
| | First | Australia | Australia | Australia | Organisation | World | Australia | Australia |
| Segment | Segment D | | × | | × | | | × |
| Segment | Segment C | × | | × | | × | | |
| Segment | Segment B | | | | | | | |
| Segment | Segment A | × | × | | | × | | × |
| Kano Drivers | Productivity | | | | × | × | × | × |
| Kano Drivers | Time | × | × | | | | × | × |
| Kano Drivers | Comfort | × | × | × | × | × | | × |
| Kano Drivers | Wellbeing | × | | × | | × | | |
| Kano Drivers | Price | × | | × | | × | | |
| Kano Drivers | Safety | × | | × | | × | × | |
| Kano Drivers | Convenience | | × | × | × | × | | × |
| Journey Stage | Leave Station Premises | × | | | × | | | |
| Journey Stage | Disembark | × | × | | | | | |
| Journey Stage | Travel | × | | | | | | |
| Journey Stage | Wait on Platform | × | × | | | | | |
| Journey Stage | Navigate | × | | | | | | |
| Journey Stage | Arrive at Station | × | × | | | | | |
| Journey Stage | Plan | × | | | × | | | |
| Opp Areas | Social Engagement | | × | | × | | | |
| Opp Areas | Technology Difference | | | | × | | × | × |
| Opp Areas | Travel + | | | × | | | | × |
| Opp Areas | On Board Experience | | | × | | | × | |
| Opp Areas | Station & Surrounds Environment | × | | | × | × | | |
| Opp Areas | Getting to the station | | × | | × | | | |
| Generator / Idea | Team Member D | × | × | | × | | | |
| Generator / Idea | Team Member C | | | × | × | | | |
| Generator / Idea | Team Member B | | × | | × | × | | |
| Generator / Idea | Team Member A | | | × | | | × | × |

**Figure 5.6:** More complex Decision Criteria Matrix.

## Evolutionary Algorithm

Evolutionary algorithms (EAs) are inspired by natural selection. Natural selection works on populations of creatures. There are groups of creatures with a range of varied traits relevant to survival. Creatures in a population compete for access to scarce resources to survive and breed. The best-adapted creatures survive longer and increase their chances of having offspring. Genes carry traits from parents to offspring. This survival of the fittest is how nature selects for superior traits in a population. Over generations, natural selection ensures creatures that are better adapted to their environment outlast the others who die out. The winners in evolution are those getting to pass on their genes. Strictly speaking, natural selection works at the level of genes not the level of creatures.[10]

Natural selection is probabilistic rather than deterministic. Meaning the creatures with superior traits are more likely to breed more. This is not guaranteed because luck plays a part. Sometimes an individual creature may be lucky and survive even though it is less adapted than its rivals. Sometimes a superior individual may be unlucky and meet its demise before being able to pass on its traits to offspring. Over many generations, the survivors tend to be better adapted on average. Every generation is potentially a little better on average than its immediate ancestors.

When animals mate, their offspring combine some traits from each parent. This combination of traits is called *crossover*. Offspring are different from both of their parents mostly due to crossover. New traits can also emerge in offspring because of imperfect reproduction. Sometimes offspring differ genetically from both of their parents. This effect is called *mutation*. Creatures evolve when either crossovers or mutations provide an evolutionary advantage. It should be apparent that natural selection is divergent due to crossovers and mutations, and convergent due to survival of the fittest. EAs are the conceptual domain analogue of how natural selection acts to solve problems in the real world.

EAs have been used to solve a range of difficult computational problems. Instead of a starting population of creatures they work on a list of possible solutions. Instead of traits/genes, computational EAs describe solutions in terms of discrete characteristics. Each generation the solution set diverges using crossover and mutation algorithms. Computational EAs replace natural selection with a fitness function. This function acts to identify which solutions should be continued to produce future generations of solutions. The best solutions in each generation are retained and the others are discarded. The process is simpler for AMP selection.

The starting population of possible AMPs are assessed first by the Go Team for aspects making them intriguing or concerning. Then this enhanced list is shared with the Consulting Group for them to add any additional intriguing or concerning considerations. Some AMPs may be neither intriguing nor concerning. Other AMPs may be both. The AMP list can then be ranked based on the net score determined from the total number of intriguing aspects less the total number of concerning ones. This creates the starting AMP population.

In each generation (or round) the first step is to pick two AMPs at random. In practice, care is taken to ensure the highest ranked AMPs are not selected together in the first round. First the AMPs are subject to crossover. This is done by taking the intriguing aspects of one AMP and modifying the other AMP to have these benefits as well. Then the counterpart AMP is modified to include any intriguing aspects. The resulting crossover AMPs are compared by the Go Team (using NGT or nominal pairs). The best crossover survives to the next generation. Similarly, both original AMPs are mutated. This is done by trying to change each AMP to reduce any concerning aspects. After this the mutated pairs are compared (again using NGT or nominal pairs). The best mutant also survives to the next generation. This process of picking a pair of AMPs, creating crossovers and mutations, then retaining the best crossover and the best mutation is repeated until there are no more AMPs in the original list. An odd number of AMPs means the last option gets automatic selection to the next round after mutation.

Some Go Teams prefer to create a fitness function based on criteria similar to the those in the simpler DCM presented previously in the Phase II section. In this case, a crossover or mutation is selected by virtue of being superior to its counterpart on more criteria. The advantage of this comparative selection approach over the basic DCM is that no subjective scale is required to assess each AMP. The decision is simply about which one of the pair is better to survive to the next round.

Each round begins with the new list of retained, modified AMPs. Each round the list neither increases nor decreases because each pair is replaced by a single crossover and a single mutation. This process of crossover/mutation/selection is repeated for successive generations. In practice it becomes apparent the process is reaching its limits after some number of rounds. The law of diminishing returns certainly applies. At this point the selection process is cut down to focus purely on convergence. This is done by selecting random AMP pairs and going directly to comparative selection without crossover or mutation. Only one AMP survives the pairing. This means over each selection round the remaining AMP list halves. The process works like a knockout tournament with round winners matched together in subsequent rounds all the way to the final. Again, any round with an odd number of AMPs results in one getting a bye through to the subsequent round. This tournament-style approach to decision making allows the best AMP to be selected comparatively over a series of rounds rather than by trying to assess using a DCM-based approach. This distinction matters because theoretically AMPs should be evaluated against criteria objectively, but the nature of this decision-making problem confounds this. Instead only subjective assessments can be made.

At the end of either the EA, DCM, or complex DCM process, a preferred adjacent market position should have been identified. The preferred AMP will be one from the original list if a DCM approach was used to converge. It will likely be quite different from all the original AMPs if an EA approach was taken. Either way, the next step is to translate the AMP into a minimum viable initiative for market testing and iteration.

## Phase III: Design Your Minimum Viable Initiative

Minimum Viable Initiative (MVI) is the Lean CX analogue of the widely used Minimum Viable Product (MVP) concept popularised by Eric Ries.[11] Lean CX focuses on MVI because CX innovation is not constrained to the territory of a product. At the same time, not all aspects of the business model canvas need to be considered for CX innovation. Because your organisation is already delivering customer experiences, any MVI must be relevant to the current business context. So an MVI can address any aspect of your organisation's engagement with a customer.

The ideal MVI establishes and articulates the combination of service/product/value/segment elements that you believe will meet your customers' CAPFUL and TERMS needs. It also needs to take account how far you can push each element in terms of newness or difference from the current state to MAYA.

It is likely that getting to MAYA will take some iteration. This makes testing your MVI the most critical part of the overall Lean CX process. This is where the most similarities with the agile design movement emanate.

Earlier chapters introduced how the Lean CX approach requires understanding customer needs and identifying elements of the overall experience to change or innovate. This is based on linking three psychographic considerations:
1. The segment's DISC profile
2. What we know about which CAPFUL need state is most important
3. What we know about the customers' TERMS that will help us focus

The design matrix (see Figure 5.7) is used together with the business model canvas template adapted for Lean CX to capture the different CX elements under consideration. As a quick recap:
1. *Segment*: Describes which customer cohort is in focus. Here this is described using the DISC framework in the design matrix
2. *CVP*: The bundle of products and services that will best align to the segment, the needs state, and the stage in focus
3. *Channels*: How the CVP is communicated, sold, and supported
4. *Relationship*: Describes the dynamic that exists between your organisation and your customer and ranges from total self-service to automated services to communities and personalised concierges
5. *Pricing*: Is the adaptation of the BMC revenue streams element (simply, what price is required to satisfy the design matrix and maximise value?)
6. *Partnership*: Describes whether there are any partners required to deliver the MVI

| DISC | CAPFUL | TERMS | STAGE | CVP | CHANNELS | RELATIONSHIP | PRICING | PARTNERSHIP |
|---|---|---|---|---|---|---|---|---|
| Dominant | Certainty | Time | Discover | | | | | |
| Influencer | Aspiration | Emotion | Compare | | | | | |
| Supporter | Prestige | Risk | Buy | | | | | |
| Conscientious | Fulfilment | Money | Use | | | | | |
| | Uncommon | Situation | Support | | | | | |
| | Love | Senses | Share | | | | | |

**Figure 5.7:** Customer needs to Minimum Viable Initiative.

You can change some of these or all of them in pursuit of a MAYA concept. So where do you start? In Lean CX our objective is to construct a MAYA concept that is innovative enough to get cut-through, but not too advanced to put potential customers off. At the start of the process we may have some ideas as to what changes we can make to the CVP, engagement channels, the kind of relationship, the price, or delivery partnerships. To confirm we need to test the proposed changes. This is done through rapid iterative testing involving customers to garner real time feedback, make adjustments, and add refinements toward our MAYA concept.

**Test Templates**

The intent is to test quickly and learn what elements of the MVI work. Other elements will need to be rethought. The MVI Summary & Test Template is a simple two-page tracking tool for this process. Adapted from the Business Model Canvas framework,[12] the MVI Template contains the MVI Summary and the MVI Split test sheets.

The first step of the process is to use the MVI Summary to describe in detail the key elements that will be constructed and tested with 'real' customers (see Figure 5.8). Pictured below, it contains seven different elements.

*Who* describes the specific audience the MVI is relevant to. Label the segment and provide a brief descriptor to help other project members understand and empathise with the target segment. Also describe the customer journey stage in focus, or multiple stages if applicable. Lastly, provide a summary of the specific customer need or desire that is the focus of the MVI. Be as specific as possible.

*What* is where you list in bullet point or short sentence form the key elements of the customer value proposition that you have developed in response to your earlier work to understand customer needs, reflect on your organisation's capabilities, and competitive offers.

Remember, the CVP is a bundle of benefits that solve or respond to a specific customer need or desire. Elements of the CVP can be quantitative and qualitative. For a mobile phone, a quantitative element could be a price benefit; a better camera; larger storage; or it might be waterproof. Qualitative benefits might include a burnished aluminium case; a beautiful felt-lined box; or the promise of an exclusive level of post-sale support. CVP elements do not always have to be 'premium' – you could just as easily have a lower quality camera, plastic casing, and a plain paper box, with the additional benefit of a significant price difference in the market.

*How* includes how your customers discover, try, buy, and when appropriate are supported. Often referred to as 'channels,' these interfaces can be analogue or digital and can be considered across the customer journey. Taking the mobile phone example, CVP interfaces might include sponsored posts by a celebrity on Instagram to raise awareness and consideration; a Facebook discussion page on the benefits and uses for the new camera capability; special zones in retailers to capture peoples'

| Who<br>[Segment Target]<br>[Journey Stages]<br>[Focus Need \| Desire] | What<br>[CVP] | | How<br>[Interfaces \| Packaging]<br>[Communications] |
|---|---|---|---|
| Why<br>[Estimated Value Potential]<br>[High Level NPV] | | Success<br>[Key Pirate Metric] | |
| Go | | Consult | |

**Figure 5.8:** Minimum Viable Initiative summary.

attention and draw them toward a demonstration; and specially selected customer service agents for the unique customer service experience on offer.

*Why* is the financial benefit you believe is possible by investing in this MVI. This can be high-level, order-of-magnitude forecasting or can be a reasonably detailed estimate of, say, cost savings to the business by delivering a better experience. The point is to ensure that the MVI and the resources invested in testing the MVI are anchored around the promise of creating new value for the organisation.

*Success* is where you track which of the Pirate Metrics (see Table 3.1) you believe will improve, and is the basis for your Estimated Potential Value uplift. Depending on your MVI, you might also include other traditional CX measures such as Net Promoter Score[13] (NPS), Customer Satisfaction (CSAT), or Customer Effort Score (CES).

*Go* and *Consult* contains the Go Team and Consult Group members. This identifies who is responsible for execution and who is required to assist with engagement with wider business.

Completing the MVI Summary is the foundation for conducting the split tests to help prove and improve the MVI concept. The *MVI Test* template describes and records the results of these market tests.

*Impacts* cover how the MVI is expected to resonate with customer needs (CAPFUL and TERMS elements). It also covers the potential pirate metric impact. If applicable, other non-financial metrics such as NPS or Effort Score can be included here.

*Test A* lists the key elements of the MVI used as the base market test.

*Test B* lists the differences defining the split test. This split test could be two different MVIs, or parts of the same MVI. The relevant elements come from the design matrix diagram table described above (see Figure 5.9).

| MVI | | | |
|---|---|---|---|
| Impacts | Test A | Test B | Learnings |
| CAPFUL | [Specific MVI element] | [Key Differences to Test A] | Positive |
| TERMS | | | Negatives |
| AARRR | | | Still Unknown |

**Figure 5.9:** Split Test Template.

## MVI Testing

*Split tests* are used to validate or adjust hypotheses about different elements of the MVI to make it a MAYA concept. Test environments can range from in-person to remote tests using video conferencing technologies. They can also be fully administered or fully self-serviced by customers. Some of the ways you can develop a prototype include:

- Paper prototyping: creating paper versions of digital experiences
- Card sorting: allowing customers to order labelled cards to signal response and preference
- High fidelity interfaces: Wizard of Oz functionality to mimic software applications
- Low fidelity interfaces: Click throughs to provide experience of interaction flows
- Box environments: Construct a physical diorama experience
- Flow testing: Role playing to test logic in particular sequences
- Direct response testing: Emails and landing pages to test click through and response

Construct split tests to vary a key element in your MVI and test differing customer responses. Ideally each split test only varies a single MVI element. However, in practice, different elements may be changed in early stages to help with faster convergence on MAYA factors.

The following design matrix example for a Boutique Travel Experience offer (see Figure 5.10) focuses on a split test for different relationship constructs: The widespread self-service experience where the customer does all the work, and a travel experience concierge where someone is paid to match the customer's needs with specific travel experience suggestions. The second test looks at alternative pricing models. One is a subscription model where, for example, you pay $1,000 per

Boutique Travel Experience

| DISC | CAPFUL | TERMS | STAGE |
|---|---|---|---|
| Dominant | Certainty | Time | Discover |
| Influencer | Aspiration | Emotion | Compare |
| Supporter | Prestige | Risk | Buy |
| Conscientious | Fulfilment | Money | Use |
| | Uncommon | Situation | Support |
| | Love | Senses | Share |

| CVP | CHANNELS | RELATIONSHIP | PRICING | PARTNERSHIP |
|---|---|---|---|---|
| A boutique travel service bringing you tailored and unique travel experiences that only a select few will ever enjoy. | | Self Service – browse and buy yourself | Subscription Fee Charged Monthly | |
| | | Travel Experience Concierge | % Fee Per Experience Booked | |

**Figure 5.10:** Boutique Travel Experience.

month and receive 3 Travel Experiences per year. The other is the more traditional approach of product costs combined with a % fee for the agent.

Simplifying the design matrix to focus on the relationship and pricing variables produces Figure 5.11. The tests will explore cohort responses to four different combinations of the relationship/pricing CX elements. Any number of MVI elements can be tested this way provided effective communications can be managed. In practice, no more than three elements are recommended to maintain manageability.

| | | PRICING | |
|---|---|---|---|
| RELATIONSHIP | Self Service – browse and buy yourself | 1. Subscription Fee Charged Monthly | 2. % Fee Per Experience Booked |
| | Travel Experience Concierge | 3. Subscription Fee Charged Monthly | 4. % Fee Per Experience Booked |

**Figure 5.11:** Relationship and Pricing.

The focus of the split tests is to collect evidence to confirm or refute predictions about the attractiveness of proposed CX innovation elements. Construct a test with two cohorts who are representative of the target segment and then let them the experience Test A or Test B conditions. Collect their emotional and rational reactions to the different elements. This includes whether assumed CAPFUL needs were satisfied. For example, has the CAPFUL need for Prestige been met with a Travel Concierge Subscription-based model? Does it also meet the segment's key TERMS need? And what signals are customers giving regarding price levels for the subscription or % fee model?

While Lean CX typically focuses at the initiative level and is therefore primarily interested in how our MVI resonates with customers in terms of their need state (CAPFUL and TERMS) and how the MVI is likely to drive value through a change in pirate metrics (Acquisition, Activation, Revenue, Repeat, Referral), depending on the MVI and the level of fidelity of any particular element you are testing, you may want to include more traditional UX metrics. These might include experience performance metrics such as task completion, time on task, error rates, and learnability through to behavioural and physiological measures such as pupillary response and skin conductance.[14]

*C+ L+ Scales: Bridging the doctor-patient gap for cancer diagnosis*
*Big Pharma[15] faced the same challenge as its competitors – how to find a meaningful way to get cut-through with the specialist doctors who decide which drug will be used to treat their patients. A firm had a range of oncology drugs available, some of which were market leading (typically identified as having better efficacy) and some of which were about the same as other manufacturers. Given the constraints in Australia from a regulatory perspective, Big Pharma deployed the same small set of marketing and sales tactics that Every Pharma typically used. In other words, they struggled to get cut-through.*

*In researching the patient and physician experience, a range of strong insights emerged that helped shape potential CX innovations and create an effective adjacent market position. One of these was the insight that during the critical consult when the physician tells someone they have a deadly cancer, there is a massive divide between doctor and patient. The physician, wanting to properly inform the person about the disease and potential treatment paths, operates in a highly rational, information-rich mode. They try to provide the person with as much information and detail as possible to support their decision making around treatment options.*

*The decision is significant and complex. Treatment options can range from aggressive treatment with a chance of survival or longer life but at the cost of well-being, to simple management treatments that provide for a better, though shorter, quality of life. This can be an extremely hard decision for patients to make. Hearing they have cancer often drops them into a kind of daze. Despite their doctor's best intentions, they become locked on the words "You've got cancer." Patients are typically incapable of fully understanding or absorbing the information physicians are presenting them with at the time.*

*Using this insight as a prime, we developed a simple kinaesthetic model to help the patient weigh and evaluate the trade-offs between treatment and quality of life. In the form of a miniature tug-of-war, there were two figurines that the patient could label with their name, and a string connecting them. These represented two versions of the patients themselves. The figurines were placed on the consulting desk, and two lines drawn at either end – one representing quality of life, the other representing quantity of life. With the physician's guidance, the patient would 'pull' the figurines in one direction or the other as they discussed different aspects of the possible treatment regimes and what was important to her life. The inherent dissociation involved in using the model helped patients get past their diagnosis shock.*

*Interacting with the model helped the patient create their own 'move toward' or 'move away' options. It also helped bridge the emotional gap between the patient and physician. This simple, very cheap and easy to implement consulting tool provided a market edge for Big Pharma, as the next appointment they had with their oncologist customers was not to talk about another drug, but to discuss a useful way for physicians to become more effective in their roles through a new technique to help patients understand and decide more effectively.*

*In MAYA terms, the concept was an advancement on the usual leaflets and pamphlets used to discuss treatment options, yet not too advanced – almost everyone understands the metaphor of a tug-of-war. The AMP created for Big Pharma was one of trusted support – no longer just another product seller.*

## Getting to MAYA

The prototyping and market testing phase is about finding a balance between 'different/newness' and 'strangeness.' This is the 'Goldilocks' version of any particular MVI element. For each MVI and each segment, this may look quite different. Continuing our Boutique Travel Experience example, we can understand our customers' response to the Travel Experience Concierge in terms of levels of intimacy they are comfortable with. Here we see that a Travel Concierge who is making recommendations based only on simple demographic and preference data might be considered a rather vanilla experience, probably not worth paying for (see Figure 5.12).

| | Level Of Intimacy | | |
|---|---|---|---|
| | Low | Moderate | High |
| Travel Experience Concierge | Knows your name, email, suburb, gender, travel preferences | Plus knows your income, typical travel expenditure, personal likes and dislikes via conversation | Plus follows you on Instagram, Facebook and Pinterest, posting regularly to your channel and making recommendations to you and people like you to build your status as a boutique travel star |
| | Vanilla | Goldilocks | Creepy |

**Figure 5.12:** Travel Experience Concierge.

However, a concierge who has a deeper level of understanding and insight derived through appropriate interactions like questionnaires or direct conversations could, for the target segment, be advanced enough relative to self-service travel alternatives that it is attractive. In Goldilocks terms, it is 'just right.' You might also test a much deeper level of intimacy where a concierge is proposed to follow their customers on different social channels and is encouraged to stimulate engagement by actively posting and other activities to build the social prestige of their client. It is possible however that customers might see that as creepy. This can be an issue when Prestige elements are pushed too far.

*P+U+ Segway – too advanced to be acceptable*[16]
*One example of a CX innovation that pushed too far was Segway. The device was first introduced around 20 years ago and finally retired in 2020 without ever having achieved its goals of revolutionising personal transport. If there was ever a poster child for a product too innovative to be successful, it would be Segway. Segways were sold for niche industrial and fleet applications. These included police departments, tour groups, warehouse workers, mall security guards, and airport maintenance staff. But the product failed to achieve mass adoption despite nearly two decades of trying.*

*Segway's designers envisaged revolutionising the personal transportation category by introducing a stand-up two-wheeled scooter. Segway was designed for quick and quiet zooming from one place to another. It was to replace walking for those with enough money and a desire to stand out. The rider simply had to step onto the Segway, stand holding the two handlebars and control speed and direction by simply moving their body weight. It sounded wonderfully exciting and simple at the time.*

*The Segway worked as advertised, but it was awkward to use. It was small enough to ride inside a building or into an elevator, but at 40+ kg was too heavy to carry. This made stairs a significant problem. In cities, Segway also faced similar adoption problems to bicycles. Most cities have streets that are designed for cars with footpaths for pedestrians. Bikes and Segways don't really work on either. Riders of both vehicles are also criticised for looking somewhat silly.*

*Cyclists in bright racing garb are mocked for being MAMLs (middle aged men in lycra). Segway riders were just mocked for looking dorky.[17] And while cycling was considered healthy, Segway riding is almost the opposite. Segway riders don't burn many calories while riding and three high profile falls damaged the device's safety reputation. President George W. Bush's fall was widely reported after being caught on camera by the press in 2003. Journalist Piers Morgan broke three ribs after falling off a Segway in 2007. Segway corporation owner James Heselden died after he accidentally steered his Segway off a cliff in 2010. The main reason for the usability problems stemmed from a lack of customer feedback.*

*Segways were kept under strict secrecy during their development for fear of being copied. The result was that product testing and consumer feedback were strictly limited. This inhibited the company from getting the product and customer experience right. This is the opposite of the Lean CX approach.*

*We can speculate about Segway design intentions based on the extensive amount written about the device. Three key need states seem to have been targeted: (1) a need for Prestige (P+), (2) a need for Uniqueness/Novelty (U+), and (3) a desire for Time savings (T in TERMS). Segway riders did enjoy an element of prestige simply because the device was relatively rare. The uniqueness of the device satisfied users wanting something new. And for riders who mastered riding the device, Segway was indeed a time saver, travelling at 2–3 times normal walking pace.*

*Lean CX testing of these CAPFUL and DISC need states may have revealed problems with MAYA design considerations. Safety (C+) may have earned a higher priority. Different DISC profiles adoption motivations were also questionable. S-types may not have seen the need to change from their current transport arrangements except to reduce walking effort. D-types would have been attracted to reduce their commute, but in practice, Segways were no faster than cars during traffic jams and slower outside of congestion. C-types had serious concerns over Segway's safety. They also were worried about how it fit with the rules. It was not clear if the devices were legal for footpaths or if they had to be registered to go on roads. C-types may have been more prepared to adopt Segways if a licence was required to operate one. I-types were attracted to stand out from the crowd. In some sense Segway was a fashion product more than a transport option. The problem here was Segway's price. Few people were prepared to pay $5000 for stand out fashion. The current rise of electric skateboards and hoverboards[18] is partly driven by their price point. Their riders also get to stand out. These products are far more affordable at $500 retail and it seems much closer the MAYA for their users than Segway ever was.*

## Phase IV: Refine and Validate

This last phase before handing the MVI over to other teams to scale involves three key steps:
1. Finalising the MVI in terms of a complete articulate of initiative with sufficient detail for the delivery parts of the organisation to understand and implement, including the likely 'size of the prize' for being successful.

2.  Ensuring key learnings from the earlier market test cycles are collated and communicated to relevant teams to support a continuous learning process.
3.  Embedding and hardening measures and data capture to track and monitor the initiative's performance as it is moved to scaled delivery.

## Finalising the MVI

Finalising the MVI and the handoff to the business to scale is one of the most critical steps and often where organisations fail to realise the benefit of CX innovation. This is where the earlier work in Phase I together with great documentation and continuous engagement start to pay off. Having effectively engaged and managed both the Go and Consult teams, you are likely to have the right level of understanding and buy-in from the parts of the organisation who now need to productise or scale your MVI. Throughout your project as the MVI starts to take shape, it is valuable to identify one or two potential sponsors for the MVI to champion it as it moves to scale.

Your MVI should now be articulated at a level of detail where the parts of the organisation responsible for delivery can understand what they need to do and how it will fit into the overall project. This can vary significantly by organisation and initiative type and can be conveyed through any number of artefacts and presentations. You might use a service blueprint,[19] target experience map, experience concept summary, and value chain maps, for example. Some organisations require a handoff via more traditional artefacts such as the dreaded Requirements Definition Document (RDD) and the even more feared Solutions Definition Document (SDD), whereas other organisations have adopted agile or non-waterfall delivery methodology in parts or all of the organisation.

Town hall or brown-bag presentations can also be an effective method for communicating the MVI vision and reinforcing how you are solving particular customer needs and creating specific value for your organisation. It is good practice to do these throughout the process, not just at the end of your MVI development.

## Unpack Key Learnings

From your early MVI hypothesis estimated potential value calculations, you will have picked up signals from your testing that support and refine your assumptions with regards to how your MVI will impact targeted metrics, whether it be higher acquisition rates due to a superior CVP, better conversion rates due to improved purchasing experience (fewer fall outs), or increased customer lifetime due to better and more relevant engagement throughout the relationship. You should be able to articulate with confidence the specific value uplift you expect to see as your MVI is scaled.

Throughout the Lean CX process you will uncover a range of learnings that can be used beneficially across the organisation. If you can maintain a Learnings Log that captures the learning and expresses it in terms of the audience (segment), the context (activity, environment), cause or trigger (the event and response), and the implication to the customer and to your organisation, you will have constructed a rich asset for other teams to leverage. It is good practice to provide a well-structured version of these learnings to the hand-over team, but to also unpack them throughout the project as a continuous learning exercise.

## Hardening Measures

The last step in Phase IV is to ensure that as the MVI is productised or scaled, the right measures are in place to track success and to rapidly adjust aspects of the product, service, or experience in response to that data. There are three key kinds:

*Measures showing customer traction.* These are basically the pirate metrics important to your specific MVI. For example, when Amazon introduced the '1-CLICK' to buy experience, you can be sure they tracked how many people used that feature and assigned a commercial value in terms of captured sales versus the previous buying experience that had more potential drop off points. This is how you ensure tracking toward the estimated potential value figure that you sold your organisation on.

*Measures proving business scale.* There are a range of these, one example being product metrics. Product metrics might be added to the analytics model your organisation uses to understand product performance (units sold, usage, time on site, uptime, etc. – whatever is important from a customer and business success perspective).

*Measures providing CX insight.* This covers how your MVI has shifted customer perceptions around what it is like dealing with your organisation. These include NPS, CSAT, and Customer Effort Score, for example, and can be easily tracked through the VOC program mentioned above.

## Scaled Agile

An increasing number of organisations around the world are adopting agile development principles and processes across their enterprise. This is commonly termed 'Agile at Scale' and 'Scaled Agile.'[20] The organisation is redesigned to facilitate initiative execution via small, dynamic cross-functional teams vs. the traditional silo-based approach still common across all sectors. There are two significant challenges with Agile at Scale. These can be resolved or reduced by the adoption of Lean CX into the operating model. The first is the cultural challenges that come with a substantial change to how an organisation works. The second is the competing agendas problem that arises when many distributed teams compete for ideas and resources.

To explain these two key challenges, we must first understand what Scaled Agile is. Scaled Agile is a way of organising resources in a decentralised, cross-functional way to federate ideation, decisioning, and initiative execution. It relies on squads comprised of specialists from different parts of the business and orchestrated by a scrum manager to focus on 'increments' of an overall solution with the objective of rapidly defining, designing, and building pieces of a larger solution. The goal is to accelerate deployment with more of a test-and-learn approach.

Scaled Agile involves a range of role types that may be entirely new to the organisation. As mentioned above 'scrum masters' are the agile version of a producer. Product owners are the new initiative owners with considerable decision-making authority with regard to product features and value construct. Sitting above this is typically high-level program management whose job it is to try and coordinate a vast array of separate and often competing agendas. Importantly, Scaled Agile involves a range of protocols and rituals like daily stand-ups and huddles.

With this context, the first challenge is common and involves a well-known psychological condition known as 'survivor's syndrome' (or guilt syndrome). Survivor's syndrome develops where people have survived a traumatic event and feel guilty for that survival. With scaled agile this is typically following a large organisational restructure involving significant role redundancies. Not for the faint-hearted, Scaled Agile is not just about changing a few work practices. It involves up-ending the organisation, changing people's roles and accountabilities, and in a real way handing decision making to teams where it was previously held tightly by managers and executives.

In this landscape, it is inevitable that people are lost from the organisation in the spill-and-fill approach to finding the most suitable people for the new agile roles. For those who survive the spill-and-fill there can be an interesting tendency to over-index the symbols and rituals of agile to demonstrate their commitment to the change agenda and justify why they survived when others didn't. This behaviour can get in the way of execution as a lot of time and energy is devoted to rituals instead of productive work. One bank client typified this negative consequence.

*C- U- Western Bank challenged by Scaled Agile move*
*Western Bank[21] was one of the earlier movers in the banking sector to adopt Scaled Agile wholesale across the organisation. Working with a large global consulting firm, plans were developed to redesign the organisation toward an agile work model. As part of the change, a range of new roles were introduced, functional models changed, and new work practices introduced.*

*Many people were directly affected by either leaving the business or being placed into new roles. Some people were completely new to the organisation. Large sums were spent on change management including education on why the change was necessary, what Scaled Agile is, and how the new model would work at the enterprise, group, team, and individual levels.*

*Despite these considerable efforts to support and transition the remaining employees to new roles, workplace survivor syndrome crept in. This was especially evident where the roles were new and unfamiliar. People placed into subject matter expert roles without the requisite experience were expected to learn on the job. Leaders were educated on the core principles and processes of agile. Both audiences tended to over-index the many rituals of Scaled Agile at the expense of pragmatic and practical work effort. To us outside consultants working with the organisation after Scaled Agile was implemented, there were many confounding interactions more like being in a church than a business. The whole environment was a bit like the Chinese proverb of the wise man pointing to the moon and the imbecile looking at his finger. People in the new operating model didn't have the ability to discriminate what aspects of organisational behaviour actually mattered. Examples included regular meetings to report no progress. A focus on the importance of sitting or standing during certain presentation stages. Reframing partial progress to move items from one column to another on whiteboards, when actually nothing had really changed. Ultimately this impeded the pace at which new ideas could be surfaced, investigated, and most importantly actioned to create value quickly.*

The second major challenge with a move to Scaled Agile is competing agendas and federated ideation and decisioning. In principle, the concept of allowing teams across an organisation to discover and develop improvement and innovation ideas seems like a good approach. In fact, this is better than a command-and-control approach that is often too distant from customers. In practice, however, the teams often do not have the resources or the capabilities to effectively do this. Even when they do, across the organisation you start to see a large collection of ideas and initiatives that eventually collide in either resource conflict or value contention. This is where Lean CX can really help.

The 'fast path to value' principle inherent in Lean CX means teams can quickly and effectively determine the likely optimal set of initiatives early in the process before applying them to the Scaled Agile hopper. This hopper is the industrial scale

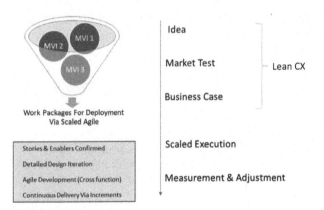

**Figure 5.13:** Scaled Agile Hopper.

deployment of features and capabilities. Typically, expensive and timely CX design efforts are not required to adequately help find and align the right initiative set across the organisation. The resources usually spent on those activities are used instead to market test and validate initiatives. Lean CX is the best filter for feeding validated initiatives into the Scaled Agile model ensuring that scarce deployment resources are focussed on initiatives that have the most value creating potential (see Figure 5.13). Lean CX's approach to quickly identifying ideas, market testing those cheaply and using that data to build reliable estimates of the value potential help the organisation to more effectively prioritise what gets focus. In the next chapter we refocus away from managing the Lean CX cycle and Scaled Agile to examine how the Lean CX approach changes for business-to-business applications.

## Endnotes

**1** Double Diamond is the name of a design process model popularized by the British Design Council in 2005, and adapted from the divergence-convergence model proposed in 1996 by Hungarian-American linguist Béla H. Bánáthy. It suggests that the design process should have four phases: Discover, Design, Develop, Deliver.

**2** Hastreiter (2018). "Preface: Reprogramming Your Corporate Immune System," in Linnhoff-Popien et al. (eds.) *Digital Marketplaces Unleashed*, Springer.

**3** Harned (2019). "How to Clear Project Confusion with a RACI Chart," *TeamGantt*. https://www.teamgantt.com/blog/raci-chart-definition-tips-and-example (accessed 09/07/20).

**4** Wikipedia "Dunning–Kruger effect" https://en.wikipedia.org/wiki/Dunning%E2%80%93Kruger_effect (accessed 09/07/20).

**5** Dew (2018). *Customer Experience Innovation: How to Get a Lasting Market Edge*, Emerald Publishing Limited.

**6** https://www.providoor.com.au/

**7** McMillan et al. (2016). "How to use the nominal group and Delphi techniques," *International Journal of Clinical Pharmacy* Vol 38.

**8** Dew and Hearn (2009). "A new model of the learning process for innovation teams: networked nominal pairs," *International Journal of Innovation Management* Vol 13.

**9** Dew (2018). *Customer Experience Innovation: How to Get a Lasting Market Edge*, Emerald Publishing Limited.

**10** Dawkins (1996). *The Blind Watchmaker: Why the Evidence of Evolution Reveals a Universe without Design*, W. W. Norton & Company.

**11** Ries (2011). *The Lean Startup: How Today's Entrepreneurs Use Continuous Innovation to Create Radically Successful Businesses*, Currency.

**12** Osterwald and Pigneur (2010). *Business Model Generation: A Handbook for Visionaries, Game Changers, and Challengers*, John Wiley and Sons.

**13** Reichheld (2006). *The Ultimate Question: Driving Good Profits and True Growth*, Harvard Business School Press.

**14** Tullis and Albert (2008). *Measuring the User Experience: Collecting, Analyzing, and Presenting Usability Metrics*, Morgan Kauffman.

**15** A multinational pharmaceutical company.

**16** Golson (2015). "Well, That Didn't Work: The Segway Is a Technological Marvel. Too Bad It Doesn't Make Any Sense," *Wired*. https://www.wired.com/2015/01/well-didnt-work-segway-technological-marvel-bad-doesnt-make-sense/ (accessed 8/7/20).

**17** McFarland (2018). "Segway was supposed to change the world. Two decades later, it just might," *CNN Business*. https://edition.cnn.com/2018/10/30/tech/segway-history/index.html (accessed 08/07/20).

**18** See https://skywalker.com.au/ for some product examples (accessed 18/7/20).

Polaine, Lovlie, and Reason (2013). *Service Design: From Insight to Implementation*, Rosenfeld Media.

**19** *Harvard Business Review*, "Agile at Scale," May–June 2018 edition.

**20** Western Bank is a 2nd tier retail bank in Australia not identified for commercial in confidence reasons.

# Chapter 6
# Business to Business

Up until now, this book has focused on Lean CX with the implicit assumption customers were consumers. Many of the concepts and tools also apply when customers are businesses. However, there are significant differences between the two groups. These differences mean applying Lean CX in business-to-business (B2B) markets varies from business-to-consumer (B2C) markets. The size of the B2B opportunity mandates customising experiences to better meet their needs.

## B2B vs. B2C

The B2B space comprises more than half of the world's economy.[1] In 2010, B2B transactions were calculated at $50 trillion globally. The figure has increased significantly since, but most of the research and media coverage about the development of commercial activity comes from a Business-to-Consumer (B2C) perspective. Analysis of US Federal Reserve data shows that in 2019 the American B2B market was worth $23.1 trillion, a significant 1.6 times larger than the $14.2 trillion B2C market.[2] This especially applies to reports about new products with the growth of social media-enabled marketing and CX. Most business school students are taught about theories and cases rooted in a B2C context. This occurs even though the demand for early career sales and/or marketing roles is often greater in B2B. Table 6.1 summarises some of the main stereotypical differences between business and consumer markets.

Table 6.1 emphasises the large transactional and offering differences between B2C and B2B markets historically. With such a massive difference between the two types of market, it is only logical that the CX in B2C and B2B environments is often profoundly different. Think how long it takes you to make up your mind about trying out an inexpensive new app, a different toothpaste option, a new restaurant or the latest movie on Netflix. It all happens in a matter of seconds to minutes. Choosing a new laptop or phone demands a higher level of personal investment. But even this is a simple decision process compared to many B2B purchasing evaluations. Now imagine you work in the rapidly changing automotive sector as part of the team selecting autonomous driving technology for Toyota or the Volkswagen Group. Both Toyota and Volkswagen each employ more than 300,000 staff globally. Their extended supply chains span the globe. The purchasing these firms undertake involves much higher stakes. You are under much more pressure to make a good purchasing decision. At the same time, a far wider range of stakeholders are involved in the evaluation process.

The car industry is currently in flux due to major shifts in consumer preferences. One shift is toward electric vehicles. Another relates to how ride sharing is reducing the need and expectation that consumers will own their own vehicle. These

https://doi.org/10.1515/9783110683929-006

**Table 6.1:** Main Differences between B2C and B2B Markets.

| Dimension | B2C | B2B |
|---|---|---|
| Orientation | Marketing promotion | Manufacturing/Tech focus |
| Customer segments | Large | Small |
| Market Complexity | Less complex | More complex |
| Value perceptions | Emotional then rational | Rational then emotional |
| Transaction size | Tends to small | Tends to large |
| Purchase time | Short | Often long to very long |
| Branding | Extensive/sophisticated | Often limited |
| Buyer/seller interdependence | Limited | Often significant |
| Relationship use | Limited | Often significant |
| Relative size of buyer/seller | Seller larger | Often similar |
| Offering complexity | Tends to be simpler | Tends to be more complex |
| Decision maker | Individual consumer/couple | Web of decision makers |
| Time period for value delivery | Often short | Often long |
| Customer experience | Individualised | Institutional |

shifts reduce industry certainty related to technology standards and market demand. Deciding on the right autonomous driving components is a decision reaching all the way up to the most elevated decision-making units in your firm. Would-be suppliers to your firm need to manage the corresponding customer experiences differently.

They have a lot riding on a deal with your company. There are orders of magnitude fewer potential customers for them to approach than in consumer tech markets. At the same time, each potential customer represents orders of magnitude more unit sales for years to come. Buyer concentration in B2B markets has changed value chains.

The current century has seen the rise of the FAANGs (Facebook, Apple, Amazon, Netflix, and Google). Most individuals consider their relationship with these powerful and disruptive mega-brands as consumers. However, these supercharged technology giants have built their success through their ability to manage both B2C and B2B activities. While the headlines about Apple might be about their new iPhone offering, or how their services are expanding to build recurring revenues, the company's success is enabled by B2B relationships with long-term suppliers. Samsung supplies Apple with integrated circuits, Infineon provides communications hardware, Primax produces its digital camera modules. Apple also has relationships with raw material suppliers such as Agnico-Eagle and American Elements. Many B2C firms find themselves in a similar situation as Apple. They increasingly have to rely on B2B suppliers to ensure that they can deliver competitive products and services in line with market trends.

In the B2C service-focused economy, physical products like phones, cookers, and cars are increasingly digitally enabled. The trend toward digitalisation compels manufacturing firms to integrate their offerings with intelligent digital systems. This enables their products to function without human intervention by connecting with other machines. Internet access also enables the efficient working of the B2B economy.

Human-machine, machine-human, and machine-machine communication is becoming the norm in B2B relationships. As firms such as Alibaba have risen in importance, suppliers have benefitted from digital platforms to automate payments, rebates, and invoices. These changes have transformed the efficiency of B2B transaction processes. This development and expectation of the constant updating of data underpins the Internet of Things (IoT). IoT is a global phenomenon relevant for both B2B transactions and B2B service delivery. Digital technologies are also fuelling globalisation in B2B markets.

The internet has meant B2B customer demand has become global. Clients can now compare and source products from across the globe with remarkably low transaction costs. This has had two effects. Most B2B firms are now facing more competition in larger markets. They are also dealing with greater variation in demand. Consumer tastes and preferences vary significantly across cultures and borders. This means global B2C organisations (like P&G, Nestle, Unilever, and Danone) must ensure that their offerings match local tastes and cultural drivers and avoid taboos. This reduces the leverage they could previously exploit from operating at global scale. It also changes the way they source from their suppliers.

The 2020s see B2B markets being influenced by four major trends and driving forces:

1. The need to focus on an increasingly global marketplace
2. The need for organic growth (rather than growth through acquisitions)
3. Dramatic increases in customer power due to digital information and manufacturing
4. The need to harness the potential of B2B big data and analytics

The big news is that the spotlight in B2B markets is moving on from products and supplier technology (the key areas of focus in recent times) to the customer-facing functions involved in Customer Experience.

## Buying Modes

With B2B buying processes changing dramatically as buyer-seller interdependence increases, the nature of buying relationships and CX has become ever more critical. Grewal et al.[3] identified three major different types of buying relationships. This increases B2B marketing complexity. Dealing with this difficulty is part of the price to pay to access B2B markets – worth over US $50 trillion globally.

Table 6.2 can help B2B firms assess the type of buying relationship they are engaged in. This is a foundational step in determining how best to structure CX activities and associated resource allocation decisions. The differences in B2B and B2C commercial activity is the impulse to planning carefully for CX success in B2B markets. Table 6.2 outlines three categories of B2B transaction: Transactional Buying Operations (TBOs), Routine Exchange Relationships (RERs), and Organic Buying Relationships (OBRs).

**Table 6.2:** Modes of Buying.[4]

|  | **Transactional Buying Operations (TBOs)** *Routine and often low-margin business with limited strategic impact* | **Routine Exchange Relationships (RERs)** *Future-focused, highly inter-dependent relationships* | **Organic Buying Relationships (OBRs)** *Future- and often innovation-focused strategic relationships* |
|---|---|---|---|
| **Key aspects** | – Tactical negotiation between vendors and buyers<br>– Price focus<br>– Periodic re-evaluation<br>– Products or services not strategic for buying organisation<br>– Frequently highly automated through e-commerce<br>– Centralised (often high volume) buying | – Centralised strategic partner selection<br>– Complex initially, with high involvement from buyer and seller teams<br>– Once contract established, implementation of buying and value delivery is routinised and often highly automated | – Strategic partner selection<br>– Deep involvement from both buyers and sellers<br>– Solution focus, solving problems together to co-create value for downstream customers and users<br>– Uncertainty of goal achievement<br>– High risk/high reward<br>– Centralised decisions<br>– Multiple seller-buyer boundary spanner interface points |
| **Complexity** | Low to Moderate | High – during negotiations | Moderate to High (can be very high) |
| **Novelty** | Moderate | Low – implementing deal | High |
| **Importance** | Low | High – high volumes and profits | Moderate to High (can be very high) |
| **Uncertainty** | Low to Moderate | Low – once the deal is done | Moderate to High (can be very high) |
| **Time pressure** | Low | Moderate to High | Low to Moderate |

## Transactional Buying Operations

TBOs occur where the commercial reward and negotiation requirements are often low and the products and services involved are commoditised and easily substituted. Buyers in these relationships have low switching costs. These customers and their CX need to be managed to maximise leads, efficiency, and speed. TBOs involve low levels of customisation at most. Most commonly they offer 'search goods.' These are products and services where fitness for use can be determined prior to purchase. Search goods are most commonly purchased on price so suppliers in TBO activities must focus on cost leadership. This contrasts with Routine Exchange and Organic Buying Relationships, which are longer term and more complex in nature.

## Routine Exchange Relationships

RERs involve higher returns than TBOs because buyers perceive higher switching costs and greater quality risks. Purchase negotiations are normally more complex. The CX aspects during both the negotiation and value delivery phases require different design and performance. RERs may involve higher levels of customisation by suppliers. Buyers typically undertake greater levels of buyer scrutiny. Negotiations typically address supply agreement durations, sunk asset investments, quality assurance, and liquidated damages provisions for performance shortfalls. RERs may be established for search goods to drive volume discounts and lower ongoing purchasing costs, however RERs also apply to 'experience goods.' Experience goods are products and services where fitness for use cannot be determined prior to purchase. After purchase, the value of future purchases is self-evident. Reputation, references, and referrals are far more important considerations for an initial purchase of an experience good. RERs are different to OBRs largely because OBRs involve 'credence goods' where future fitness for use is not determinable even after initial purchase.

## Organic Buying Relationships

OBRs are the most complex, uncertain, and highest reward group of B2B activities. Value is often co-created in these relationships, as organisations collaborate on future-oriented projects where the focus is uncertain. For example, as Netflix developed its streamed entertainment offerings to consumers, it relied on its collaboration with AWS (Amazon Web Services) to create and manage the cloud-based computing capacity to make streaming the go-to entertainment experience of the late 2010s and 2020s. Simultaneously, it had to develop co-creative relationships with program makers (often small- to medium-sized operations that collect around film and program series projects) to create the content that grabs audiences and builds subscriber numbers.

Table 6.2 outlines considerations for both sellers and buyers to manage their B2B relationships. OBRs may be strategic, deep, personal, and co-creative. At the other extreme, TBRs can be highly automated. Each of these relationship groupings will demand different types of customer experience, and they will be looking for different types of value. But make no mistake, organisations need to segment their customers effectively so that they can develop the CX for each customer group accordingly.

Designing for Lean CX in the B2B space is dependent on the dominant buying relationship you will have with your customers. Once the dominant transaction mode has been identified, CX development needs to consider a range of areas:

- Identifying the customers who will help your firm grow the most over time
- The value these B2B buyers are looking for
- The different types of buying journey that a spectrum of customers undertake
- How buying processes are likely to change over time
- Structuring for Lean CX

A key CX element of B2B involves eCommerce.

## eCommerce

B2B eCommerce refers to the exchange of goods and services between companies through an electronic platform. Companies operating in the B2B eCommerce space follow either the direct model or the marketplace model to conduct their business. The direct model involves companies setting up their own platforms and selling directly to the buyers. A marketplace, on the other hand, is a platform where many companies sell their products alongside their competitors.

A recent Statista report indicates that global B2B eCommerce was worth $US 12.2 trillion in 2019, up from $5.83 trillion in 2013.[5] The B2B media industry alone was worth $128 billion.[6] Amazon, Alibaba, Rakuten, Mercateo, Global Sources, Walmart, and IndiaMART are the major players in the global B2B eCommerce market. Amazon rebranded its B2B eCommerce operations from AmazonSupply to Amazon Business in 2015 and achieved sales of over US$ 1 billion in the following year. Alibaba has a share of about 30% in China. It is now expanding its operational base to India, Europe, and the US. The company's vast network of low-cost suppliers enables it to dominate the market. Its nearest competitor in China is Global Sources.

Despite B2C eCommerce achieving widespread adoption in China, the rapid evolution and boom of B2B eCommerce is having an even greater impact on buyers, sellers, and investors globally. Cloud platforms are growing in market share and influence due to the strain on legacy platforms struggling to deal with the fast growth of levels of eCommerce transactions. B2B eCommerce firms are integrating their systems and platforms to establish an omnichannel relationship with their customers. Despite this, there are barriers to eCommerce growth.

Personalisation efforts are being hindered by the lack of quality customer data. This stems from structural issues. B2B eCommerce markets have fewer buyers and hyperspecialised service suppliers. In addition, the significant scale and complexities of B2B – including larger order size, variable prices, big product ranges, and more demanding delivery deadlines – are placing great demands on existing supply chains. Another barrier to B2B eCommerce growth is that organisations often simply extend their ERP solutions, placing major demands on their legacy platforms. With B2B companies now required to be flexible and match the B2C shopping experience, the importance of flexible and interoperable eCommerce architectures is becoming increasingly important.[7] This aspect of CX improvement is not just limited to eCommerce transactions.

## Changing Customer Value

Peter Drucker asserted that the true purpose of a business is to create and keep customers.[8] Most managers will nod in agreement to the sentiment, whatever discipline they work in. The unfortunate fact is that few businesses actually act on Drucker's advice. The root cause of this is short-termism. Commercial staff in particular are regularly under pressure to deliver quick profits through compromising the quality of the offering, charging for services, imposing penalty clauses, and short-changing their customers. Over time, this short-termism ends up reducing the value customers receive and correspondingly create for supplier organisations.

Managing customers for the short term is not a good decision. Earning and building customer loyalty is absolutely in the interest of both managers and shareholders. Research shows that firms maintaining superior Net Promoter Scores for at least three years increase revenues roughly 2.5 times faster than industry peers.[9] The return to shareholders is two to five times greater over the subsequent decade.

*L+ Amazon's B2B customer focus*
*"Rather than ask what we are good at and what else can we do with that skill, you ask: Who are our customers? What do they need?" said Jeff Bezos of Amazon's customer-centric innovation process "And then you say we're going to give that to them regardless of whether we currently have the skills to do so, and we will learn those skills . . ."[10] Research shows that growth leaders are much more likely than more conventional firms to report that all of their senior-level leaders were attuned to the voice of the customer.[11]*

*Key to the growth of Amazon since the firm was established in 1994 has been the mantra that it is always 'Day 1' for the firm, with 'Day 2' being characterised by Bezos as "Stasis. Followed by irrelevance. Followed by excruciating, painful decline."[12] Analysis of Jeff Bezos's letters to shareholders between 1997 and 2018 reveals that three themes have driven Amazon's extraordinary growth in both B2C and B2B markets including the current profit engine, Amazon Web*

Services (AWS): Customer obsession, willingness to fail, and patience to think long term.[13] Much of Amazon's success has come from understanding the customer experience desired by customers in the wide range of B2B categories that the firm has moved into, such as advertising (now the world's third largest online advertising platform after Google and Facebook), infrastructure, SMB loans and cloud-computing – a new market that it dominates.

While Amazon's commercial success has been built through leadership capabilities and much more, its customer obsession is to be respected. Significantly for the digital era, the firm is data driven, identifying the customer-journeys of B2B and B2C customers alike, confirmed by the fact that in 2018 'third-party' sales made up 58% of sales on the Amazon platform.[14] Customer obsession has driven the development and delivery of Lean CX to its long-term B2B partners.

While the data supporting the benefits of developing customer loyalty might not come as a surprise, the conditions and capabilities to support a relentless focus on customer loyalty have only recently started to come together. New accounting tools and technologies, and far-reaching changes in the way that firms organise work, such as agile project methodologies, are creating corporate environments aligned to the prioritisation of customer loyalty. Investors are also coming around to the idea that customers are the most compelling source of corporate value. A crucial piece of the puzzle confirming the prioritisation of customer-centred activities came in August 2019, when the Business Roundtable, made up of many of the biggest US firms, issued a statement signed by 181 CEOs who committed to lead their companies for the benefit of all stakeholders – customers, employees, suppliers, communities, and shareholders.[15]

As organisations look for growth, it's useful to consider their relationships:
- Big customers and intermediaries (Alibaba, eBay, Amazon, etc.) are getting bigger
- They are trying to reduce the number of suppliers
- Customers are becoming more sophisticated in how they buy
- RER mode and OBR mode customers demand tailor-made solutions
- The people and technology costs of serving customers is increasing
- Success with customers is increasingly about the human side of how they work together
- Customers are demanding more data sharing using digital technologies
- Sustainability considerations are supporting the growth of circular economy markets
- Ecosystems are being established by focal customers as a response to global competition
- Collaboration is being demanded across networks combining companies and regulators

The concentration of buying activity at a global level has increased the focus of selling firms via global account management. At the same time, increased buyer knowledge and power have moved the balance of power away from sellers. The most important buying organisations (in terms of growth, volume, profitability, and opportunities to co-create value) are usually the most sophisticated and demanding buyers.[16]

Buying teams are growing in size and now include a wider set of roles/specialties, with greater involvement from nonprocurement functions than before. On one side, this suggests that buying organisations should be positioned to benefit from a wider range of skills and knowledge within the customer-based decision-making unit. However, both buyers and sellers have a big problem. Customers are deluged with information and choice, and they prevaricate when making decisions.

### U+ A+ Intuit involves customers

When working with contacts from a customer's organisation, it is important to seek out individual responses from a range of roles – and then make sure that the information is available to every member of the account team. Follow-up calls should be made to probe for specific complaints, priorities, and desires. Disciplined follow-up activity gives great opportunities to demonstrate understanding of the customer's needs, and to explain how your firm can solve problems for them.

When Intuit started to seek feedback on a regular basis from new customers for their accountancy software, they rapidly learned that many of those customers did not understand the full capabilities of the company's accounting software, nor were they aware of the webinars and other onboarding services that were available to them. Intuit's Pro Tax Group swiftly set up a New Client Services team to bring fresh customers on board, connecting them with major product features, all with the express aim of matching the software to the workflow of the users as easily and quickly as possible. Intuit saw that customers who engaged in the program were 49% more likely to engage and renew their subscriptions. Lean CX is not just about acquiring customers, it is about onboarding to create value – and reduce the loss of customers in the future.

Recurring customer issues needed to be raised within the firm, as Lean CX cannot be secured without mobilising the wider enterprise. The problems that get in the way for users can involve a mix of policies, IT systems, or digital experiences than can only be corrected with the intervention of higher level staff or by additional functional groups. Internal follow-through and project work is key to changing the customer and user experience, and creating a clear focus on customer issues by making feedback visible, resources can be secured to drive through change.[17]

The B2B relationships that underpin growth are dynamic, and continue over time. When buying groups, and the users that they support see that a supplier is gathering feedback, and using it to improve the customer experience, trust grows. Listening to customers is not enough, they need to see positive change across the elements of value identified by Eric Almquist et al. in the B2B Value Pyramid.[18]

The key to cut-through in B2B is to have a clear focus on the value customers are prepared to pay for. Bain and Company has invested heavily in a multi-year project to identify fundamental components which they call the 'Elements of Value.'[19] The elements are structured in four categories: functional, emotional, life changing, and social impact. The main driver of the project was Eric Almquist, who has spent 40 years examining why customers buy. His motivation was to take advanced techniques to measure customer behaviour out of the academic sphere and into the mainstream, enabling organisations to make use of his insights day by day. Bain's value pyramid[20] is the B2B analogue of the CAPFUL framework introduced in Chapter 4.

The base layer of the pyramid centres on the essentials. These order qualifiers are similar to the hygiene factors previously presented as part of the Kano quality framework. They relate to table stakes like fitting within budgets, ensuring regulatory compliance, and achieving minimum quality standards. The next level sees functional elements aligned with supporting the buying organisation's economic or performance needs such as cost reduction or scalability. In the world of manufacturing, these have long been priority areas, and both sellers and buyers have traditionally focused much of their activity on these functional elements (see Table 6.2).

While the elements of value at the base of the pyramid are the functional elements that have been at the centre of offering development for decades, the elements higher up the pyramid are often the ones that matter the most. It is these higher-level, subjective elements that many companies fail to focus on sufficiently, particularly when developing Organic Buying Relationships. Getting organisations to focus on the softer aspects of their value propositions is often hard, particularly when considering the 40 elements included in the B2B pyramid. Identifying the elements of value that matter the most takes offering development teams and the organisational hierarchy into new areas of activity.

Almquist's work supports individuals and teams focused on the more complex B2B environment, helping them to understand the full spectrum of customer priorities, and prioritise what matters most to buyers.[21] While the buying process in B2B is far more complex, B2B and B2C decision making increasingly show some similarities.

B2B sellers need to keep their prices competitive, conform with regulations, specifications, and ethical guidelines. Buying teams continue to scrutinise vendors and assess cost-of-ownership by taking objective data around price and performance into account. But meeting these requirements just gets your firm into the group of vendors being considered. Bain's research demonstrates reduction of anxiety is a dominant factor for many buying decisions. Identifying the full spectrum of both rational and emotional factors involved in B2B purchases enables firms to shape their value propositions and associated CX approaches. Selling teams need to conform with the technical requirements that get them to the negotiation table and focus in on the higher level elements of value relevant to winning business. Delivering the highest impact elements of value matters when strategic partners are being selected through the periodic in-depth evaluation and negotiation phases at the centre of Routine Exchange Relationships. Focusing on the elements of value prioritised by buying teams helps sellers to avoid the commodity trap. Lean CX offers a way to finding the most valuable emotional factors involved in B2B purchase decisions.

Survey research with more than 2,300 corporate decision makers in IT infrastructure and commercial insurance helps to bring to life the positive impact of delivering on multiple elements of value.[22] The average Net Promoter Score of companies who delivered on six or more of the elements was 60% higher than that of companies who only delivered between one and five of the elements of value. Contrary to traditional notions that B2B is all about price, the strongest predictors of customer loyalty were product quality, expertise, and responsiveness. Seven of the top 10 elements of value in the study were concerned with ease-of-doing-business such as simplification, transparency, and reducing effort (to boost productivity), the availability of a variety of staff that fits with the needs of customer buying teams (access), supported by expertise, stability, and responsiveness amongst others.

Based on Bain's extensive research, it is difficult to argue against building a CX approach that focuses in on the full spectrum of the elements of value, and especially those concerned with increasing the ease of doing business.

Research[23] shows that those involved in buying decisions are stressed and unsure about how to move from exploring supplier options (easy) to making decisions that work for the multiple stakeholders within the organisation impacted by the buying decision (difficult). When you add in how a buying decision can affect strategic partners within the firm's wider ecosystem, life gets even more complicated. This results in decisions getting stuck. Decision makers can be drawn into circuitous learning loops as they learn more and more. Paradoxically, learning may increase confusion. Buyers can find the buying process growing in size and inertia. Greater knowledge leads to more questions, and purchase decisions get pushed back or shelved. The number of individuals in an organisation engaged in B2B solution purchases grew from an average of 5.4 in 2015 to 6.8 in 2017.[24] With more people involved, and a wider range of organisational priorities in the mix, it is tricky for buying teams to move beyond obvious motivations such as "be careful," "reduce costs," and "let's not try too much that is risky and new." Such motivations are too imprecise to adequately guide decision making.

The work of Sheena Iyengar[25] shows how a greater range of choices slows down decision making. The increased range of options that B2B buyers are typically contemplating demands more time for consideration. Analysis increases as members of the decision-making unit negotiate trade offs. The increasing range of options slows down the purchase process and causes anxiety after B2B contracts have been approved. The anxiety arises as members of the decision-making unit continue to ruminate individually and collectively as to whether the correct decision has been made.

Solution purchases regularly take double the time that customers expect that they will. Around 65% of customers spend as much time as they had planned for the completed purchase process just preparing for direct engagement with commercial staff from the vendor.[26] So what should supplier organisations do?

The answer would seem to be obvious: simplify the buying process, making it easier for buyers to buy. The answer is not as straightforward as it sounds. Sellers have been focusing on designing and executing sales processes since the art and science of selling was invented. Surveys show that most commercial staff think giving customers *more* information will help to advance the sales process. They try to flexibly respond to buyer queries and help decision-making units to consider widening options. Sales staff are doing their best to be as responsive as possible, stretching themselves to deliver all the information that is requested. For most sales staff trying to deliver a great customer experience, the natural response is to be customer-centric by providing data, cases, and testimonials that stack up in the customer's in-box, while options are tweaked and nuanced. But the feedback from B2B buyers is that more information decreases ease of purchasing by 18%.[27] Increased information and more options make buying even tougher to do. All this customer-centricity is expensive, with major professional services firms, like accountants, regularly spending over $US 500,000 on bidding for major contracts. All this cost is limiting the capacity to develop sales in both core and adjacent arenas.

A review of the impact of selling tactics on the buying process delivers a surprising sting in the tail. While the customer-centric, hyper-responsive approach reduces purchase ease, a more prescriptive sales process can increase purchase ease by 86%.[28] Suppliers adopting a prescriptive approach to their customers provide defined recommendations to buyers supported by a clear set of arguments. The offering is more limited but is very clear in terms of their capabilities. The complicated phases of the buying process are explained simply.

This book focuses on Lean CX. In the B2B space where complex solution sales are the order of the day, simple and cost saving approaches increase the rate at which sales are closed. This approach helps business customers feel happier about their experiences. Easing purchases requires assertive communications to customers. Explaining the major problems customers tend to face when buying demonstrates insight and market penetration. Showing how customers are helped to solve these problems demonstrates experience and success. Customers can see prescriptive sales staff as being ahead of the competition when they can anticipate and remove problems.

The business results are also clear. Vendors that simplify buying are 62% more likely than their competitors to win sales in arenas that demand premium offerings.[29] Research shows that purchase ease is the biggest factor in terms of deal quality. Reassuringly, the buyers who have closed prescriptive, simplified sales processes are 37% less likely to regret their purchases.[30] This also makes it easier for suppliers to build on positive commercial relationships across other offering categories.

There may be a disconnect between purchase ease and how suppliers manage their sales and marketing functions. Typically sales and marketing staff have developed and managed their teams with greater emphasis put on individual performance. This is often different from performance management in other functions in the organisation. However, research has shown that between 2002 and 2012 the impact of an individual's task performance on business unit profitability at the organisational level decreased from 78% to 51% on average. During the same period, the impact of an employees' network performance increased from 22% to 49%. Network performance relates to how much individuals give to and take from their colleagues. Even in the sales area, network performance now makes up around 44% of individual impact.[31]

With customers increasingly well-informed about the problems that they are trying to solve within their organisations, compliance with highly process-dominated approaches to sales and customer experience delivery have become outmoded. Building on the insights summarised in the B2B Elements of Value pyramid (Figure 6.1), to deliver great CX to customers, the staff managing connections with their B2B customers

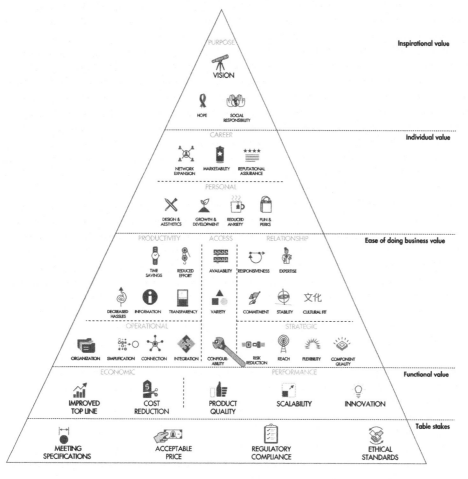

**Figure 6.1:** B2B Value Pyramid – Used with permission from Bain & Company (www.bain.com).

need to invest their time in validating which elements of value are most important to the buying decisions. Rather than grinding through a sales process, Lean CX prioritises focusing in on the things that matter the most. If the customer values functional value delivered at the right price, then don't waste time and money on justifying complex offerings for Transactional Buying Operations. However, when it comes to Routine Exchange Relationships and Organic Buying Relationships (see Table 6.2) with complex negotiations, engage a wider range of roles in exploring the elements of value that matter most. The key is to learn where to deploy the resources of the selling organisation to support the qualification and prioritisation of opportunities at the right time. Lean CX is not all about driving the efficiency of a standardised sales process, it is about focusing at the right time on the key stages of increasingly complicated customer journey at the right time. It is about learning and satisfying the buyers' jobs-to-be-done.

## Jobs-to-Be-Done

At its core, the concept of jobs-to-be-done (JTBD) is delightfully simple: focus in on the objectives of people and organisations independent of how they seek to accomplish them. The approach resonates because most people in business know that great offerings and customer relationships are built around solving problems. The key points at the heart of the jobs-to-be-done approach are:
– People and organisations buy offerings (products and services) to get jobs done
– Completed jobs means specific measurable outcomes are achieved
– Customer segments are defined by customer-desired outcomes rather than demographics
– Value creation activities are linked to customer- and user-defined metrics

The JTBD approach first gained traction in the area of product and service development. It lies at the centre of the popular Business Model Canvas and Value Proposition Design approaches.[32] B2B teams (in companies including Philips) and B2C teams (in companies including P&G) have rapidly adopted the JTBD methodology to develop differentiated offerings to solve the problems mattering most to their customers and users. It is important to deliver solutions for precisely identified customers, users, and occasions within deeply understood workflows to really get the best results from focusing on jobs-to-be-done.

Through mapping the success criteria associated with jobs in both B2C and B2B environments, the development of an offering is centred on the significant detail that customers and users value above all else. The critical importance of delivering an offering that covers the social, emotional, and functional aspects of the job should not be underestimated, and this connects directly with the Elements of Value pyramid.

The introduction of JTBD is important to the development of Lean CX with B2B customers as the approach helps teams to work through what jobs buying teams, and the individuals within those teams, are trying to complete through the buying journey. Before we identify what buying tasks customers must complete before finalising a purchase, let's examine how B2B buyers are researching vendors. Through understanding digitally enabled customers and their customer journeys, we can move toward some recommendations on how best to use Lean CX approaches to both win customers and build ongoing customer value for both buyers and sellers through multi-year relationships.

*A+ Adobe innovated around JTBD*

*An interview with Shantanu Narayen, the Chairman CEO of Adobe reveals how a tight focus on customer experience has underpinned the transformation from a packaged software centred organisation to one that now has around 90% of revenue coming from recurring sources, as compared to less than 5% before the move to a subscription model.*

*Narayen highlights the importance of taking a long-range view when building a sustainable and resilient company. Taking the long-range view is particularly important when every decade or so firms need to adapt to major disruptive shifts in technology. As with many businesses, the move to cloud computing and mobile delivered a requirement for change. Adobe saw that the cloud could be mobilised to improve CX in two major ways: location independence and collaboration. For the first time, a creative professional could have permanent access to all of their tools: fonts, brushes, presets, and project files. The firm also identified how users could be released from their desks to use flagship products like Acrobat/PDF and Photoshop so that mobile devices can be used for creative work – not just consumption.*

*Even profitable market leaders like Adobe have to make tough decisions about where to focus, and what to invest in. While the rise of platform-based business models is well documented, it is still easy to focus on solving the wrong problems through a platform. Adobe chose to invest in deep technology innovation that will pay off over the long run. Aligned to jobs-to-be-done thinking, Adobe sought out hard problems so that they could build positive customer experience for many years into the future through intertwining their solutions into the workflow of their users.*

*Adobe was well-connected with designers and creatives before their shift to cloud-based solutions. But they recognised that they could connect in to both the intelligence AND the creative clicks of designers to improve the entire workflow of a customer, becoming more mission-critical for users and customers in the process. Adobe stretched their ambition to not just enhance content creation, but to facilitate content delivery and monetisation as well. The company's approach is built on long-termism, and the incorporation of data-centricity into designing a customer experience that saves their users time AND increases creativity at the same time.*

*Narayen explains: "We had core hypotheses that led us through the transition from a product-oriented business to a subscription model: that we could deliver a better experience long term. Our hypothesis stated that understanding how people are using our products online would enable us to tailor our offerings quicker than the traditional 12- or 18-month product development cycles allowed us to do." Through innovating with users and with a steely focus on their customers' digital experience, 27% of current revenues come from new growth areas beyond the core.[33]*

Most B2B organisations are dealing with buyers who do not expect or often want to deal with a salesperson until it is time to close a deal. More than 75% of all B2B purchasers, including both enterprise buyers and small businesses, have only limited contact with salespeople.[34] These buyers increasingly rely on digital resources including buyer reviews, blogs, social media, videos, and suppliers' and third-party websites. The laptop is being eclipsed by the smartphone to seek out information, especially through social media and search engines. In this pervasive digital environment, pushing products or services onto customers does not work well. Marketing and sales need to work closely together to become more pull-oriented.

The experiences that B2B buyers have as B2C consumers means that they expect the same level of online and mobile experience that they enjoy with Netflix or eBay. At the very least, they expect enhanced search functionality, reviews, personalised service and product recommendations, ratings, and most importantly a consistent experience. CX can be defined as the quality of all of a buyer's encounters with a company's products, services, or brand, and increasingly the CX is digital. The Value Pyramid (see Figure 6.1) gives us a robust and proven guide to the elements of value that might be involved in understanding a buying teams' jobs-to-be-done, particularly when it comes to the ease-of-doing-business elements.

Most B2B CX-focused marketing plans aim to deliver the right content to the right person at the right time.[35] However, nailing down what's right has become more complicated. B2B customer journeys weave in and out of online and offline channels and can last months and sometimes years.

These journeys usually involve a selection of business owners, analysts, decision makers, researchers, procurement professionals, finance executives, and technical specialists who work together to plan, research, and make purchases. The buying teams connect with operational staff within their business and wider ecosystem to enable the appropriate staff to mobilise whatever offering has been procured to play its role in creating value within their organisation.

Google and Boston Consulting Group undertook research to explore the increasingly multichannel and digital nature of current B2B customer journeys.[36] The majority of B2B buyers stay online throughout most of their journey, comparing process, checking product specifications, and assessing options, while in many cases then connecting with a third-party or direct sales representative to conclude the purchase. Their research found that on average two-thirds of B2B buyers indicated that purchase decisions had been significantly influenced by their digital search process.

B2B buyers are tech-savvy, with a Google study indicating that millennials (people under 35 years old) constituted almost half of B2B researchers in 2019. This is a huge shift from just two years earlier when only a quarter were millennials. Millennials spend more than six hours a day on their phones. This is twice the time spent by people over 45 years old. Millennials are beginning to exert their influence over the purchases their organisations make. They are ready to buy digitally, with more than 50% having used suppliers' websites to make purchases. Almost 20%

have used Amazon to make purchases for their businesses. These trends are going to accelerate as millennials mature and move into more senior roles, and as Gen Z progressively enters the workforce and takes control of more buying decisions.[37]

Buyers are extending their investigations before involving their suppliers' people. More than three-quarters of all B2B purchasers ranging across small business and major corporations have only limited interaction with sales staff.[38] The 2020s see buyers relying on digital resources – including suppliers' and third-party websites, videos, buyer reviews, blogs, and social media to narrow their choices. The current B2B buyer expects the same online and mobile experiences and features that they experience as consumers, including:
- Enhanced search functionality
- Ratings and reviews
- Personalised product and service recommendations
- A consistent experience

A firm's marketing content needs to tell a story about a vendor's products and services through the stages of the research process to get cut-through. The need for content coverage applies from awareness through purchase and retention stages of the buyer journey. These stories need to be consistent across:
- All digital media (website, video, interactive)
- Different channels (landing pages, print magazine, webinars, point of sale)
- Many devices (laptop/docking station, tablet, smartphone)

The fact is that buying journeys have changed significantly over the last ten years mirroring changes in B2B buying behaviour. In the past, efficiency-focused sales and customer experience initiatives were based around the idea of a linear step-by-step process. To work through how best to help customers progress through a complex purchase, they need to complete six B2B buying tasks to secure purchases:
1. Problem identification
2. Solution exploration
3. Requirements building
4. Supplier selection
5. Offer validation
6. Consensus creation

It is helpful to connect the buying tasks with the B2B buying journey because these requirements do not progress sequentially, but often simultaneously, as shown in a Figure 6.2.[39]

Each of the phases and decision points in Figure 6.2 can cause looping, revisiting, or re-evaluation. The high level of repeat work inside the buying organisation is demonstrated by the fact that buying groups are revisiting each the four core buying jobs (problem identification, solution exploration, requirements building, and

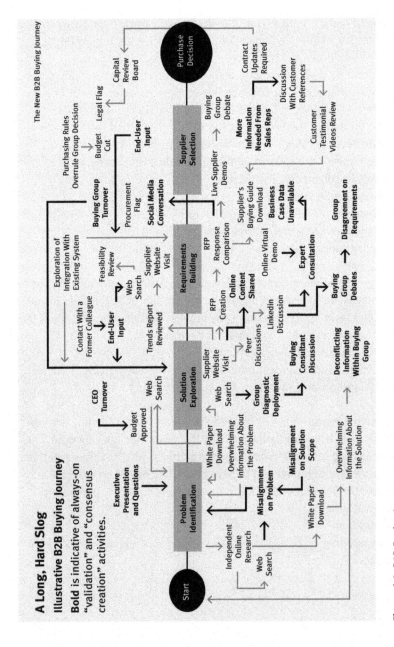

**Figure 6.2:** B2B Buying Journey.
Source: https://www.gartner.com/en/sales/insights/b2b-buying-journey.

supplier selection) as the level of complexity grows. Customers are sucked in to repeating each job again and again until all jobs are seen to be completed at the same time. Let's add back in the increase in the number of individuals engaged in B2B solutions purchases growing from an average of 5.4 in 2015 to 6.8 in 2017, and the sense of frustration is high. So modern B2B buying and CX has moved on from progressing through a funnel, it is now about often-diverse individuals and work groups completing a distributed set of tasks. Through taking a jobs-to-be-done perspective, selling organisations are better able to understand what individual sellers and their colleagues are trying to achieve within this complex buying scenario. It is useful to consider the buying process[40] as three stages of different durations:

1. *Early stage information challenges*: Customers have trouble distinguishing between meaningful, conflicting, and irrelevant information. Matching information needs without overload is challenging.
2. *Middle stage people problems*: Team members have competing priorities, with different criteria for purchase. This phase often sees conflicting views on the need for change and reveals hidden concerns.
3. *Late stage option issues*: Customers have too many purchase options and are overwhelmed. As vendors push to secure business, new and confusing offers are introduced. Anxiety can build if the implementation plan for different options is unclear.

## Organising Around Customer Journeys

B2B seller organisations must respond to the expectations that members of the customer decision-making unit have for their buying experience. While customer-centricity is a term that is used regularly, selling organisations also need the structure to deliver to their target audiences. Leading organisations will align structurally around their audiences, and this will direct both their technology and organisational design decisions. We are 20 years into the era of marketing automation and digital marketing, but most B2B commercial operations still design their customer engagement programs around key geographies, products, or industry events. Research has[41] found that 47% of organisations said that customer needs drove their marketing strategies, but only 40% said that they prioritised solving customers' problems over promoting their products.

The challenges don't seem to be around mindset (customer-centricity) or vision, but firms still cling to structural strategies of the past: 36% organise around industry segments; 43% organise by channel-specific domain expertise such as email, advertising, or social;[42] and the work that gets done to secure customers and deliver outstanding customer experiences is driven by the structures and metrics guiding the routines and behaviours of staff engaged in creating those customer experiences.

While a persuasive 73% of marketing leaders have indicated that they had adopted journey maps as a planning approach within their departments, only 35% reported that journey maps are the basis for planning the work and the associated structures of their marketing organisations.[43] So it would seem that the analysis is being completed - but then ignored. The challenge is the big chasm remaining between research and practice. Many B2B companies still fall short of delivering the outstanding customer experience capable of winning, retaining, and referring customers.

Changing structures to deliver customer experience can take many forms. While it can include organisational charts and titles, it is much more about the matrices that work in each firm – how work actually happens within increasingly agile teams in increasingly networked organisations. Agile working, bringing together a broad range of skills and capabilities to solve customer-driven problems, is being adopted in diverse spheres such as banking (ING), music (Spotify), and most software-enabled businesses. However, the flexible working approaches that fit and mobilise each business need to fit the specific contexts that each team is working in. The main considerations for each stage of the B2B customer journey are shown in Table 6.3.

**Table 6.3:** B2B Purchase Stages.

| Customer purchase stage | Activities to prioritise |
| --- | --- |
| **Early stage: Information challenges** | – Deliver 100% consistent messages through joined-up digital marketing approaches<br>– Most early consideration of an offering will be online – and increasingly mobile – so prioritise CX spending accordingly<br>– Make it easy for customers to move from the information phase to purchasing online – as contact with people is frequently a switch-off<br>– Connect up sales and marketing staff into customer-centric commercial units<br>– Train sales staff to connect with customers through social media |
| **Middle stage: People problems** | – Use the jobs-to-be-done approach to deep dive into understanding the people-centred barriers within the customer's business<br>– Look for patterns that reveal the few higher-order obstacles that cause a disproportionate amount of buying difficulty<br>– Focus on customer ease<br>– Attack a small number of big problems, helping selling staff inundated with new tools and systems<br>– Uncover all stakeholder concerns |
| **Late stage: Option issues** | – Support the customer's purchase decision-making process<br>– Guide customers through a prescriptive approach to increase purchase ease<br>– Do not offer too many options |

## Key Player Impacts

Large technology-enabled companies have grown faster than organisations in more established offering categories. A highly persuasive current story of an established firm moving into an adjacent market and sustaining high growth and great margins is Amazon - including through the COVID-19 pandemic. The firm's growth story mixes vital ingredients for growth in the modern economy:
- Amazon is a born-digital firm
- Time and again, the organisation has moved into new categories, from the early days of books, into devices (Kindle, Alexa), and services (Amazon Web Services)

Some of the Amazon growth story was presented in Chapter 3. However it is not the only large technology-enabled success. February 2020 saw four of the biggest technology-centred organisations all exceed $1 trillion in valuation at the same time – Microsoft, Apple, Amazon, and Alphabet. Even when demand for core products has slowed, these turbo-charged companies have changed lanes by growing or buying subsidiaries that can diversify revenues and keep top and bottom line growth rising. These mega-businesses seem to keep moving into adjacent market opportunities. While Amazon already has large and still growing businesses, it is also scaling its advertising business. Google is a giant in the advertising space and moving into cloud services. Apple, Google, and Amazon have all decided to build subscription-based streaming services to compete with Netflix and Disney.

The difference between the US$ 1 trillion+ players and the rest is that they have established the strategic and operational routines to move into adjacent spaces.[44] In addition, in 2020's year of business dislocation due to the COVID-19 pandemic, Big Tech's dislocation from the circumstances faced by the majority of firms is underlined by the fact that at the outset of the pandemic they were fortunate to have combined net cash reserves of around $350 billion.[45] From their positions of relative strength, many companies are going to be competing with large tech companies able to tighten their grip on major areas of digital activity, while sustaining their drive into new categories. This demonstrates the increasing range of large highly competent players that can move into core and adjacent market spaces. Smaller rivals for established and emerging market spaces can leverage the technology and service capabilities of major platform players such as Amazon and eBay to play in previously settled markets. Companies of all sizes can use the major platform players to secure market and capability reach that could not have been imagined ten years ago.

## Building CX Beyond the Core

Building on the work of Grewal and Nagji and Tuff, we can consider how different B2B buying modes apply to the running of a portfolio business (see Table 6.4).

**Table 6.4:** B2B Buying Modes.

| | |
|---|---|
| **Core Market** | **Transactional Buying Operations (TBOs)**<br>Routine, and often low-margin business with limited strategic impact<br>No focus on collaborative, innovation-centred activity<br>CX requirements can be standardised, guided by the elements of value concerning table stakes and functional value |
| **Core Market** | **Routine Exchange Relationships (RERs)**<br>Future-focused, highly interdependent relationships<br>Sometimes extensive collaboration, established through complex negotiations; a wide range of buyer and seller capabilities (e.g., technology) can be involved before agreements are negotiated<br>CX requirements need to be considered in two parts:<br>**Pre-contract:** CX to particularly focus on ease of doing business elements of value<br>**Contract implementation:** CX to major on productivity, functional and table stakes elements of value |
| **Adjacent opportunities** | **Organic Buying Relationships (OBRs)**<br>Future- and often innovation-focused strategic relationships<br>Vendors working with existing partners or new partners in adjacent product, technology or CX spaces; a wide spectrum of buyer and seller capabilities can be involved, with boundary spanners key to joint problem-solving<br>CX to focus on the elements of value concerned with access and relationship that support the ease of doing business between organisations |
| **Transformational opportunities** | **Organic Buying Relationships (OBRs)**<br>Innovation-focused strategic relationships explored through working with existing partners or new partners in new to the company and new to the world product, technology, or CX spaces<br>High risk and high reward<br>CX to centre on relationship elements of value along with individual value elements such as network expansion, design, personal growth, and anxiety reduction |

- *Transactional Buying Operations (TBOs)* fit into core market activities, where selling firms support buying firms through transactional relationships, with an acceptance between both organisations that the level of engagement is low. The focus is on table stakes (e.g., price and specifications), and delivering economic functional value (e.g., cost reduction and improved sales for the buying firm). The jobs-to-be-done are well understood, and so are the CX expectations.
- *Routine Exchange Relationships (RERs)* support the evolution of the process or offering of their customers in core markets. However, the focus is on incremental innovation, and supports core market activities. All 40 of the elements of value are

involved, so focusing on the jobs-to-be-done is critical to avoid wasting effort on irrelevant activities. The demands of the customer journey to secure a contract are high, with collaborative working a key part of the mix. Once the deal is done, delivery of the offering is highly automated, and the CX expectations are well-defined.

– *Organic Buying Relationships (OBRs)* are future-focused and see vendors operating beyond their established markets in adjacent (technology, existing and new customer) arenas. Because of the emergent nature of the problems that the vendor and buying organisations are trying to solve together, boundary spanners with high-level T-shaped thinking capabilities are needed, along with a range of specialist knowledge. Adjacent opportunities are usually progressed within established ecosystems, but success often involves working with new partners and insights. The CX requirements here overlap with what's needed for success in agile teams, with the elements of value concerned with access and relationship that support the ease of doing business between organisations. When it comes to transformational opportunities in B2B arenas, none of the collaborators fully understand the problems that they are trying to solve, or the jobs-to-be-done. Boundary-spanning activity will be needed to connect multiple players, with diversity in knowledge (all types) and collaborative working needed to frame problems and join the dots.

The CX requirements when organisations are collaborating on transformational innovation and business projects include everything covered above regarding success in adjacent arenas, along with individual value elements such as network expansion, design, personal growth, and anxiety reduction – because transformational innovation is stressful and risky for an individual's reputation.

In this chapter, we have come a long way from considering the main differences between B2C and B2B business, and the CX elements required for success in B2B environments. We have looked to the future, and to how organisations can collaborate within B2B relationships, as they co-define the jobs-to-be-done in transformational innovation spaces. IDEO, a renowned leader in design thinking, emphasises the significance of the cross-pollination of ideas when developing new offerings. Cross-pollinators can see patterns that are not evident to the majority of individuals and can identify key differences. They often think in metaphors, helping them to see relationships and connections that others miss. IDEO describes cross-pollinators as T-shaped people, who usually have a depth of knowledge in at least one area of expertise. What makes them different and highly impactful is that they also bring a breadth of knowledge across a range of themes, and they are great at connecting the dots. Effective cross-pollinators can jolt an organisation into action, as they bring in big ideas from the outside.[46]

It is important for organisations to bring in cross-pollinators from outside, with different knowledge sets and skills, to mobilise their established staff in the search for new CX approaches. T-shaped thinkers can shake up thinking. They connect ideas inside the firm as well as bringing pro-active linkages with outside individuals and partners. The significance of T-shaped thinkers is also emphasised by Jeffrey

Dyer, Hal Gregersen, and Clayton Christensen as they considered what makes up 'The Innovator's DNA.'[47]

Firms often risk being limited in their search and select activities through a lack of collaboration both internally and externally,[48] with boundary-spanning a high-impact capability both individually and at the level of the organisation. Through connecting companies and individuals with knowledge from outside core markets, collaborating firms secure access to the different skills, perspectives, and networks that they need to search for, and select a balanced portfolio of options beyond the core. The next chapter provides an insight into the way organisations in the future may organise to take advantage of T-shaped thinkers to innovate and grow.

## Endnotes

**1** Lilien (2016). "The B2B Knowledge Gap," *International Journal of Research in Marketing* Vol 33 No 3.
**2** https://b2bard.com/which-is-truly-bigger-b2b-or-b2c/ accessed 24/11/2020.
**3** Grewal et al. (2015). "Business-to-Business Buying: Challenges and Opportunities," *Customer Needs and Solutions* Vol 2 No3. https://doi.org/10.1007/s40547-015-0040-5.
**4** Ibid.
**5** Clement (2020). "B2B e-commerce in the United States – Statistics & Facts," *Statista*. https://www-statista-com.uoelibrary.idm.oclc.org/topics/4884/b2b-e-commerce-in-the-united-states/.
**6** Guttman (2019). "B2B Marketing – Statistics & Facts," *Statista*. https://www-statista-com.uoelibrary.idm.oclc.org/topics/2495/b2b-marketing/.
**7** Ibid., footnote 187.
**8** Drucker (1954). *The practice of management,* Harper & Row.
**9** Markey (2020). "Are you undervaluing your customers?" *Harvard Business Review* Vol 98 No 1. https://doi.org/10.1016/0169-2070(88)90019–2.
**10** Lyons (2010). "The Customer Is Always Right," *Newsweek*.
**11** Day and Shea (2019). "Grow Faster by Changing Your Innovation Narrative," *Sloan Management Review* Vol 60 No 2.
**12** Economist (2020). "And on the second day . . . ." *The Economist*.
**13** Osterwalder et al. (2020). *The Invincible Company: How to Constantly Reinvent Your Organization with Inspiration from the World's Best Business Models*, Wiley.
**14** Ibid., footnote 194.
**15** Business Roundtable (2019). "An Economy That Serves All Americans." https://www.business roundtable.org/business-roundtable-redefines-the-purpose-of-a-corporation-to-promote-an-economy-that-serves-all-americans.
**16** Grewal et al. (2015). "Business-to-Business Buying: Challenges and Opportunities," *Customer Needs and Solutions* Vol 2 No 3. https://doi.org/10.1007/s40547-015-0040-5.
**17** Markey (2016). "Run B2B Sales on Data, Not Hunches," *Harvard Business Review Digital*. https://hbr.org/2016/09/run-b2b-sales-on-data-not-hunches.
**18** Almquist et al. (2018). "The B2B Elements of Value," *Harvard Business Review* Vol 96 No 2.
**19** Ibid.
**20** Bain (2018). "Explore the B2B Elements of Value," Bain & Company. https://www.bain.com/insights/explore-the-b2b-elements-of-value-interactive/.

**21** Almquist (2018). "How Digital Natives Are Changing B2B Purchasing," *Harvard Business Review*. https://hbr.org/2018/03/how-digital-natives-are-changing-b2b-purchasing.

**22** Almquist et al. (2018). "The B2B Elements of Value," *Harvard Business Review* Vol 96 No 2.

**23** Toman et al. (2017). "The New Sales Imperative," *Harvard Business Review* Vol 95 No 2 http://search.ebscohost.com/login.aspx?direct=true&db=bsh&AN=121396370&site=ehost-live.

**24** Ibid.

**25** Iyengar (2010). *The Art of Choosing*, Abacus.

**26** Ibid., footnote 205.

**27** Ibid., footnote 205.

**28** Ibid., footnote 205.

**29** Ibid., footnote 205.

**30** Ibid., footnote 205.

**31** Adamson et al. (2014). "Why Individuals No Longer Rule on Sales Teams," *Harvard Business Review Digital Articles*. https://hbr.org/2014/01/why-the-individual-no-longer-rules-in-sales.

**32** Osterwalder and Pigneur (2010). *Business Model Generation: A Handbook for Visionaries, Game Changers, and Challengers*, John Wiley and Sons/Osterwalder, Pigneur, and Bernarda (2014). *Value Proposition Design: How to Create Products and Services Customers Want*, Wiley/ Osterwalder et al. (2020). *The Invincible Company: How to Constantly Reinvent Your Organization with Inspiration from the World's Best Business Models*, Wiley.

**33** Anthony et al. (2019). *The Transformation 20*, Innosight/Narayen and Michelman (2019). "Key Words for Digital Transformation," *Sloan Management Review* Vol 60 No 2/Bell and Schwartz (2019). Innosight

**34** Andersen et al. (2017). "How Digital Leaders Are Transforming B2B Marketing," *Boston Consulting Group*. https://www.bcg.com/de-de/publications/2017/marketing-sales-how-digital-leaders-transforming-b2b.aspx.

**35** Arguably some sales and marketing efforts are aimed at convincing customers to make a poor purchase decision in favour of the supplier firm. The error of this short-termism has previously been presented.

**36** Archacki et al. (2019). "Capturing the Offline Impact of Online Marketing in B2B," *Boston Consulting Group*.

**37** Ibid., footnote 216.

**38** Archacki et al. (2017). "Mobile Marketing and the New B2B Buyer," *Boston Consulting Group*.

**39** Gartner (2018). "New B2B Buying Journey & Its Implication for Sales." https://www.gartner.com/en/sales/insights/b2b-buying-journey.

**40** Ibid., footnote 205.

**41** Forrester (2020). "Predictions 2020: B2B Marketing and Sales Report." https://go.forrester.com/blogs/b2b-marketing-should-organize-around-the-customer-in-2020/.

**42** Ibid.

**43** Ibid.

**44** Moore (2020). "So much for the techlash," *Financial Times*. https://www.ft.com/content/a49b002a-4997-11ea-aee2-9ddbdc86190d.

**45** Waters (2020). "Big Tech has the cash to expand after crisis," *Financial Times*. https://www.ft.com/content/27fdaf5c-f4ab-4a0f-ba9e-038911b49fe8.

**46** Kelley (2006). *The Ten Faces of Innovation*, Profile Books.

**47** Dyer et al. (2019). *The Innovator's DNA*, Harvard Business Review Press.

**48** Hansen (2009). *Collaboration*, Harvard Business Review Press.

# Chapter 7
# Explore and Exploit

Normally the final chapter in a book like this would be about how expand beyond managing the Lean CX cycle as presented in Chapter 5 to consider how to scale a preferred Lean CX initiative. The contents of such a final chapter typically would describes some version of change management requiring top down support to execute. Two highly recommended topics to cover in this regard are John Kotter's Eight-Step Change Process[1] and Eli Goldratt's Change Matrix.[2] We don't really have anything new to add to this topic. So instead of rehashing some other frames around how to scale, this chapter expands beyond the Scaled Agile concept introduced previously. A different approach to solving the innovation selection and execution problem is outlined. This novel approach suggests how swarm algorithms could deal with the so-called ambidexterity problem.

## Ambidexterity

Charles O'Reilly and Michael Tushman published findings showing 90% of ambidextrous organisations achieved their goals in 2004.[3] The same year, Julian Birkinshaw and Cristina Gibson published findings showing a high correlation between a firm's performance and its level of ambidexterity.[4] Ambidextrous firms both *exploit* their existing market opportunities and *explore* for new opportunities simultaneously. The dual nature of ambidexterity provides a definition for the difference between a start-up and an established firm.

Start-ups have no choice but to explore markets for new opportunities because they are on a search for a profitable sustainable market. According to McKeown, the only strategy a start-up should pursue is not to be one.[5] This contrasts to the common behaviour of established firms who have found their profitable sustainable market. These established firms tend to avoid exploration in favour of exploitation. Exploitation is characterised by implementing systems and processes to increase the ability to deliver consistent quality at greater scale. Established firms also exhibit a 'corporate immune system.' This system treats innovations and entrepreneurial initiatives as threats to the organisation's survival.[6] McKeown explains how the maturation stages of an organisation tend to result in a systemic aversion to exploration after the firm's first rapid growth period.[7] He describes the stages as Early Struggle, Fun, Whitewater, Predictable Success, Treadmill, the Big Rut, and Death Rattle.

https://doi.org/10.1515/9783110683929-007

## Business Life Stages

The commencement stage of every organisation is Early Struggle. In this stage, the start-up is trying to replace funding from seed partners with free cash flow from sales to customers. Its founders are focused on opportunity. While most start-ups fail in this stage, those who survive enter the Fun stage. During Fun, the firm achieves rapid growth and paradoxically sows the seeds of its own potential future demise; and the business sees the solution to most problems as getting more sales. At some point, Fun transitions to Whitewater as the level of sales exceeds the firm's capability to reliably deliver. This occurs when the scale and complexity of the business makes it impossible for the organisation to deliver consistent quality.

At this point, the business needs to either contract back to the Fun stage, or institute systems and processes to overcome the complexity problem – without such systems and processes, the business cannot effectively scale. The managers of the business must change their management style for the business to continue to grow. This requires a transition from an opportunity focus to more administrative behaviours. Stevenson and Gumpert described this difference in management approach as a spectrum. At one end are the entrepreneurial, opportunity-focused Promoters. At the other end are the administrative, risk-averse Trustees.[8]

Promoters pursue opportunities assuming their current resources are irrelevant. They believe the resources required for a worthwhile opportunity can be attracted and organised as required. Promoters tend to be more comfortable with game changing innovations and are happier to bet on growth. These bets are often made in small stages to manage risk. They like the exploration arm of ambidexterity. Trustees are almost the perfect opposite.

Trustees are more concerned with protecting the pool of resources they already control. They are more averse to loss and strive to retain what they already have. Trustee innovation efforts tend to be focused on increased efficiency and producing incremental improvements. Trustees don't like betting on growth. They will carefully analyse the risk of an investment in extensive detail before committing. However, somewhat paradoxically, when they do commit, they often invest more than Promoters because they need to achieve change at scale. They also prefer owning assets Promoters would happily lease or barter for to use as needed without ownership. Trustees prefer the exploitation arm of ambidexterity. McKeown asserts businesses cannot achieve scale without incorporating Processors into the organisation. Trustee is essentially a different name for Processor. Trustees are necessary to achieving consistent quality delivery at scale. This is hallmark of McKeown's Predictable Success stage.

Organisations achieving the Predictable Success stage undergo a power transfer. Managing complexity at scale changes the organisation's culture and climate. Often the visionary founder(s) of the original start-up can become disenfranchised with these changes. They may withdraw from the day-to-day management of the business or exit their shareholding completely. This tilts the balance of power in favour of the process-oriented Trustees. These managers can then further divert the firm's culture to overvalue the status quo and undervalue new opportunities. This tips the firm into the Treadmill stage.

Treadmill is characterised by the organisation compelling compliance to procedures without regard for why the procedures were established in the first place. Organisations in Treadmill are strongly bureaucratic. This is very stabilising for the organisation and drives consistency, however it also tends to stifle vision, initiative, and innovation. If firms stay too long in Treadmill, they can lose their ability to self-diagnose and fall into the Big Rut stage.

The Big Rut stage occurs when firms lose perspective on the changes required to remain competitive. McKeown suggests this stage can be lasting because the firm is supported by its accumulated tangible and intangible assets. Firms in the Big Rut have typically achieved a scale and market position somewhat insulated from direct competition. Despite this position, ultimately firms who fail to recover from entering the Big Rut become obsolete. This may be a gradual loss of price/performance competitiveness against known rivals or because of disruption by a new market entrant. Either way, the firm is consigned to the Death Rattle stage without the possibility of return. In Death Rattle, firms are restructured or broken up and sold for parts, having failed to sustain the integrity of their balance sheet.

The behaviours of an organisation in Treadmill are what gives rise to Christensen's Innovator Dilemma as presented in the opening chapter. Firms who have overshot beyond the Predictable Success stage find innovation hard to do. The have the exploitation arm of ambidexterity sorted, but at the expense of losing their original start-up exploration capability.

## Systemic Business Errors

The overshoot into Treadmill can be characterised as an error relating to cause and effect. In statistical correlation studies, errors are classified as either Type 1 or Type 2. Type 1 errors are committed when correlation or causality between two variables is concluded even though there is no underlying objective relationship. An example of this is the study of Astrology. While many people attest to their belief in the position of the stars as significant in their personality development and the way their lives are unfolding, Astrology has been debunked by science.[9] Believing in Astrology is a Type 1 error. In business, a classic Type 1 error is the pursuit of the latest business fad espoused by a self-styled management guru. Often a successful executive will create a range of maxim-based recommendations for business success without conducting the necessary research to validate their causality or generalisability. This is common with books about business leadership, for example. The problem is not that the maxims are not a useful perspective. The problem is how they are presented as absolutes without adequate correlation evidence. These Type 1 errors are more critical to avoid than Type 2 errors.

A Type 2 error is committed when a lack of correlation or causality between two variables is concluded despite an underlying relationship. An example of this relates to how couples argue. Psychologist John Gottman was able to predict divorce with 93% accuracy from the analysis of the results of a 14-year study of 79 couples by the way they handled conflict.[10] Sadly, 21 of the relationships ended in divorce. All couples experience some level of disagreement or conflict. What matters is how the conflict is conducted. Gottman found showing contempt and criticism toward your partner were significantly correlated with relationship breakdown. Believing you can show contempt for or criticise your partner without damaging the relationship seems like a Type 2 error. Generally, Type 1 errors are more serious than Type 2 because the second error is likely to be due to a smaller statistical relationship.

There is also a Type 3 error defined by Ian Mitroff.[11] A Type 3 problem is a classification error. Mitroff defines Type 3 errors as solving the wrong problem perfectly. An example relates to 'fail safe' versus 'fail secure' locks. A fail safe lock on a house is one able to be unlocked without a key from inside a house. In the event of a fire it is safe because the people inside can unlock the door to escape. The problem with this locking system relates to breaking and entering. A thief who enters the house through a window when its occupants are out can also open the fail safe lock once inside without a key. This makes it easier to steal high-value large items like TVs, computers, and stereos. Fail secure locks like deadbolts are unable to be opened from inside without a key. The problem is in the event of a fire they can prevent or delay people from escaping. Installing a fail secure lock becomes a potential Type 3 error if there is a fire because people's safety is more important than the security of their possessions.

Mitroff asserted managers may identify the wrong problem when faced with a challenging business situation. In business, digital security can become a Type 3 error. Many customers find it difficult to deal with password requirements designed to make guessing a password more difficult. This includes forcing the customer to set a password with a minimum number of case-sensitive digits and special characters. Some organisations will even force users to change their passwords from time to time. While this may improve security, it also tends to frustrate customers. Having frustrated customers is the opposite of what most businesses would want to achieve. Hence the Type 3 error. A better solution would be to ensure customers are not frustrated in the first place and then work out how to implement the minimum level of necessary security.

Mitroff's Type 3 error is commonly observed when linear relationships are incorrectly assumed. This normally manifests as the idea that if something is good then more of it is always better. The digital security example above highlights how more is not always better. For many business situations there is a range of optimal performance. There can be either too little or too much of a good thing. Edward De Bono described this situation as a 'salt curve.'[12] The overemphasis

Trustees place on exploitation, efficiency, and consistency at the expense of exploration, effectiveness, and innovation is a salt curve problem. It can be a Type 1 error – not realising exploration is required for the organisation's long-term survival in a changing environment. It can be a Type 2 error – believing consistency and risk avoidance are the correct behaviours for continued success. It can be a Type 3 error – where the problem of how to have more control to deliver consistently at scale is not the correct problem to solve. Lean CX is one approach to solving this problem of not enough exploration and too much exploitation.

Nassim Nicholas Taleb described the problem of overexploitation in *Antifragile*.[13] Typically increased business efficiency comes at a trade-off to durability. Efficient businesses tend to be more fragile than other businesses. An example of fragility is taking an intercontinental flight with a transit stop between connecting flight legs. The ideal situation is to take a single flight from your origin to your destination. This is not always possible and sometimes there is a requirement to take two or more flights instead. The most efficient use of time for a traveller in this situation is to have no waiting time in transit between the arrival of the first flight and the departure of the second connecting flight. The problem with this is if the first flight is delayed then the traveller will miss their connection. The fragility of this system for the traveller is inversely correlated with the length of their stopover. The longer their wait in transit, the less likely they will miss their connection due to their first leg arriving late. Increasing efficiency tends to increase fragility in business in a similar way. Avoiding exploration is one example of this.

Established organisations seem to overlook the problem of fragility because they are so focused on exploitation. The reason for this is because their historic experience suggests success is more likely and faster when a firm is focused on exploitation. Taleb characterised this error of problem definition as the Turkey Problem:[14]

> Consider a turkey that is fed every day, every single feeding will firm up the bird's belief that it is the general rule of life to be fed every day by friendly members of the human race 'looking out for its best interests,' as a politician would say. On the afternoon of the Wednesday before Thanksgiving, something unexpected will happen to the turkey. It will incur a revision of belief.

This creates an inherent conflict for organisations to operate ambidextrously. The following quotes from O'Reilly and Tushman[15] describes this conflict and the bias to exploitation:

> ". . . the fundamental tension at the heart of an enterprise's long-term survival . . . was to engage in sufficient exploitation to ensure its current viability and, at the same time, to engage in sufficient exploration to ensure its future success. In our view, organisational ambidexterity is about survival."
>
> ". . . To make these transitions required these companies to simultaneously compete in mature businesses and to orchestrate firm assets to allow them to develop the requisite new capabilities to compete in new businesses."
>
> ". . . In the short term, ambidexterity is intrinsically inefficient in that it requires the duplication of efforts and the expenditure of resources on innovation, not all of which will be successful."

## Partial Ambidexterity Solutions

Three approaches to achieving ambidexterity inside organisations have been identi-
fied by researchers:[16]
- Sequential ambidexterity
- Structural ambidexterity
- Contextual ambidexterity

*Sequential ambidexterity* is compatible with the McKeown's stages of the firm outlined above. Over time firms can shift from exploration to exploitation and then
back to exploration in a cycle to better fit with external conditions. This means alternating between McKeown's Predictable Success and Treadmill stages. The challenge is working out when and how to switch.

*Structural ambidexterity* takes a different approach. The firm separates into different divisions instead of separating exploration and exploitation into different time
stages. The exploitation division is the cash cow responsible for business as usual. The
exploration division is expected to develop innovations for the mainstream business to
take up. Structural ambidexterity is different from sequential ambidexterity because exploration and exploitation are conducted simultaneously. The theoretical value in this
approach is that the company can run two different operating models. In practice the
innovation division will have a different strategy, reporting lines, incentives, skill sets,
culture, and processes to the mainstream business. This is true for both small-scale
'skunkworks' like the team who developed the PC for IBM despite limited funding and
large-scale centralised R&D units like those in Philips. About 50% of all private R&D
activities in the Netherlands were undertaken by the 'Big Seven' during the 1990s.
These firms were Philips, Akzo Nobel, ASML, DSM, Shell, Unilever, and Océ.[17] These
companies traditionally centralised their R&D efforts. Now it is becoming more common for businesses to leverage more forms of decentralised R&D and open innovation
approaches. This change has come because the challenge with separating out the innovation function is to integrate innovations into the mainstream business. Decentralised
R&D can reduce the internal innovation take-up problem. The case example below
shows how innovation approaches at Philips have changed over its corporate history.

---

*U+ Innovation and ambidexterity for Philips over its life stages*[18]

*The multinational company Philips was founded in 1891 to produce carbon-filament lamps and
other electro-technical products. The company's early struggle lasted until 1895. After avoiding
near bankruptcy, the two founding brothers brought in their much younger brother Anton
Philips. He had an engineering degree, but initially worked in the business as a salesperson.
Anton is credited with having a visionary impact on the company. In the 1920s Philips started to
manufacture other products. The company seems to have gone beyond the Fun and Whitewater
stages into a period of Predictable Success with Anton involved. The first half of the firm's corporate history includes the introduction of successful innovations interspersed with significant*

*gaps. It is likely that the company was alternating between exploration and exploitation in an early form of sequential ambidexterity up until approximately 1960.*

*After producing lighting products from start-up, exploitation lasted until the end of the 1930s. It was not until 1939 that the company released their Philishave electric razor. The Philishave brand survived until 2006. After the World War II in the late 1940s and early 1950s, the firm resumed exploration. In 1949, the company began selling television sets. Philips also redeveloped the Stirling engine as a low-power portable generator for valve radios. However, after producing only 150 'Bungalow sets' the company realised the product was too expensive to produce and not relevant for transistor radios. By 1951, the company had abandoned the generator product. Philips did use the Stirling engine in cryocoolers. In 1950, Philips Records was formed. The record company merged with Siemens' record division to become PolyGram in 1962.*

*Philips then seems to have entered a period of exploitation for a decade up until the early 1960s. In 1963, it brought out the audio Compact Audio Cassette tape. Several different market applications of the cassette tape were introduced. This suggests the firm had increased its R&D efforts. Separate divisions for innovation, production, and marketing meant the company was probably operating as a structurally ambidextrous firm from the early 1960s. Cassette tapes were used in many different market applications including dictation machines, as alternative to vinyl records, in answering machines, and in radio cassette players. In 1972, Philips launched the world's first home video cassette recorder only to be overtaken by Sony Betamax and later VHS format machines. Japanese manufacturers were able to achieve greater scale because they produced for NTSC, SECAM, and PAL standards. Philips only produced for PAL and later joined the VHS consortium instead of retaining its own standard. In hindsight, the decade leading up to 1980 may have been a Treadmill stage for Philips.*

*By the early 1980s Philips was nearing the end of the era of tape as a storage media. Computers began to replace tape for storage with solid state media including Compact Discs. Philips and Sony partnered in 1982 to release CDs. CDs went on to evolve into a range of formats for use in different devices. For example, Philips' CD-i was released in 1991 as a combination media player, education platform, and game console. The device was finally withdrawn in 1998 after it failed to achieve cut-through against more powerful, cheaper rival game consoles. Philips had also developed the LaserDisc early on for selling movies. This CD development culminated in DVD in 1997 and ultimately Blu-ray in 2006.*

*In the 1980s, Philips's profit margin dropped below 1%. It seems the firm was entering a Big Rut. Many of its innovations at the time were incremental market applications rather than fundamental breakthroughs. Its corporate strategy seems to have become increasingly dictated by trustees rather than promotors. For example, it delayed the commercial release of the LaserDisc to avoid cannibalising sales of video recorders. In 1984, mergers and acquisitions seemed to take precedence over innovation. The company transferred integrated circuit production into a joint venture called AMSL and purchased around a third of German firm Grundig. Resorting to acquisition to grow is symptomatic of an executive team preferring exploitation to exploration. Acquisitions seem like faster, less risky solutions to innovating in-house for revenue growth. The irony is, in practice, most acquisitions fail. Troubles for the company continued into the 1990s as its status as a leading electronics company declined.*

*Early in the 2000s, the firm was mired deeply in its Big Rut. The first decade of the new century saw no large-scale successful market innovations. Instead, Philips continued to invest in mergers and acquisitions. In 2004, Philips switch from the slogan "Let's make things better" to "Sense and Simplicity." This is indicative of the risk avoidance focus inside the firm. By 2010, the Philips physics laboratory had been scaled down. The firm had retreated from innovating in consumer electronics.*

*Philips cut 4,500 jobs to meet financial targets after an 85% net profit reduction in late 2011. It went on to lose €1.3 billion that year. In 2012, the firm sold off its TV manufacturing division and continued to cut 2,200 more jobs in 2015. After two decades in decline and then major re-structuring, the company shifted from electronics to healthcare. This represented a major new exploration phase for the firm. Five years on, Philips seems to be thriving again with this change in focus. Perhaps it is one of the few large firms to return from the Big Rut stage.*

*Contextually Ambidextrous*: Both sequential and structural ambidexterity are company level approaches. In contrast, contextual ambidexterity operates at the level of the individual. Contextually ambidextrous businesses are more flexible. They allow employees to use their own judgement as to how they allocate effort between work for adaptation activities (exploration) and work for alignment activities (exploration).[19] Companies like 3M allow their employees to take time out from their scheduled work to invest in projects they think are worthwhile.

**U+ 3M's 15% and 25% rules support contextual ambidexterity**[20]

*The 3M Company has grown exponentially since its early days. During 1914 to 1966, the compound annual growth rate of sales was 17.1% per year to achieve $1.2 billion revenue in 1966. 3M continued its exploration behaviour to become substantially diversified. Two corporate rules underpin 3M's innovation strategy. 3M's 25% rule mandates the firm must earn 25% of total sales from products less than 5 years into market. In 2015, the 3M company achieved sales of $US 30 billion up from $20 billion in 2004. More well-known is 3M's 15% rule.*

*The 15% rule permits employees to spend 15% of their work week on experimental projects offering the potential for new products. This idea was promoted by William McKnight in 1948 after he had been general manager for seven years. McKnight was famously quoted to say: "Encourage experimental doodling. If you put fences around people, you get sheep. Give people the room they need." The firm now sells more than 60,000 products with operations in more than 70 countries. Blockbuster product successes include Scotch Tape and Post-it Notes. However, the company has a remarkably diverse product range. In 2012, one employee project yielded a wireless Bluetooth stethoscope. The product allows doctors to listen to patients' lungs and hearts during their rounds. The system automatically stores the data for deeper software analysis and better diagnosis.*

Companies like 3M are counter-conventional to the way most companies approach employee management. According to Daniel Pink, the most common motivational approaches organisations use to manage employees reduces autonomy.[21] This in turn prevents contextual ambidexterity.

## Swarming for Innovation

Executives will commonly say the reason their organisation does not innovate more is due to a difficulty with alignment. They believe the scale and complexity of their firm prevents them from pursuing exploration and exploitation simultaneously.

A system perspective casts doubt on size and complexity as barriers to ambidexterity. Markets are observed to be ambidextrous despite being at least an order of magnitude more complex and larger in scale than the firms they are comprised of. Regardless of the reticence of current major market players to innovate, there are always start-ups prepared to try and shake up the status quo. New entrants are always hoping to disrupt incumbents and are prepared to invest on spec to do so. Start-ups and new entrants are the way markets explore. Our contention is that organisations who do not at least match the dynamism of the market they operate in are certain to experience an untimely and avoidable demise. Requiring alignment in a business at the expense of innovation is a Type 3 error.

Markets can operate ambidextrously despite their size and complexity because they do not start with an axiomatic requirement for alignment. Markets are more decentralised and tend to be controlled from the bottom up. The most successful firms have the greatest market share as the result of many individual customer choices.

In contrast to markets, companies are more centralised and controlled from the top down. This control structure is embedded in the company's DNA from the moment it starts up and typically continues for the firm's entire life span. Founders typically start firms to enjoy more working autonomy and are compelled to explore to escape from the Early Struggle stage of their business. They take charge of their firm until the Whitewater stage of development compels them to systematise. Systematisation switches the firm from entrepreneurial management (Promoter style) to administrative management (Trustee style). Trustees are prone to build in layers of hierarchy for accountability. They perceive the need for checks and balances to deal with risk and prevent variability. As businesses scale, the central control originally imposed by the founders of the firm is replaced by a top down management structure with various levels of authority. Partly this has to do with the concept of Dunbar's number (the maximum limit of people who can work together directed by a single leader).[22] Partly it has to do with trying to ensure consistency at scale through increased management controls. Controlling people causes them to reduce their predisposition to explore and restricts ambidexterity.

There are social structures in nature capable of ambidexterity. These groups work even though their members are very stupid compared to humans. Their group size can dwarf the number of employees in most businesses. These are the social structures of creatures like ants, bees, wolves, antelope, fish, and birds. The groups are variously known as colonies, hives, packs, herds, schools, and flocks. This book will use the term swarm to describe a social structure in nature capable of organising its members to act as an ambidextrous group. Swarms have four key characteristics:[23]

1. Self-organisation
2. Diverse knowledge
3. Indirect collaboration
4. Adaptive mimicking

*Self-organisation* is inherent in the mechanism the swarm uses to solve its colony's key survival problem. Instead of being organised by a single, central leader from the top down, the colony's organisation emerges from the bottom up. The pattern of organisation arises from simple principles of behaviour every member adheres to. There is no leader in a flock of birds or school of fish who directs the others in the group. Yet birds and fish band together to find food more efficiently and to be safer from predators. The queen in a hive of bees or ants is not in charge. Yet ants and bees can split their food gathering activities between harvesting known sources of food and searching for new sources of food very effectively. Self-organisation is a principle of markets not evident in most companies.

Markets act as an ambidextrous system to manage and distribute scarce resources effectively. The market economy of the US was able to prevail against the competing centrally planned system of the USSR. Ultimately, the USSR broke up after they were unable to continue to economically compete with the US. Despite the advantages of improved efficiency and alignment a single central authority should theoretically enjoy, the USSR could not win against the self-organisation arising from the US market.

China is now opening its economy up. The Chinese government is experimenting with different zones to allow more decentralised market factors to catalyse growth. Most companies don't operate this way. Companies control scarce resources of cash, people, and ideas. Rarely do companies allow formal internal market structures for the allocation of these resources to emerge. Cash is allocated in budgets from the top down. People are selected and promoted by others higher up in the hierarchy. Ideas are not formally traded within organisations between different areas. Investing in an innovative idea requires approval from higher up the management chain. Lack of internal markets for cash, talent, and ideas hinders organisations from leveraging their diversity of knowledge.

*Diverse knowledge* is a critical component of a swarm's success. Charles Talleyrand is credited with saying, "There is one body that knows more than anybody, and that is everybody." Swarms have evolved to automatically share information an individual colony member has for the benefit of the group overall. This sharing is the primary 'herd effect.' It is common for swarms to exhibit various herd effects related to food or danger. If one member senses danger, the whole group reacts as one. Examples include stampedes of herding animals, flocks of birds suddenly taking flight, or a school of fish scattering. These reactions can be triggered by a single member of the swarm. The nature of the swarm allows the early warning to benefit all members – then the swarm reacts. Similarly, when one member of a swarm finds food, the rest of the swarm takes advantage of the discovery. This arrangement benefits all swarm members because the search for food becomes more efficient.

Leveraging diverse knowledge is becoming more prevalent in organisations. Some firms use cross-functional teams, others are increasing open innovation efforts to solve problems, and some are using crowdsourcing techniques to inform decisions. These are all direct collaboration methods. Information is shared directly between company employees. Swarms don't work this way. Instead they collaborate indirectly.

*Indirect collaboration* is a natural extension of self-organisation and diverse knowledge in swarms. Termites do not have a supervisor-level termite directing workers to build or repair their hive. The workers do not interact with each other to agree on what each should do. Instead, every worker follows rules about how to respond to their environment without needing to have a meeting about it. There are no direct interactions. If a termite mound is damaged, larger soldier termites arrive to stand guard. These soldiers respond instinctively to the changes in temperature, humidity, and light inside the mound. Similarly, workers arrive bringing soil grains coated with saliva to patch up the hole. The saliva contains a pheromone to attract other workers with soil grains to the same spot. Each worker knows to add their soil grain to the work in progress because of what they smell, not because of a direct communication with a colleague or any superior.

In business this is similar to the way companies organise customer service team members to deliver omni-channel support. The backbone of the system is a database allowing the service agent to know what has happened before. The database eliminates the need to talk directly with the last person who helped the customer, and instead they learn indirectly what is needed next based on what is stored in the system.

Customer journey maps are also useful for organisations in this way. A journey map allows people in different silos of the organisation to understand how their role fits into the customer's overall experience. Ideally, this means they can specialise in their piece of the puzzle and deliver customer satisfaction without having to do a personal handover with the previous team member in the fulfilment process.

Indirect collaboration permits high quality with efficiency because individual agents do not need an overview of everything to do a good job. They just need to know how they should fit in with the process at their station. If they know this and are intrinsically motivated to do their jobs there is no need for direct supervision. Employees can learn how to do their jobs by observing their peers and copying what works. This is like adaptive mimicking.

*Adaptive mimicking* is the final characteristic of swarms. Birds flying in a flock stay together without colliding because they reference each other's positions. Research into how starlings flock showed the birds have simple positioning rules. First, they try to keep their nearest neighbours on either side of them, where they can see them. They ignore birds in front or behind them. This makes sense because starling's eyes are on the sides of their heads. What is surprising is the second rule. It might make sense to try and have a set distance between each bird and its nearest neighbours. In practice, starling flocks seem to be elastic. Sometimes birds can be a meter apart and other times five metres apart in their flock. Intense analysis showed that the birds are not trying to keep their neighbours at a set distance. Instead they try to keep the same average distance between their nearest six to seven neighbours. This makes the birds extremely sensitive to the density of the flock. Should a hawk dive to attack the flock, this sensitivity allows all birds to effectively scatter rapidly without colliding into each other. In effect, each bird is copying all the others somewhat idiosyncratically. This is adaptive mimicking.

In business, adaptive mimicking governs many of the ways people maintain their informal positions inside their organisations. One obvious method is how managers dress. In some corporate environments there is a uniform men wear based around the suit and tie.[24] In more creative environments this uniform becomes jeans, jacket, and no tie. Lawyers dress differently than teachers, even though both work in communications fields. Trade workers on a mining site tend to dress differently than their counterparts on building sites in both overt and subtle ways. Workers exhibit adaptive mimicry in dress and speech with their peers on the same site. The overt site differences (like wearing high visibility vests and use of site-specific jargon) are often important to job function. Mimicking helps with safety and efficiency. Other site differences (like size of belt buckles, style of safety glasses worn, and how people greet each other) are more subtle. Mimicking more subtle aspects helps workers to fit in socially. Consumers also exhibit adaptive mimicry behaviour in many different markets.

In fashion the latest trends are pure adaptive mimicry. Perhaps teenagers are among the most focused in this regard. Every teenager needs to express a difference in their attire to their parents as part of establishing their independence and identity. At the same time, teenagers want to fit in with their social peer group. The combination of these needs and wants results in teenage fashion. To express their individuality, adolescents wear remarkably similar clothes, sport similar hairstyles, and listen to the same music as their friends. They mimic their group's style to fit in, with a little bit of adaptation to be unique.

Adaptive mimicry also happens at the organisational level. It is common for businesses to copy other successful businesses. Many firms attempt to compete on price instead of working out how to effectively differentiate themselves. Some businesses simply mimic other businesses' strategy, value proposition, and/or positioning to avoid risk. There seems to be a correlation where the higher the level of regulation in a market sector, the more the players will mimic each other. Sectors like aged care, insurance, banking, and air travel are filled with companies offering customer value propositions barely distinguishable from their rivals.

Firms mimic each other to a lesser extent in less regulated markets. This happens across different industries. Many software firms present End User Licence Agreements designed to limit their liability and/or increase their rights beyond those automatically granted by copyright law. Often construction companies attempt to purchase services from contractors with provisions for unlimited liquidated damages. Their contractors attempt to cap or remove these provisions. The opportunity to adjust prices based on contract conditions is simply not considered even though it could provide a valuable differentiation. Even in unregulated aspects of business, firms tend to mimic each other. This results in the emergence of informal market standards.

Hotels most commonly have a 10 a.m. check out and 2 p.m. check in. Consumer products often come with a 12-month manufacturer's warranty. Retailers selling these products offer warranty extensions at an extra price. Blister-packed fast moving consumer goods are generally difficult to open. These packages are designed to prevent sampling, shoplifting, and transport damage. These examples suggest markets operate to reduce risk through adaptive mimicry of the businesses they are comprised of. Swarms are similar.

## Ant Colony Optimisation

Swarming creatures solve problems at a group level they could not effectively or efficiently solve at an individual level. At the heart of each swarm's problem-solving capability is an algorithm honed by evolutionary forces. Each algorithm is specific to the swarm species using it and the problems past generations have had to solve. Various swarm algorithms have been adapted for use in solving computational problems difficult to solve with traditional means. For example, Ant Colony Optimisation (ACO) has been applied to the so-called 'Travelling Salesman Problem.'[25] This problem relates to the issue of working out an efficient route for any sales, service, or delivery agent who must attend multiple sites. The computational difficulty stems from complexity. As the number of stops increases, the possible number of route combinations increases factorially. Searching through all the combinations for the fastest or shortest is not feasible in many commercial applications. Even with powerful computers, the problem takes too long to solve. ACO provides a faster option. The ACO algorithm uses virtual agents, who like ants finding the best path to food, work out a superior route to take. ACO does not always find the best solution. Instead it commonly finds a good enough solution much faster than traditional computing methods can.

*C+ Air Liquide uses swarm algorithms for route planning*
*Air Liquide in Texas has saved an estimated $US 20 million by applying a version of ACO.[26] The firm has around 100 separate plants making various gases. They must deliver these products to thousands of customers by truck and pipeline. Optimising manufacturing is further complicated by a deregulated electricity industry where prices change minute by minute. Air Liquide built an algorithm based on how ant colonies harvest food after complexity scientists shared insights about how ACO works. The Air Liquide program runs each night to create production plans and delivery schedules. It has been a source of sustainable competitive advantage for the firm.*

In an ant colony, the workers involved with gathering food need to split resources between scouting and harvesting activities. Workers are employed in one of three roles – as scouts searching for new sources of food, as harvesters collecting food from a known source, or as onlookers waiting for the right stimulus to become either a scout or harvester. Unlike a company where workers are allocated roles or tasks by a manager, in an ant colony each ant assumes a role and they switch between roles based on what they smell.

Ants in the scout role are tasked with finding food. They leave a trail of pheromones behind them on their search so they can find their way back to the hill. Ants do not see very well and find their way around mostly using their sense of smell. Finding a food source triggers them to change their role from scout to harvester. They pick up some of the food and follow their own pheromone trail back to the nest. They continue to lay down more pheromones on their trail during their return journey. The pheromone quantity they produce is proportional to the quality of the food source. A bigger and better food source is more stimulating because it has a greater and more attractive smell. This in turn excites the harvester to excrete more pheromone. As the ant returns to the hill, the initial stimulus from the food fades and it releases less pheromone. The result is a pheromone trail to the food source with a strength proportional to the size, quality, and distance to the food source. The pheromone strength acts as a signal for other workers. This signal adjusts dynamically as the food source diminishes with harvesting.

Onlooker workers back at the nest and wandering scouts may smell a food trail and be triggered to follow it to help harvest. The trigger response is not a threshold response – it is a probabilistic response. This means strong trails are more likely to trigger additional harvesters and weak trails are less likely to attract more workers. But both strong and weak trails can still attract workers. An ant may smell a trail but choose to ignore it and continue as an onlooker or scout, regardless of how intense the pheromones detected are. Once a worker becomes a harvester, they stay in that role until their specific food source is depleted and then switch to either scouts or onlookers.

Trail strength is not only proportional to food source quality. Harvesters attracted to a trail add their pheromones from each trip to those already laid down by previous workers. This makes their trail more attractive to other workers. So the more ants harvesting from a trail the more likely other ants will also join in. This counteracts the natural reduction in signal strength due to the diminishing food source. In this way, the best food sources attract the most harvesters from the hive. The relative attractiveness of each trail changes dynamically as food sources are gradually depleted, more ants are attracted to a specific trail, and new trails are made with additional food source discoveries.

One of the more important results to emerge from this system is the ability to find the shortest route to a food source. Imagine two ants are returning as harvesters from the same source by different routes. The ant who travelled the shortest distance will produce a trail with relatively more pheromone. This will tend to attract more additional harvesters than the other longer route. As more harvesters are attracted to the shorter route it will become even more preferred. In this way the colony can find the most efficient path to each food source. This emergent property resulted in using the ACO to solve the Travelling Salesman Problem such as Air Liquide in the case example above.

Ant colonies are inherently ambidextrous. They have evolved over many generations to optimise the balance between harvesters, scouts, and onlookers. Ant hills will have some scouts out exploring for new opportunities, some harvesters exploiting current opportunities, and some onlookers available to take advantage of changes in the overall opportunity set. Importantly, each ant selects their role without being directed by a supervisor ant. There is no hierarchy in the colony. Individual ants make a choice based on what they have learned about what else is going on around them. ACO can be adapted to the problem of allocating resources between exploitation and exploration activities in companies.

---

**A+ Making movies and video games like an ant colony**

According to Rob Brown,[27] movie making has changed since the top down approach of the 1930s. Originally studios would own the equipment and employ the actors and others required to create a production. Now films are made when enough of the players required come together believing a film project is a good idea. This could start with an actor or their agent thinking a movie has promise. They talk to other contractors required to get the project to come to life – camera operators, casting companies, producers, special effects providers, producers, directors, and so on. The more people interested, the more compelling the project becomes for those asked to fill the final roles. Just like ants being attracted to a strengthening food trail, as more people commit to a film project, it becomes more attractive for those still needed to join. Valve Corporation goes one step further.

Valve Corporation makes computer games and runs the online platform called Steam. Their first game was released in 1998 to critical acclaim and commercial success. Steam was launched in 2003 to issue upgrades to users. The platform evolved to distribute other games soon after. By 2011 Steam had grown to account for approximately half of all digital PC game sales. Valve was reportedly worth more than US$ 3 billion by 2012. At the time it had only 250 employees. That valuation meant Valve was more profitable per employee than any other US firm at the time, including Facebook and Google.

Valve is a remarkable success story because the company uses an extremely decentralised management approach. Their website proclaims the firm to 'Boss-free since 1996.' The firm's employee handbook explains to team members how Valve goes beyond the percentage of self-directed time at companies like 3M and Atlassian. At Valve, people get to spend all their time on self-directed projects. The firm apparently structures around a rule of three. Anyone who has an idea for a project can pursue it if at least two other coworkers agree it is worthwhile. The result is some workers end up working on multiple projects and then dropping those less worthwhile to commit more to projects as their success becomes more certain. All of this happens without traditional top down direction. Valve organises a lot like an ant colony.

Adapting the ACO algorithm to the ambidexterity problem in business could work as follows:

1. Set up a pool of self-directed workers.
2. The workers must be able to search for opportunities (explore) and scale them up (exploit).
3. Allow these agents to choose how they spend their time.
4. In the searcher role, workers seek new opportunities.
5. Others in the doer role will work on scaling business as usual.
6. It may be ok for a third cohort in a watcher role to see how things go before committing.
7. Searchers and doers should report on their progress at intervals.
8. Workers can change roles to searching, doing, or watching with each new report.
9. Attracting workers to a project will naturally depend on how good the progress looks.
10. Good projects will attract more support and expand.
11. Projects are discontinued as they lose their doers to other projects.

This self-directed approach requires a culture of trust and self-accountability to succeed. The system could fail if people do not act in the best interests of the organisation. This requires the right information sharing, incentives, and values to guide the firm to the right balance between searchers, watchers, and doers. The firm will also have to find employees who can both search and scale opportunities.

ACO is one innovative way firms may organise for ambidexterity. However the 'no free lunch theorem'[28] logically proves no swarm optimisation technique is superior for solving all optimisation problems. Other swarm algorithms will work better in other company contexts. Many businesses would not be able to successfully organise like Valve Corporation. A lack of hierarchy could be untenable for many established firms who are not familiar with decentralised controls. The next section presents the Grey Wolf Optimisation (GWO) as an alternative to ACO.

**Grey Wolf Optimisation**

The two main differences between GWO and ACO are hierarchy and swarm size. GWO includes levels of authority just like most companies. It also operates with fewer agents than ACO usually needs. GWO is different from ACO because wolves have different issues to deal with than ants do. A wolf pack needs to track, surround, and attack much larger prey than ants.

Wolves prey on grazing animals like deer and buffalo. Their prey is far more dispersed than the food sources ant colonies exploit. So most of the time the pack is out tracking prey. As a result the hunting ground for a wolf pack covers far more area than the scouting field of an ant colony. The pack has far fewer scouts available for the food search than ants. This makes effective and efficient tracking the key problem the wolf pack must solve.

Typically the pack forms into small teams to track potential prey. When one team finds prey, their team leader howls to let the other teams know. At this point, the pack must correctly decide if closing in on this primary target is worthwhile or if they should keep tracking other secondary prey. This decision is critical because the secondary prey will be alerted to the pack's presence should they attack the primary target. The secondary prey will likely be long gone when the pack are finished with their primary target. If the primary target is too big to bring down or too small to be worth the effort or somehow gets away, the pack will go hungry.

Ant colonies do not have the same criticality to managing their scouting function. They do not need to focus carefully on when to switch from scouting to harvesting. Ants tend to operate continuously and simultaneously in their activity phases (scouting, harvesting, and onlooking) because their food sources are more plentiful. The ratio of scouting to harvesting is the opposite of wolves. Ants spend much more of their efforts on harvesting than scouting. Wolves spend much more of their time on tracking than closing in and attacking. This creates the differences between how GWO and ACO work.

One major difference is that wolf packs establish a hierarchy to organise their activities.[29] They give various pack members different levels of authority. There are Alpha, Beta, Delta, and Omega level wolves in every grey wolf pack. Alphas are the overall leaders of the pack. They decide when to track, surround, and/or attack prey. They also choose the general area the pack will search. The Alpha pair are the only wolves allowed to mate. The pack chooses Alphas based on their ability to manage the pack. This is surprising because other animals with hierarchical social structures normally end up with the strongest members being dominant.

Under the Alphas are the Betas. Beta wolves support the Alphas in managing the pack. On a hunt both Alphas and Betas will lead small teams of Deltas and Omegas. The Betas lead their teams to flank the Alphas and search parallel regions for prey. Betas use their discretion to choose how far to locate away from the rest of the pack. Too close and the pack cannot cover as much ground. Too far away and the pack cannot converge fast enough to bring down prey before it escapes. A Beta will howl to alert the rest of the pack when their team is close enough to some prey.

It is the Alphas who decide if the rest of the pack should close for the attack. Alphas may howl in response to a Beta to summon the rest of the pack. They may also howl if their own team finds suitable prey. Then the pack closes in. The pack will attack on the Alpha's command. Alphas only initiate an attack when they can see the prey and have enough pack close by to support bringing it down. Success means the pack can feed.

Wolves eat in order of hierarchy. Alphas first, then Betas, and then Deltas. Omegas eat last because they are at the bottom of the pack social structure. Being an Omega is not much fun, they are the scapegoats of the pack and must submit to the dominance of all the other wolves. Omegas are necessary because they provide an outlet for venting frustration within the pack. Packs who lose their Omega are prone to infighting.

Alphas do not seem to assign the roles of their fellow pack members. It is likely this is more of an emergent classification arising from social interactions among pack members. This makes the hierarchy in GWO different from the way organisations are typically structured. The other difference to human organisations is the way the wolf pack is organised in teams to search for prey in parallel. Wolf packs exhibit a kind of sequential and structural ambidexterity. During tracking they are essentially exploring in semi-independent small teams. On the command of their Alphas they switch to single unit to surround and attack prey. The pack changes from exploration to exploitation. Simultaneously, their structure changes from small teams to a single larger unit. This organisation is similar to the way Sony pursued market opportunities for mobile phone content from 2001 on.

---

*C+ U+ Sony Ericsson searches mobile markets for success*[30]

*In 2001, Sony and Ericsson formed a joint venture called Sony Ericsson Mobile Communications (SEMC) to leverage the best of Ericsson radio technology and Sony consumer electronics design capabilities. At the time, mobile phones were starting to become a new channel for content. Initially ring tones, but then wallpapers (static images to customise your home screen) to in-built games and later music. The first substantive commercialisation of content through mobiles was ringtones.*

*Consumers proved willing to pay to personalise their phones and at one point ringtones were selling for £3-£4. Each tone was typically a heavily truncated version of a popular song and sounded only roughly like the original. This avoided copyright infringement and eliminated licencing costs. The marginal cost to Sony to provide a ringtone was almost nothing. Games were the next substantive content space for mobiles after ringtones. A range of simple games were developed and embedded in the factory and sold as part of a phone's feature set. An early example was the game Snake embedded in Nokia phones. Nokia was one of Sony's main rivals in mobile.*

*Sony Ericsson had a dedicated focus on developing mobile content channels (specifically Sony assets) for use in Sony mobile phone handsets. The objective was simply to create point of sale differentiation and value add via branded assets. Each of the Sony sister companies had their own programs and were trying to maximise profits from their content brands. Some of the most important included Sony Pictures Entertainment with movies, Sony Computer Entertainment with the Playstation, Sony Music with music and Sony Ericsson with mobile games. The Sony Group tasked each of the different companies to explore the new 'rivers of gold' mobile content promised at the time.*

*SEMC developed a mobile game business model. Each game's theme leveraged other copyrighted assets and branding for cut-through. The first levels of a game were embedded in the phone for free. SEMC created the back-end technology to allow the rest of the game to be downloaded for a fee. This had the dual effect of improving the Sony Ericsson handset value proposition upfront and creating the potential for additional revenue after the handset had been purchased. This made SEMC the logical partner for the other Sony businesses to work with despite its relatively low market share. SEMC had content development and innovation capability. Most importantly, it could accelerate market growth via seeding content in handsets. SEMC wanted Sony sister companies to leverage its capabilities on favourable commercial terms. Sony Europe convened the EuroTop initiative in Salzburg to find synergies between Sony sister companies.*

*Eurotop's objective was to find new ways of creating additional value and competitive advantage in the Sony group. A key focus was mobile as the emergent media and entertainment channel. The intended cooperation did not emerge for mobile content applications. Instead each Sony business built its own separate content development, sales, and marketing functions. Sony Music for example purchased 550DMV and integrated that business to kickstart its music licensing and content development. The result was visible crossover in the search for new concepts to exploit as each division rigorously pursued their own agendas.*

*For some managers inside the group the approach seemed inefficient. The response to these concerns from one Japanese corporate VP was framed around Sony's need to explore for the next great product, service, or business to ensure continued market leadership. Different teams were tasked to find opportunities in similar market spaces because at group level it was not certain who would find an opportunity or how quickly they could capitalise on it. The group executives believed the duplication was worth the investment. Having more scouts out looking for the next big thing improved Sony's chances of staying ahead of rivals. The cost of multiple resources was far outweighed by the payoffs from success.*

*This parallel search approach in separate teams after a top down directional guidance from the group executive is analogous to parts of the GWO algorithm. The Alpha command was to search the mobile content space for opportunities. Each sister company was then like a Beta leading its team of Deltas. However, the example also falls short of GWO in some other ways. First, the crossover problems should not have occurred. Beta wolves are careful to keep their distance from other teams. In this case, competitive rivalry between the sister companies resulted in search overlaps. Second, the Sony group executive never decided when it was time to circle in on a single opportunity and switch from separate exploration to shared exploitation. Ideally as each of the sister companies reported the results of their marketing and development efforts the best opportunity would have become apparent. Then all sister companies could have been directed to align around this preferred initiative to maximise synergies. It seems Sony got the exploration partly right and then stopped short of switching phases from exploration to exploitation.*

Majdi Mafarja points out one of the key issues with applying search algorithms is how to weight the exploration and exploitation functions. As the search progresses, the relative importance of exploration decreases and the need to invest more in exploitation increases. Search options are selected close to those found in the previous phases to increase the probability of discovering better solutions.[31] This would not work for grey wolves because their prey is relatively scarce; they need to track prey over a wider area. GWO deals with this issue by setting up an Alpha to decide when to switch from tracking to closing in on prey. Adapting the GWO algorithm to the ambidexterity problem in business could work as follows:

1. Determine the Alpha and Beta executives in the firm.
2. Assign the remaining employees as Delta team members under the Alpha and Betas.
3. The Alpha determines a key market opportunity to pursue with their team.
4. The Betas choose adjacent market opportunities to pursue in parallel.
5. Each market opportunity is simply a Lean CX minimum viable initiative.
6. Betas share their results with the Alpha at each pivot point in their Lean CX process.

7. Teams continue pivoting until the Alpha signals a superior MVI has been found.
8. The selected MVI can be from the Alpha's team or any of the Beta teams.
9. Then the firm's activity shifts from 'searching' to 'closing in.'
10. The team already on the target MVI continues to pivot to find the best target solution.
11. Other teams converge by pivoting to close the gap between their MVI and the target.
12. The Alpha monitors the results all teams are getting from their pivots.
13. At some point, the Alpha decides one team is close enough and the activity shifts again.
14. The business shifts to exploitation by aligning resources to scale the target opportunity.
15. This is the equivalent of the firm's attack as a wolf pack to bring down prey.

GWO is expected to fit with more established firms because they can retain some hierarchy. This lessens the difficulty of change management. GWO is also more appropriate for markets with sparse new opportunities. In these conditions, sequential ambidexterity can be a better fit than simultaneously exploring and exploiting. Valve Corporation's market context for games seems to provide a lot more opportunities for scalable growth than mobile content exploitation offered Sony at the start of the century (see cases above). The advent of casual mobile games and online distribution channels like Steam substantially reduced the cost to develop and market each new game for Valve Corporation. The swarm algorithm analogy for Valve's market context is that there is lots food everywhere. So it makes sense for Valve to use a version of ACO. In contrast, Sony in 2001 had much higher development and marketing costs to develop revenue streams from mobile content. This meant they had to be more circumspect before committing to scale an opportunity and could not explore as quickly or cheaply as Valve could a decade later. The swarm algorithm for Sony's market context has to take into account that larger meal possibilities are relatively sparse – so it makes sense for Sony to use a version of GWO.

Both ACO and GWO are swarm algorithms applied at the level of the organisation. The limitation of both algorithms is that they ignore the impact of competition. The final swarm algorithm presented here deals with the issue of competition using a different algorithm.

### Bird Swarm Algorithm

The Bird Swarm Algorithm[32] is a simplification of how flocks of birds behave. It also known as Particle Swarm Optimisation (PSO). PSO mimics birds' foraging behaviour, vigilance behaviour, and flight behaviour. Flocking has evolved in birds because of the benefits it offers. Birds inside a flock are safer because the birds on the edge of the flock are more likely to be targeted by predators. This applies equally in the air (against hawks, eagles, and other hunting birds) as on the ground (for small hunters like cats). However, even the edge of the flock is safer than flying solo. The flock has many pairs of eyes and is much more likely to detect a predator before a single bird could. Further, when the flock scatters in response to a threat it becomes harder for a predator to fix on a single target. The flock's many pairs of eyes also allow members to find food more efficiently than a single bird alone.

Flocking does have some drawbacks. The major issue for birds in a flock is to maintain separation to avoid collisions. A secondary issue is the trade-off between safety and sustenance. The core of the flock is safer than the edge, and the edge of the flock offers the first chance at food. Inside the core there is much more competition for the remaining food left after the edge of the flock has had first pickings. This means the ideal position for each bird in the flock is neither in the middle of the flock, nor on the edge of the flock. The ideal position is near the edge, but not quite on it. Birds have evolved simple rules to ensure they can flock effectively.[33] The cohesion comes from four behavioural rules:
1. Stay with the group to keep the flock together
2. Keep your distance from others to avoid a collision
3. Be close to the centre of the flock for better protection
4. Be close to the edge of the flock to eat first

The same principles apply to schools of fish and herds of grazing animals. These rules can also be applied to market positioning decisions for firms. In this case, the product suppliers and service providers in the market make up the flock. Revenues are the food the flock seeks. The newest and smallest firms in the market can be thought of as on the edge of the flock. They have the most differentiation from the main market. They also have the highest mortality risk. The most established firms with the least differentiation compete at the core of the flock. They have the lowest short-term mortality risk. They also face the most intense competition from other established players for revenue. It is common to see flocking behaviour in both commercial markets and the government sector.

*C+ Governments flock around taxes*
*Taxes are the largest source of funding for most governments around the world.[34] Figure 7.1 shows how taxes have increased for four countries over more than a century. This trend is common across all developed nations. There are some striking similarities in how western democracies impose taxes. The commonalities suggest herd effects. Governments seem to be a somewhat mindless flock when it comes to tax policy.*

*Developed countries impose taxes of around 32% of GDP. Transitional countries rake in only 25% of GDP in taxes. Developing countries collect around 16% of GDP in taxes. This corresponds respectively to the core, near edge, and edge of the flock for this cohort. Lower taxes mean more equity is available for private investment. Transitional countries' lower tax rates mean they can*

## Tax revenue, 1868 to 2008
Taxes (including social contributions) as a share of national income.

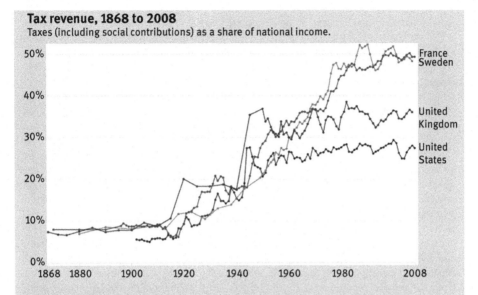

**Figure 7.1:** Tax Revenues as Share of GDP.

grow their economies faster than developed nations. However, lower taxes reduce government's ability to provide services, protect property rights, and enforce contracts. Developing nations are less economically 'safe' than transitional and developed countries and this inhibits their GDP growth.

According to a recent Forbes article[35] the world has dramatically reduced poverty and improved health, freedom, and education over the last two centuries. The root cause is economic growth. The challenge for developed countries is to move away from the core by reducing and simplifying taxes. This is a counter view from the popular media and academic commentary. Few think the world is getting better. The prevailing belief seems to be that imposing higher taxes is important to compel a less differential distribution of wealth in modern society. This position may be sophomoric because history suggests economic growth benefits everyone. The problem is that developed nations have imposed high taxation rates and these are increasing.

Most OECD tax regimes are characterised by complicated tax laws, with many different types of tax imposed, structural differences for individual and company taxation, and different levels of taxation imposed based on earnings and retained wealth. The starting point is so-called 'progressive' tax rates imposed on income. Progressive taxes are misnamed because they disincentivise growth. Progressive tax rates apply when increased earnings are subject to a higher tax rate. The assumption is higher earners can afford to pay more tax.[36]

The counter argument is that higher tax rates disincentivise higher earners to work more and increase economic growth. One alternative is to impose proportional income taxes equally to all taxpayers. Higher income earners still pay more tax under proportional income taxes because they earn more. Instead, most developed countries impose proportional taxes on expenditure on top of progressive income taxes. Examples of these consumption taxes include VAT in Europe, sales tax in the US, and GST in Australia. Consumption taxes are considered 'regressive' because the proportion of tax paid by lower income earners when purchasing the same good is higher than someone else who earns more. To help lower income earners, developed nations *fund welfare programs targeted at the disadvantaged. The OECD national average for total net social spending was 20.9% of GDP in 2015.[37] France topped the list at 31.7%. One consequence of this systemic approach to high taxation has been the emergence of tax professionals.*

*These accountants and lawyers help their clients with tax compliance to minimise their individual tax burdens. Generally tax advice is a service purchased by wealthier taxpayers. It is rational for each taxpayer to do this to maximise deductions. No developed country has implemented a simple tax system to eliminate the demand for tax professionals. The result is wasted resources. The use of tax professionals is an overcorrection to a tax system which itself is already an overcorrection. A Type 3 error in response to another Type 3 error.*

*At the country level, a complicated and high tax system is irrational. It wastes money on compliance and advice, permits some taxpayers to leverage system complexity to pay less tax and disadvantages those who cannot afford tax advice. Perhaps the most important irrationality is that complex tax systems divert smart professionals to deal with tax issues at the expense of focusing on productivity improvement. Every tax professional could better serve their national economy by providing advice on how to run businesses better or how to manage personal client finances more sensibly. Instead they are wasted on dealing with tax compliance. Few developed countries have been prepared to achieve a national competitive advantage by significantly simplifying their tax system and reducing the amount of tax they collect. As a result, it is the transitional nations who are growing faster. They are nearer to the edge of the flock with lower taxes, but not right at the edge with the least developed nations.*

Flocking behaviour has been observed in many markets. Some early examples include the 1848–1855 California gold rush and the Dutch Tulip speculation during 1636–1637. More contemporary examples include trends toward offshoring to take advantage of cheaper labour, digital platform implementations to improve productivity, software as a service (SaaS), social media as a customer touchpoint, and search engine optimisation strategies. The case below outlines how a focus on data is emerging as a key market focus in many different verticals.

**A+ U+ Cultivated data is the new gold rush for SparkLabs[38]**

*In 2014, SparkLabs Global Ventures began to seed fund start-ups generating data on customer behaviour, usage patterns, and company information. The fund was focused on firms collecting millions of data points and particularly those exploring how to monetise the Internet of Things. At the time they found most companies were reticent to pay for data. Their investments were at the edge of the flock. By 2019, the core value of data had become well known in many industries. The vanguard was financial services companies. Those firms are built on data and information. Now many larger companies are willing to pay for cultivated data to access insights. The market has moved beyond industrial manufacturing monitoring, search data, and social media information plays. SparkLabs now has more than 250 start-ups in its portfolio leveraging data and analytics. The importance of cultivated data is growing as more consumer, corporate, and government activities involve the digital world.*

*Cultivated data is information gathered from existing sources and value added with analysis to increase usability. Opportunities include both big data analysis and more novel techniques to get actionable intelligence from smaller data sets. Sources include client data (from management information systems and ERPs), publicly available data (like maps, demographics, and health statistics), and third-party commercial data (like Google Analytics).*

*42 Technologies leverages internal client data. The firm started by analysing point-of-sale data to help large retailers identify undervalued inventory items. They evolved to provide additional insights for retailers from wholesale sales data, warehouse inventories, and other data sets. Firms are also creating value from new external data sources. Inscape has a large source of content preference data for sale. The information was collected from smart TVs made by its $3 billion parent firm Vizio. In contrast, Populus is a data aggregator leveraging public data sets. City planners use Populus' cultivated data built from sharing services utilisation, public transport, and traffic information. SparkLabs asserts few cities have the capability to match Populus' value proposition. In Korea, Chartmetric has become a trusted data aggregator in the music industry by standardising how music labels and bands report their sales numbers. Korea is an emerging hot spot for data firms because of government support for data innovations. Since 1993, the Korea Data Agency has been developing a data marketplace. They pay to take private data and open it up to the public. They have tried to standardise data structures in different verticals including healthcare, finance, and transportation.*

*SparkLabs believe the data and analytics market space will only heat up in the coming years. Their position is that data is the current gold rush for start-ups. If they are correct, this will mean some data start-ups will survive, mature, and migrate closer to the centre of the market flock. In the meantime, many are struggling to survive on the fringe while more established firms jostle to get in on the action.*

Over time markets move in line with trends. This movement results in the core of the market shifting as customer preferences change and supplier value propositions evolve. Firms must move with the market in the same way birds have to stay with the flock. The market is drawn in the direction of successful explorers at or near the edge. The most successful firms are those near the edge who manage to survive and draw the rest of the market around them. Other firms seem to be able to move from the core to near the market edge as second movers.

**C+ A+ Microsoft positions near the edge of the flock**
*Microsoft has traditionally been a successful second mover in many computing applications markets. Microsoft Word mimicked rival WordPerfect. Microsoft Excel was a copy of Lotus 1-2-3 and Visicalc before it. Microsoft Internet Explorer overthrew the dominant usage share enjoyed by Netscape Navigator in the mid-1990s. However, Microsoft has struggled since then to leapfrog incumbents in several other markets. The Surface device has not dominated the Apple iPad and Android tablets. Apple shipped 11.6 million iOS tablets in Q2 2018 (28% of worldwide market share). Android shipments were 23.6 million units for the same period (58% worldwide market share). Microsoft shipped only 5.8 million units in Q2 2018 (14% market share).[39] Bing is a poor second to Google in search engines. Bing had 2.44% share and Google had 91.54% share in 2019.[40] Microsoft operating system for mobile phones has performed even more dismally. It has 0.14% market share in behind Android (74.59%), iOS (24.18%), kaiOS (0.44%), and Samsung (0.19%).[41]*

*Microsoft may have stumbled into Treadmill or the Big Rut with some its market offerings since Office. But the giant is not in the Death Rattle stage. Microsoft Teams was claimed as the fastest growing app in Microsoft company history in 2018 after the company abandoned Skype.[42] Teams is competing with first mover Slack. Slack had more than 500,000 company users in September 2018. Teams was up to 329,000 from 200,000 users six months earlier. This is just 18 months after Teams was launched. In 2019, Teams overtook Slack on user base for the first time.[43]*

Google corporate history can be analysed through the lens of the flock. It was a second mover in the internet search market. Google positioned itself away from the core of main players in the market at the time with its PageRank algorithm. The company has continued to be a second mover in many large contemporary markets like Microsoft. The company has a browser, office applications suite, and operating system in direct competition with Microsoft. However Google has tended to acquire other promising firms instead of building products from scratch. The company acquired Motorola to get access to its patents before selling the handset division to Lenovo. Google has even been prepared to cannibalise its own products. The company was a late mover for GPS applications. Google Maps enabled it to leapfrog companies like Tomtom and Garmin. Later it went on to acquire Waze because that firm had a better approach to mobile navigation. Firms like Microsoft and Google seem to pursue growth strategies with some elements of PSO. Adapting the PSO to help find adjacent market positions could work as follows:

1. Define the market as a CX space using the business model canvas.
2. Each element of the business model canvas is a potential separate dimension.
3. Cut down the dimensions in the multi-dimensional market space (MDMS) by relevance.
4. Plot rivals' offerings as points in the MDMS.
5. Plot current offerings as points in the MDMS.
6. Repeat the steps above for previous periods.
7. Determine the flock trajectory from current and previous plots.
8. Calculate the average density of the flock in the current plot.
9. Position away from rivals using average density.
10. Avoid positions too close to the edge of the flock.
11. Avoid positions too close to the core of the flock.
12. Ensure positioning is updated as the flock moves through the MDMS.

PSO is most useful for firms with many competitors. In highly fragmented markets, PSO provides a process to find a white space in the flock. In other markets with rivals ranging from small to large, PSO offers a new perspective. For large firms it provides a way to find adjacent market positions away from the core with the potential for cut-through. For small firms it provides a way to move away from the dangerous edge of the flock.

At the time of this writing, swarm algorithms have not been applied to the strategy/innovation/ambidexterity problem. The only reference we could find about using swarms in strategy was a paper about how artificial swarm intelligence (ASI) was used to help with decision making.[44] The paper explains how to use a novel approach to aggregate multiple decision maker preferences in real time through a graphical user interface.

*ASI provides the means for networked individuals to combine their explicit and tacit knowledge in real time and to work synchronously to make predictions, to assess alternatives, and to reach decisions about known unknowns. When enabled by ASI, human swarms form a collectively intelligent system that can outperform traditional methods of dealing with known unknowns.*

ASI is not specifically relevant to strategy. It applies more generally to group decision making. It may not formally be a swarm because it only meets three of the four defining swarm criteria. ASI does help a group of decision makers self-organise and aggregate diverse knowledge to decide from a predetermined range of options. The ASI interface provides a system for indirect collaboration. Decision makers direct a virtual magnet with their mouse to pull a virtual hockey puck on screen toward their preferred choice. They can see all the choices available and must react to how the puck moves due to unseen other decision makers' efforts to assert their own preferences. However, no part of this process includes adaptive mimicking. Regardless, ASI is interesting because it suggests the use of swarm algorithms is expanding from computational problems to other domains. The future will reveal whether swarm algorithms become more important for resource allocation, decision making, strategy, and/or innovation.

# Endnotes

1 See Kotter Inc. "8-STEP PROCESS," https://www.kotterinc.com/8-steps-process-for-leading-change/ (accessed 24/5/20); and Kotter (2014). *Accelerate*, Harvard Business Review Press.
2 Goldratt Research Labs, "Overcoming resistance to change with the Goldratt Change Matrix," https://www.youtube.com/channel/UCaI2xkxHvkOUROzRWcQnG5g (accessed 24/5/20).
3 O'Reilly and Tushman (2004). "The Ambidextrous Organisation," *Harvard Business Review* Apr 2004.
4 Birkinshaw and Gibson (2004). "Building Ambidexterity into an Organization," *Sloan Management Review* Vol 45 No 4.
5 McKeown (2015). "The 7 Lifecycle Stages Every Business Experiences," *Entrepreneur.com*. https://www.entrepreneur.com/video/253312] (accessed 24/5/20).
6 Birkinshaw and Ridderstrale (1999). "Fighting the corporate immune system: a process study of subsidiary initiatives in multinational corporations," *International Business Review* Vol 8.
7 McKeown (2010). *Predictable Success: Getting Your Organisation on the Growth Track and Keeping It There*, Greenleaf Book Group Press.
8 Stevenson and Gumpert (1985). "The heart of entrepreneurship," *Harvard Business Review* Vol 63 Iss 2.
9 Andrei (2018). "Astrology doesn't work and never worked. Here's why," *ZME Science* https://www.zmescience.com/other/feature-post/astrology-doesnt-work-and-never-worked-heres-why/ (accessed 25/5/20).
10 Brodwin (2015). "4 Behaviours Are the Most Reliable Predictors of Divorce," *Business Insider*. https://www.businessinsider.com.au/4-behaviors-can-predict-divorce-2015-1?r=US&IR=T (accessed 25/5/20) for an overview. The full academic paper is Gottman and Levenson (2000). "The Timing of Divorce: Predicting When a Couple Will Divorce Over a 14-Year Period," *Journal of Marriage and the Family* Vol 62.

**11** Mitroff (1995). *Smart Thinking for Crazy Times: The Art of Solving the Right Problems*, Berrett-Koehler Publishers.

**12** De Bono (1994). *Parallel Thinking*, Vermilion p137–138.

**13** Taleb (2012). *Antifragile: Things That Gain from Disorder*, Random House.

**14** Taleb (2007). *The Black Swan: The Impact of the Highly Improbable*, Penguin Books.

**15** O'Reilly and Tushman (2013). "Organizational Ambidexterity: Past, Present and Future," *The Academy of Management Perspectives* Vol 27 Iss 4.

**16** Ibid.

**17** Gilsing and Erken (2002). "Trends in corporate R&D," *Ministry of Economic Affairs, The Hague.* https://www.google.com.au/url?sa=t&rct=j&q=&esrc=s&source=web&cd=&cad=rja&uact=8&ved=2ahUKEwi9xKXjudDpAhXaxzgGHQeKCFUQFjADegQIBxAB&url= http://s%3A%2F%2Fwww.oecd.org%2Fsti%2Finno%2F33720448.pdf&usg=AOvVaw0vjZ_mJLcmifB3o7Cacj5h (last accessed 26/5/20).

**18** Wikipedia: "Philips," https://en.wikipedia.org/wiki/Philips (last accessed 26/5/20).

**19** Birkinshaw and Gibson (2004). "Building Ambidexterity into an Organization," *MIT Sloan Management Review* Vol 45 No 4.

**20** Black (2016). "How the 15% Rule Became a Stepping Stone for 3M's Innovation," *Market Realist.* https://marketrealist.com/2016/06/15-rule-became-stepping-stone-3ms-innovation/ (last accessed 26/5/20).

**21** Pink (2009). *Drive: The Surprising Truth About What Motivates Us*, Riverhead Books.

**22** Wong (2007). "What is the Monkeysphere?" *Cracked.* https://www.cracked.com/article_14990_what-monkeysphere.html (last accessed 26/5/20) has a humorous and informative take on the implications of Dunbar's number.

**23** Miller (2010). *Smart Swarm: Using Animal Behaviour to Organise Our World*, Collins.

**24** Apologies to female readers for the male gender focus of this example. There are probably rules for female executive attire but as a male it is harder to explicitly describe these accurately.

**25** Dorigo et al. (1996). "Ant System: Optimization by a Colony of Cooperating Agents," *IEEE Transactions on Systems, Man, And Cybernetics-Part B Cybernetics* Vol 26, No 1.

**26** Miller (2010). *The Smart Swarm*, Collins, has various references throughout chapter 1 and 2 presenting this case.

**27** Brown, "The benefits of creating a hive mind," *Said Oxford Business Review.* https://review.sbs.ox.ac.uk/The-benefits-of-creating-a-hive-mind.html (accessed 1/6/20).

**28** Wolpert and Macready (1997). "No free lunch theorems for optimization," *IEEE Transactions on Evolutionary Computation* Vol 1 Iss 1.

**29** Mirjalili et al. (2013) "Grey Wolf Optimizer," *Advances in Engineering Software* Vol 69.

**30** This case was recounted by Cyrus Allen (one of this book's author team) who was an executive for SEMC at the time.

**31** Mafarja (2018). "Binary dragonfly optimization for feature selection using time-varying transfer functions," *Knowledge-Based Systems* Vol 161.

**32** Meng et al. (2016). "A new bio-inspired optimisation algorithm: Bird Swarm Algorithm," *Journal of Experimental & Theoretical Artificial Intelligence* Vol 28 Iss 4.

**33** Mirjalili (2019). "Chapter 2 Particle Swarm Optimisation," *Evolutionary Algorithms and Neural Networks Theory and Applications*, Springer.

**34** Ortiz-Ospina and Roser (2016). "Taxation," *OurWorldInData.org.* https://ourworldindata.org/taxation (accessed 10/6/20)

**35** Denning (2017). "Why the World Is Getting Better and Why Hardly Anyone Knows It," *Forbes.* https://www.forbes.com/sites/stevedenning/2017/11/30/why-the-world-is-getting-better-why-hardly-anyone-knows-it/#210025757826 (accessed 12/6/20).

**36** Horton (2020). "The Difference Between Regressive, Proportional, and Progressive Taxes," *Investopedia*. https://www.investopedia.com/ask/answers/042415/what-are-differences-between-regressive-proportional-and-progressive-taxes.asp (accessed 10/5/20).

**37** Wikipedia: "List of countries by social welfare spending." https://en.wikipedia.org/wiki/List_of_countries_by_social_welfare_spending (accessed 10/6/20).

**38** Moon (2019). "Cultivated data is the next Gold Rush," *Techcrunch*. https://techcrunch.com/2019/08/08/cultivated-data-is-the-next-gold-rush/ (accessed 11/6/20).

**39** Surur (2018). "Windows 10 tablets gained market share in Q2 2018, and Surface Go may continue gains into Q3," *MS Power User*. https://mspoweruser.com/windows-10-tablets-gained-market-share-in-q2-2018-and-surface-go-may-continue-to-gains-into-q3/ (accessed 11/6/20).

**40** Berry (2020). "2020 Search Market Share: 5 Hard Truths About Today's Market," *WebFX*. https://www.webfx.com/blog/seo/2019-search-market-share/ (accessed 11/6/20).

**41** StatCounter (2019). "Mobile Operating System Market Share Worldwide Mobile Operating System Market Share Worldwide – May 2020," *StatCounter*. https://gs.statcounter.com/os-market-share/mobile/worldwide (accessed 11/6/20).

**42** Schwartz (2018). "Microsoft declares Teams fastest growing app in company history," *CIOdive*. https://www.ciodive.com/news/microsoft-declares-teams-fastest-growing-app-in-company-history/533403/ (accessed 11/6/20).

**43** Warren (2019). "Microsoft Teams overtakes Slack with 13 million daily users," *The Verge*. https://www.theverge.com/2019/7/11/20689143/microsoft-teams-active-daily-users-stats-slack-competition (accessed 11/6/20).

**44** Metcalf et al. (2019). "Keeping Humans in the Loop: Pooling Knowledge through Artificial Swarm Intelligence to Improve Business Decision Making," *California Management Review* Vol 61 Iss 4.

# Conclusion: Our Future is Lean

This book started with mice, monkeys, and gazelles. Then it finished with ants, wolves, and birds. In Chapter 1, we discussed the reasons the current approach to investing in CX was not as successful as it could have been in large firms. CX offers the potential to both increase revenue and reduce costs. Despite this, most CX initiatives failed to move the needle because they prematurely ran out of steam. Some of this had to do with measuring the wrong outcomes, but mostly it had to do with the habitual front-loading of costs traditional corporate managers deal with to make waterfall investments go. The result was often a waste.

Chapter 2 introduced the foundations of Lean Management with the Toyota Production System. Large corporates are not the only organisations suffering from waste. New product failure in an established firm is similar to start-up mortality. The only difference for the established firm is it is unlikely to be betting the farm on a single product. Most start-ups have to succeed with their first product in some form or go out of business. The only way many of them can get through their Early Struggle stage is to apply lean management to the start-up search for a profitable sustainable market. One of the most interesting observations of modern business is why start-ups can even exist. There are almost always better resourced incumbents who could pursue any start-up's market opportunity at much lower risk. The established firm has the money, talent, customers, and brand to launch much more easily. The problem is the way established firms operate – they almost always pursue cost reductions before revenue growth. They choose incremental improvement over disruptive innovation to grow. The tendency for established firms to avoid big changes is one of the reasons Lean CX is a good idea. Lean CX provides a path to innovation beyond incremental improvement. Lean CX is about creating cut-through.

Cut-through was defined in Chapter 3 after an overview of how the strategy problem has changed. In the same way markets evolve, competitive strategy has advanced over time. Formulating business strategy has shifted in the last two decades. In the 1980s competitive strategy was based on picking attractive markets to get a monopoly or oligopoly position. In the 1990s strategy shifted from outside to inside. Strategy was working out how to leverage uniqueness to create sustainable competitive advantages. These approaches to strategy were grounded in a slowly changing world. Contemporary strategy has shifted to deal with VUCA environments. Instead of trying to find a winning position or formula and prevent things from changing, companies are having to develop dynamic capabilities. The Three Horizon Model provides a framework for classifying change over different time periods. Horizon 2 in the model defines the most attractive types of innovation. Horizon 1 innovations tend to be incremental and fail to achieve much cut-through even though they are low risk. Horizon 3 innovations are moon shots – great when they

https://doi.org/10.1515/9783110683929-008

work but extremely high risk. Horizon 2 innovations focus organisations on adjacent market positions. The Business Model Canvas was overlayed on the Three Horizon Model to unpack what the sweet spot for innovation might cover. The final concept introduced was the goal of Lean CX. This was to create MAYA solutions – most advanced yet acceptable.

Different design tools to find MAYA innovations were presented in Chapter 4. These included human-centred design, design matrix, Kano diagrams, and value stream maps. These tools leveraged experience insights and customer psychology. Human brains are complex but can be simplified into three layers. The Lizard brain layer controls instincts. The Labrador brain layer relates to emotion. The Leader brain layer relates to cognition. In combination, these different brains motivate what we do, how we feel, and what we think about. Experience insights combine doing/feeling/thinking into motivations. Most customers experience motivation contextually. They act, are affected, and assess in the moment. Underneath all of this is a drive to survive. The CAPFUL needs and DISC personality types expand beyond experience insights to consider deeper customer needs. At the core of Lean CX is a focus on improving perceived customer value through better design.

Chapter 5 presented how to execute Lean CX to validate and refine minimum viable initiatives. This included four critical phases for market testing MVIs. Phase I involved the necessary preparation required for Lean CX. It turns out most firms already know a lot about their customers and can leverage their understanding to get designing CX innovations. This first phase also suggested an effective way to structure the people involved. Two cohorts were proposed. The Go Team works in the engine room of Lean CX and the Consult Group provides an external perspective and links to the wider organisation. Phase II covered different options for converging on an adjacent market position. Building on the decision criteria matrix approach, Lean CX can utilise both nominal group technique and evolutionary algorithms to find more effective ways to harness Go Team diversity. Phase III presented how to take the design tools presented in Chapter 4 and code testable MVIs into tracking templates. Phase III activities includes using split testing to find MAYA customer experiences. Phase IV discussed how to harden the findings into a scalable business proposition. Scaled Agile was also introduced as an alternative to the standard approach to roll-out changes in larger firms.

Chapter 6 redirected the focus from consumer customers to B2B markets. The differences between consumers and businesses are significant and lead to a range of varied CX considerations. Multiple buyers, longer purchase times, greater value delivery durations, and deeper supplier/customer interdependency give rise to a different value pyramid in B2B. Three buying modes (transactional/routine/organic) determine key CX considerations. In particular, B2B firms need to organise differently around business customer journeys to get cut-through with CX innovation.

Finally, in Chapter 7 swarm algorithms were presented as a solution to the basic innovation problem for all established firms: how to be ambidextrous. Established firms have a requirement to exploit their current market opportunities. They also must invest in exploring new revenue streams before their existing customer value propositions become obsolete. The requirements for a firm to evolve from Early Struggle to Predictable Success results in many large firms implementing systems and processes. This change inhibits exploration. Markets are intrinsically ambidextrous, companies are not. The difference seems to be due to decentralised (bottom up) controls in markets and centralised (top down) controls in firms. Swarm algorithms were presented as alternative organising approaches for companies to help them achieve ambidexterity. Ant Colony Optimisation, Grey Wolf Optimisation, and Particle Swarm Optimisation are already used to solve various computational problems. Methods to adapt these algorithms to help firms organise to both exploit and explore market strategies were outlined. Only a few companies seem to be currently utilising anything like swarm-based approaches.

Underpinning all the frameworks and tools was the belief success in business is based on a search to provide superior value to customers. It is not enough to simply ask customers what they want, in many cases they cannot say. It is not enough to simply copy the other firms in a market, this does not create cut-through. Lean CX is about designing and testing innovation cheaply. These testable innovations are neither trivial nor moon shoots. They may extend the value proposition currently presented to customers. They may be targeted at nearby groups of customers previously ignored. Many Lean CX initiatives will do both. All Lean CX initiatives are validated and improved with agile market testing before they are scaled. The lowest risk way to discover the future of your market is to design it yourself with Lean CX.

# Bibliography

37 Signals (2006). *Getting Real: The Smarter, Faster, Easier Way to Build a Successful Web Application*, self-published.

Ariely (2008). *Predictably Irrational, Revised and Expanded Edition: The Hidden Forces That Shape Our Decisions*, HarperCollins.

Averwater (2012). *Retail Truths: The Unconventional Wisdom of Retailing*, ABB Press.

Ayers (2011). *Engagement Is Not Enough: You Need Passionate Employees to Achieve Your Dream*, Advantage Media.

Banksy et al. (2010). *Exit Through the Gift Shop*, Mongrel.

Barney (1991). "Firm Resources and Sustained Competitive Advantage," *Journal of Management*.

Breuer and Lüdeke-Freund (2016). *Values-Based Innovation Management: Innovating by What We Care About*, Palgrave.

Christensen (1997). *The Innovator's Dilemma: When New Technologies Cause Great Firms to Fail*, Harvard Business Review.

Cooper and Vlaskovits (2010). *The Entrepreneur's Guide to Customer Development: A Cheat Sheet to The Four Steps to the Epiphany*.

De Bono (1996). *Sur/petition: The New Business Formula to Help You Stay Ahead of the Competition*, HarperCollins Publishers.

De Bono (2017). *How To Be More Interesting*, Penguin Life.

Gigerenzer and Todd (1999). *Simple Heuristics That Make Us Smart*, Oxford University Press.

Gladwell (2004). "Choice Happiness and Spaghetti Sauce," *TED Talks* [accessed 2018] https://www.ted.com/talks/malcolm_gladwell_on_spaghetti_sauce.

Goldratt (1994). *It's Not Luck*, North River Press.

Goldratt (2004). *The Goal*, Gower Publishing.

Gray et al. (2010). *Gamestorming: A Playbook for Innovators, Rulebreakers, and Changemakers*, O'Reilly Media.

Handy (2016). *The Second Curve: Thoughts on Reinventing Society*, RH Books.

Hansson and Fried (2010). *Rework*, Amekad Books.

Harford (2009). *The Logic of Life: The Rational Economics of an Irrational World*, Random House.

Kahneman (2013). *Thinking Fast and Slow*, Farrer, Straus and Giroux.

Kay (2010). *Obliquity: Why Our Goals Are Best Achieved Indirectly*, Penguin Books.

Keeley et al. (2103). *Ten Types of Innovation: The Discipline of Building Breakthroughs*, Wiley.

Kerpen (2011). *Likeable Social Media: How to Delight Your Customers, Create an Irresistible Brand, and Be Generally Amazing on Facebook (And Other Social Networks)*, McGraw-Hill.

Kim and Maugborne (2005). *Blue Ocean Strategy*, Harvard Business Review.

Klaff (2011). *Pitch Anything: An Innovative Method for Presenting, Persuading, and Winning the Deal*, McGraw-Hill.

Koch (1999). *The 80/20 Principle: The Secret to Achieving More with Less*, Doubleday.

Koch (2001). *The Power Laws of Business: The Science of Success*, Nicholas Brealey Publishing.

Koch (2013). *The 80/20 Manager: The Secret to Working Less and Achieving More*, Little, Brown and Company.

Lambert and Dugdale (2011). *Smarter Selling: How To Grow Sales by Building Trusted Relationships (2nd Edition)*, Pearson Education.

Levitt, T. (1960). "Marketing Myopia," *Harvard Business Review*.

Littauer (1992). *Personality Plus*, Fleming H Revell.

Maister (2008). *Strategy and the Fat Smoker: Doing What's Obvious But Not Easy*, Spangle Press.

Maister et al. (2000). *The Trusted Advisor*, Free Press.

https://doi.org/10.1515/9783110683929-009

Marshall and Koch (2013). *80/20 Sales and Marketing: The Definitive Guide to Working Less and Making More*, Entrepreneur Press.

Mason (2009). *The Pirate's Dilemma: How Youth Culture Is Reinventing Capitalism*, Free Press.

McGonigal (2012). *Reality Is Broken: Why Games Make Us Better and How They Can Change the World*, Vintage.

Micalko (2006). *Thinkertoys: A Handbook of Creative-Thinking Techniques (2nd Edition)*, Ten Speed Press.

Michelli (2008). *The New Gold Standard: 5 Leadership Principles for Creating a Legendary Customer Experience Courtesy of the Ritz-Carlton Hotel Company*, McGraw-Hill.

Partridge (2015). *People Over Profit: Break the System, Live with Purpose, Be More Successful*, Nelson Books.

Porter (1980). *Competitive Strategy: Techniques for Analyzing Industries and Competitors*, Free Press.

Porter (1985). *Competitive Advantage: Creating and Sustaining Superior Performance*, Free Press.

Press (2010). *Toxic Talk: How the Radical Right Has Poisoned America's Airwaves*, Thomas Dunne Books.

Ricketts (2007). *Reaching the Goal: How Managers Improve a Services Business Using Goldratt's Theory of Constraints*, IBM Press.

Ries (2011). *The Lean Start-up: How Today's Entrepreneurs Use Continuous Innovation to Create Radically Successful Businesses*, Crown Business.

Rock (2009). *Your Brain at Work: Strategies for Overcoming Distraction, Regaining Focus, and Working Smarter All Day Long*, HarperCollins.

Sutherland (2009). "Life Lessons from an Ad Man," *TED Talks* [accessed 2018] https://www.ted.com/talks/rory_sutherland_life_lessons_from_an_ad_man.

Ross (1995). *Total Quality Management: Text, Cases, and Readings*, St. Lucie Press.

Hogshead (2016). *Fascinate, Revised and Updated: How to Make Your Brand Impossible to Resist*, HarperCollins.

Sarasvathy (2001). "What Makes Entrepreneurs Entrepreneurial?" *Harvard Business Review*.

Sernovitz (2015). *Word of Mouth Marketing: How Smart Companies Get People Talking*, PressBox.

Sorensen (2009). *Inside the Mind of the Shopper: The Science of Retailing*, Pearson Education.

Taleb (2005). *Fooled by Randomness: The Hidden Role of Chance in Life and in the Markets (Incerto)*, Random House.

Taleb (2007). *The Black Swan: The Impact of the Highly Improbable*, Random House.

Taleb (2014). *Antifragile: Things That Gain from Disorder (Incerto)*, Random House.

Thaler and Sunstein (2009). *Nudge: Improving Decisions About Health, Wealth, and Happiness*, Penguin Group.

Thompson (2012). *The $12 Million Stuffed Shark: The Curious Economics of Contemporary Art*, St Martin's Press.

Tidd and Bessant (2013). *Managing Innovation: Integrating Technological, Market, and Organizational Change, 5th Edition*, Wiley.

Wright (2015). *Fizz: Harness the Power of Word of Mouth Marketing to Drive Brand Growth*, McGraw-Hill.

# Index

https://doi.org/10.1515/9783110683929-010